Politics of Citizenship and Migration

Series Editors
Willem Maas
Department of Political Science
York University
Toronto, ON, Canada

Justin Gest
George Mason University
Arlington, VA, USA

The *Politics of Citizenship and Migration* series publishes exciting new research in all areas of migration and citizenship studies. Open to multiple approaches, the series considers normative, conceptual, comparative, empirical, historical, methodological, and theoretical works. Versatile, the series publishes single and multi-authored monographs, short-form Pivot books, and edited volumes. Broad in its coverage, the series promotes research on citizenship and migration laws and policies, voluntary and forced migration, rights and obligations, demographic change, diasporas, political membership or behavior, public policy, minorities, transformations in sovereignty and political community, border and security studies, statelessness, naturalization, integration and citizen-making, and subnational, supranational, global, corporate, or multilevel citizenship.

More information about this series at
http://www.palgrave.com/gp/series/15403

Nora Siklodi

The Politics of Mobile Citizenship in Europe

palgrave
macmillan

Nora Siklodi
Politics and International Relations
University of Portsmouth
Portsmouth, Hampshire, UK

Visiting Fellow in Democracy and Citizenship in Education
Norwegian University of Science and Technology
Trondheim, Norway

ISSN 2520-8896   ISSN 2520-890X (electronic)
Politics of Citizenship and Migration
ISBN 978-3-030-49050-8   ISBN 978-3-030-49051-5 (eBook)
https://doi.org/10.1007/978-3-030-49051-5

This Palgrave Macmillan imprint is published by the registered company Springer Nature
Switzerland AG
The registered company address is: Gewerbestrasse 11, 6330 Cham, Switzerland

Acknowledgements

I would like to express my deepest gratitude to the students who participated in the focus groups in Stockholm and London. Their relentless enthusiasm despite the, at times, bumpy debates painted a vivid portrait of mobile citizenship—a source of immense inspiration for my work then and now.

My sincere appreciation goes to friends and colleagues—I feel fortunate to call the people listed below as both—without whom this book would not have happened. Be it because they provided me with help, constructive feedback or a listening ear at the different stages of the research and writing progress. In particular, I would like to take this opportunity to thank Nicholas Allen, Angela Crack, James Dennis, Mark Field, Robert Frith, Carine Germond, Wolfram Kaiser, Karen Heard-Laureote, Claudia Lueders, John Oates, Olivia Rutazibwa, Susana Sampaio-Dias, Anke SF, James Sloam, Aleksandra Sojka, Trond Solhaug and Annabel Tremlett.

The research phase for this book was funded by a Ph.D. studentship from Royal Holloway, University of London, and parts of it were hosted by Stockholm University. The writing phase was supported by the Jean Monnet Centre of Excellence (CESTE2) at the University of Portsmouth and the Democracy and Citizenship in Education (DACED) research group at the Norwegian University of Science and Technology.

I am grateful to the series editors, Willem Maas and Justin Gest, the reviewers and colleagues at Palgrave, Anca Pusca, Kumaravel Senbagaraj and Katelyn Zigg, for their support with this book project.

Last but not least, I would like to thank my non-academic circle of family and friends for their support and extraordinary patience. Thank you.

CONTENTS

LIST OF FIGURES

LIST OF TABLES

CHAPTER 1

Introduction: The Politics of Contemporary Citizenship: What's Going On?

In the light of heightened concern—especially among young people—with global challenges, from the climate emergency to widening income gaps, some of us might be tempted to believe that the time for a "one world community" is finally upon us. But, if we consider the only instance of a 'global community' so far—the European Union (EU)—we are likely to find a community where "all passports are equal, but *some* are more equal than others" (Castles 2005: 691, emphasis added). It is precisely this paradox which serves as the departure point for my book.

Specifically, this book investigates two related issues in the politics of contemporary citizenship. First, it examines the issue of community building processes, including differentiation and exclusion and the role assigned to and realised by citizens in the course of these processes. It is expected that these processes grant contemporary citizenship models their distinctively political function (Bosniak 2008; Isin and Nielsen 2008).

As we focus on the EU example, we notice that legal and policy discourses categorise citizens and non-citizens based on their intra-EU mobility status, country of origins and prospective economic contributions—in this order—and rather than merely on the basis of their nationality (Hansen and Hager 2010; O'Brien 2016). Accordingly, 'first-class' 'Eurostars'—the EU-15 mobiles—visiting European and international students as well as high-flying economic migrants and highly skilled third country nationals (TCNs) seem to make up the most 'desired'

© The Author(s) 2020

N. Siklodi, *The Politics of Mobile Citizenship in Europe*,
Politics of Citizenship and Migration,
https://doi.org/10.1007/978-3-030-49051-5_1

segment of a novel EU community.[1] The 'second-class' group, for now, refers to Central and Eastern European (CEE) mobiles. While desired for their potential economic contributions, they are projected as the principal members of the EU's very own 'welfare' tourist flows. These two, intra-EU mobile groups expected to interact with national and nationalist stayers and, following the refugee crisis, third class individuals; the members of a growing number of asylum seekers and refugees. If we take the first two categories as evidence of an exciting EU community emerging, the last two undoubtedly highlight the continued relevance of national communities. To explore the informal ways in which the role of citizens and non-citizens are changing in the light of these arrangements, this book investigates young peoples' experiences of their dual memberships in the budding EU (mobile) and their (home) national communities.

Second, the book turns to the addressing two models of citizenship as present in the EU today—the national and EU models. Accordingly, citizens from 28 member states (at the time of writing) are placed as part and parcel of an all-encompassing EU citizenry (at least from a formal, legal perspective), who enjoy distinct EU rights and entitlements. Under EU citizenship, these nationals are encouraged to move, study and reside freely across the EU—the ultimate confirmation of their 'fundamental' legal status as transnational citizens (Olsen 2012). In fact, EU citizenship seems to be *all about* intra-EU mobility. And EU mobile citizens *are* increasingly present. Yes, the actual number of member state nationals—'active' EU citizens—who embark on EU mobility might seem low, making up circa 3.4% of the EU's total population (Eurostat 2019a). Yet even this number is larger than the population of 20 of the EU's 28 member states and has grown exponentially, by nearly 290%, following the Eastern enlargement rounds in the mid-2000s (see Table 1.1). This number is also likely to be an underestimate, with temporary intra-EU mobility flows from cross-border shopping, holidays and seasonal work—all of which occur at a larger scale—notoriously difficult to trace (European Commission 2011).

Signalling the first time an attempt has been made to realise a political community above and beyond the nation state (Maas 2007), EU citizenship also changed the expectation that, once citizenship as status is bestowed upon an individual, it is all about senses of identity and political engagement (Bellamy 2008). Not in the case of the EU.

Table 1.1 Intra-EU mobility per host country (2003–2018)

Year/Host country	EU-25 movers		EU-27 Free movers			EU-28 Free movers	
	2003	2004	2006	2007	2013	2014	2018
1 Germany	2,329,788	2,331,984	2,144,648	2,467,157	2,693,259	3,179,670	4,205,194
2 United Kingdom	1,009,591	1,030,820	1,280,000	1,456,900	2,456,864	2,624,313	3,860,237
3 Spain	519,027	621,750	854,761	1,634,597	2,060,653	1,991,093	1,930,905
4 Italy	167,124	189,998	223,537	606,188	1,240,157	1,441,706	1,562,147
5 France	1,237,849		1,110,000	1,299,028	1,407,901	1,466,185	1,542,653
6 Belgium			612,000	632,243	807,920	826,938	902,706
7 Austria	172,497	182,124	218,746	263,174	416,022	518,670	693,855
8 Netherlands	222,942	224,285	233,867	244,918	380,540	403,028	525,626
9 Ireland				351,874	396,954	406,062	434,988
10 Sweden	206,919	206,977	213,168	225,487	281,975	289,225	318,263
11 Luxembourg			155,000	170,940	206,119	214,390	244,400
12 Czech Republic	59,122	63,298	87,144	109,866	160,626	173,279	219,350
13 Denmark		66,550	71,994	81,219	147,075	160,014	213,465
14 Greece			88,000	157,700	196,114	192,642	211,155
15 Portugal	66,672		81,000	95,556	100,930	100,595	136,887
16 Cyprus		44,800	55,000	77,900	112,587	110,871	114,536
17 Finland	32,762	34,558	37,923	42,471	76,328	83,990	98,212
18 Hungary		17,347	24,879	101,046	79,835	80,817	77,998
19 Romania					19,528	20,618	56,750
20 Slovakia		12,202	14,041	19,218	55,909	45,174	55,949
21 Malta					12,846	15,210	38,563
22 Poland	1,829			23,928	26,162	27,710	30,098
23 Slovenia		1964	2540	3006	6925	16,318	19,540
24 Estonia			5000	6700	7707	7830	18,890
25 Croatia					8662	9816	16,598

(continued)

Table 1.1 (continued)

Year/Host country	EU-25 movers			EU-27 Free movers			EU-28 Free movers	
	2003	2004	2006	2007	2013	2014	2018
26 Bulgaria					11,762	12,139	13,105
27 Latvia	3386	4407		6264	5590	6035	6192
28 Lithuania	2868	3200	3426	3491	3248	3711	6129
EU Total	6,032,376	5,036,264	7,516,674	10,080,871	13,380,198	14,428,049	17,554,391

Source Eurostat 2019a; Grey cells: data missing or non-EU member state

A growing number of empirical assessments, albeit from a European integration studies angle, has found that intra-EU mobility *is* a key factor influencing senses of national and European citizenship, notably senses of identity (especially relevant for my book in this respect are the assessments by Bruter 2005; Favell 2008; Van Mol 2014; Recchi 2015; Ross 2015, 2019). The resulting politics of *mobile citizenship in Europe* is then partly responsible for the highly contextualised and multifaceted character of citizens' attitudes and behaviour today. This is expected to be the case for contemporary youth citizenship especially, given young peoples' susceptibility to changes in their citizenship attitudes and behaviour (Sloam and Henn 2019). To explore the associated changes in senses of citizenship, this book examines the perceptions of young EU mobiles and stayers of their national and EU citizenship across three dimensions—identity, rights and participation.

This book accordingly offers a more politically embedded reading of contemporary national and EU community building processes and models of citizenship as practised in the context of heightened intra-EU mobility. The book applies the conceptual approaches advocated by scholars working in the field of citizenship studies to the empirical case of the EU. Doing so can advance our understanding of citizenship and migration politics in the EU and beyond, with some novel conceptual and empirical insights.

Specifically, the book illustrates that the majority of citizens in the EU—and beyond, with the United Kingdom (UK) on course to exit the bloc—hold varying senses of national and EU affiliations using secondary survey analysis (EB 89.1 2018) (Chapter 3). Once the issue of mobility is introduced to the equation, even the young and highly educated segment of the EU's population show varying national and EU attachments—the group expected to be ideal national *and* EU citizens, the ultimate 'winners of European integration' (Kriesi 2014; De Vreese et al. 2019).

In order to investigate contemporary notions of community building processes and senses of citizenship specifically, this book relies on original focus group evidence with young (18–30 years old) and highly educated EU mobiles and stayers in Sweden and the UK. In the course of interrogating novel community building processes as emerging along the mobile/stayer and EU citizen /TCN distinctions, it proposes revising the dichotomy of active/passive citizen categories in *both* models of national and EU citizenship (Chapter 4). Furthermore, by comparing EU mobiles' and stayers' perceptions of the dimensions of national (Chapter 5) and EU

(Chapter 6) models of citizenship—identity, rights and participation—my book offers an original empirical assessment of what these models signify today.

The rest of this introductory chapter is structured as follows.

The first part considers some of the key citizenship and learning mobility developments in the EU, with a specific focus on the UK and Sweden—the cases selected to illuminate some of the likely implications long-standing national similarities and differences likely to have *within* a 'global community'. The second introduces relevant theoretical approaches from citizenship and EU studies prisms, while the third touches upon the key research questions and the methods adopted to studying the issue of mobile citizenship. The final part offers an overview of the key themes across the chapters from the rest of this book.

1.1   A Snapshot of What Is and Isn't Going on with Citizenship in the EU

The European project was initially launched through popular notions of a 'permissive consensus' in the 1950s; an abstaining but consenting public (Lindberg and Scheingold 1970: 277). Yet, recent years have clearly marked the arrival of a 'constraining dissensus'; an increasingly engaged and sceptical public (Hooghe and Marks 2009), especially where the issue of 'an ever-closer Union among the peoples of Europe' is concerned. And so, while EU actors retained their objective of turning a chiefly economic project into a political one (recently in von der Leyen 2019), growing popular discontent has ensured the slowing down of the European integration project. The latter has even gone as far as to deliver the most glaring example of 'European disintegration'—'Brexit'.

These developments may force us to gloss over the EU's achievements and instead focus on its failures—not least in the realm of its citizenship and migration policies.

Traditionally indicating a locus of contestation (cf. Bauböck 1994; Castles and Davidson 2000; Isin 2009), the nexus between citizenship and migration has become 'complementary' through the introduction of EU (or European) citizenship in the 1993 Maastricht Treaty (Declaration 2 and Article 8, Treaty on European Union [TEU] 1993). EU citizenship not only marks the earliest—and to date the *only*—example of transnational citizenship model but also the first *genuine* attempt at establishing a transnational political community and transnational democracy (Checkel and Katzenstein 2009; Bauböck 2019). Furthermore, EU citizenship is unique in its reliance on cross-border migration specifically. Derived from the EU's long-standing free movement provisions, its institutional framework *only* extends the scope of member state status through the intra-EU mobility of citizens (Maas 2020).

This point has been reinforced in every EU treaty so far, placing citizens' EU mobility at the heart of EU citizenship and *prior to* their EU-level political participation (most recently in Article 20 of the Lisbon Treaty (Treaty on the Functioning of the Union, [TFEU]). Even more, until recently, EU treaties made no mention of the rights of EU stayers.[2] Instead, they have only expanded and defined the rights enjoyed by EU mobiles. Moreover, official EU discourses equate intra-EU mobility with *active* EU citizenship (Siklodi 2015). EU mobility facilitates citizens' exercising of EU rights, including non-discrimination on the basis of nationality as well as some of their political rights, including the right to vote in the EU and the municipal elections at the country of their residence (Guild et al. 2014).

Importantly however, intra-EU mobility also facilitates the redefining of national models of citizenship in Europe. EU mobiles do this *formally*, via participating in EU, national and local politics whilst staying abroad (Recchi 2015: 105–122). They also do so through less formal channels of participation, e.g. increased presence in the socio-economic life of local sending and host communities (Favell 2010) or by taking up membership in or engaging across *informal* networks, including an emerging EU-wide community (Van Mol 2014: 66–90).

Such developments challenge the popular belief that citizenship can only function within nation states, or that the granting of citizenship *must* be made on the basis of birth right or a fixed residency status (Turner and Khondker 2010). In fact, popular beliefs on citizenship and migration are under increased pressure due to the *mere* presence of the EU mobile citizen. The latter often dominates news and political headlines across the EU's member states. Most notable among these is the 'politicisation' of the free movement of CEE citizens following the 2004 enlargement (McMahon 2015). The difficulty states have faced in implementing the EU's equal treatment provisions when EU mobiles' access to non-contributory welfare provisions are concerned is also noteworthy (Schmidt et al. 2018).

These issues have affected EU nationals' attitudes to national and EU politics considerably. The large majority of stayers—the non-mobile, 'passive' EU citizens whose first reference point remains squarely within the confines of the nation state (Duchesne et al. 2013; Van Ingelgom 2014)—are far removed from EU debates. They have felt increasingly 'forgotten' and 'overlooked' by some members of the political elite (Clarke et al. 2017). Infused with nationalist and antagonistic ideals, their sentiments served as a fertile ground for populist ideas to flourish. Indeed, the appeal of the latter has been so extensive that, by 2018, one in four Europeans had already cast *at least one* vote for populist politicians (Lewis et al. 2018).

Although EU mobiles and external migrants have been easy scapegoats, the actual level of migration has not been as enormous as the hype in support for anti-migrant, populist politics would have us believe. To illustrate this issue, Table 1.1 summarises the level of intra-EU mobility since 2003.

Specifically, Table 1.1 shows the number of EU mobiles resident semi-permanently in a host EU state in three key points in time between 2003 and 2018, namely around the EU's most recent and most contested enlargement rounds (cf. Moravcsik and Vachudova 2003). The countries are ordered according to the number of EU mobiles each country hosted in 2018—the most recent available data.

According to these figures, 17.5 million EU mobiles live in a host country—from a pool of just under 513 million (Eurostat 2019a). In the context of long-standing EU provisions on free movement (Maas 2007), the EU mobile segment is extremely small. However, Table 1.1 also reveals that there was in fact a steady and substantial increase in the number of free movers. Despite the economic, financial and migration crises, as well as the accompanying growing hostility and restrictive integration policies towards, mainly CEE mobiles, their total number increased threefold in the 15-year period. It is not surprising that most CEE countries are at the bottom of the list, while EU-15 countries are at the upper half of the table, with the Czech Republic serving as a notable exception. There is also a striking difference in the number of EU mobiles hosted by the 'big five' EU countries—Germany, the UK, Spain, Italy and France. They not only rank 1st to 5th at the top of the table, but host almost three-quarter of *all* EU mobiles.[3]

The numbers and ranking of Sweden and the UK, where the focus groups were conducted for this study—and the context of which will be used as indications of host country context impact—are highlighted in the table. These countries were originally selected as case studies because of their initial willingness to allow free movement from CEE states after the 2004 'big bang' enlargement. Their subsequent contradictory approaches towards EU mobiles are indicative of the ever-changing state of *internal* European politics.[4] Indeed, by 2007, Sweden was the only EU-15 country with an open border policy. Therefore, Sweden is the only EU-15 state where *all* EU citizens can and have been able to exercise their EU citizenship rights without any *formal* restrictions.

According to Table 1.1, both countries have seen a gradual growth in their EU mobile population and, by 2018, the UK ranked 2nd and Sweden 10th as host states. While they seem relatively close in their ranking, there has been a substantial difference in their overall number of EU mobiles—a gap that has only expanded over time. Sweden started off 2004 with just under 207,000 EU-25 (EU-15+EU-10) mobiles. Even with the larger, EU-27 pool, this number grew to just under 290,000 in ten years. Nonetheless, due to its open border policy, Sweden has seen some growth in the number of new EU mobile year-on-year arrivals, from 16,500 in 2004 to 29,000 in 2017 (Eurostat 2019a). By contrast, the UK already had over a million EU mobiles, almost five times that of Sweden, in 2004. By 2018, this number reached over 3.8 million peoples. This figure is *ten times* that of Sweden for the same year (at 318,000). In fact, EU mobiles now represent nearly six per cent of the UK's total population. While their year-on-year estimates decreased after the Brexit referendum, the previous 15 years saw a quadrupled growth in year-on-year arrivals to the UK (from 65,000 in 2004 along and to 230,000 in 2018) (Migration Watch UK 2019).

Of course, the actual number of EU citizens who have had some opportunity to enjoy EU free movement is likely to be much higher than Table 1.1 indicates, after all it does not reflect upon short-term intra-EU mobility. Some estimates suggest that this figure is considerably higher—and had already included at least 20% of the EU's total population ten years ago (European Commission 2011). Nonetheless, given the differentiated approach to further integration EU actors decided to adopt (von der Leyen 2019), member state differences are set to remain for the foreseeable future. Previous academic studies have underscored just how important these contexts can be for aggravated senses of citizenship (Heath et al. 2019), including senses of youth citizenship specifically (Motti-Stefanidi and Cicognani 2018).

The focus groups will be able to complement these ongoing conversations by providing an indication of whether and to what extent the ideal segment of the EU's citizenry is affected by such variations. The evidence will also be indicative of whether and how such contexts shape young citizens' perceptions of the "other", the non-EU citizens. Accordingly, UK focus groups are expected to demonstrate the *negative* impact host country contexts can have for young citizens' senses of EU citizenship and the *positive* impact country contexts might carry for citizens' senses of nationality. By comparison, the Swedish case is expected to show the *positive* impact for EU citizenship and *negative* impact for senses of nationality country contexts are likely to offer.

I am not suggesting that the surge in pro-nationalist policies across the EU did not weaken the pro-nationalists positions in Sweden (Halikiopoulou 2018). Contrary to what idealised discourses on 'Swedish exceptionalism' would have us believe (Schierup and Ålund 2011), Sweden has been no exception when recent changes in EU attitudes are traced against the backdrop of the EU's economic and refugee crises (Elgenius and Rydgren 2017). Their adverse impact is perhaps most obvious in the rising vote for the right-wing, populist and anti-immigration Sweden Democrats (SD) party. The share of 5.7% facilitated the SD entering the *Riksdag* in 2010 for the first time. By 2014, the party more than doubled its votes to 12.9% and, by 2018, its vote increased to 17.6% (SCB 2019a).

The SD's presence in the highest levels of Swedish policy making has had significant repercussions. It brought about "a jolt of unprecedented magnitude" for the Swedish political system and party setup (Neuding 2018), and for the country's international reputation as a 'safe place' for immigrants (Brown 2018). Even attitudes towards migrants have seen a marked shift to the right of the political spectrum after 2015 (Ericsson 2018). For instance, making his case for the re-introduction of internal border controls and the turning away of all refugees with Syrian passports, the centre-left Prime Minister, Stefan Löfven, recently described the country's previously progressive approach to immigration as 'naïve'. With processes of exclusion informing official procedures *and* unofficial discourses (Norman 2018), a United Nations (UN) official likened Swedish developments to the fall of "the last bastion of humanitarianism" in Europe (Crouch 2015).

While similar trends have not quite taken hold of the UK's migration politics (Blinder 2015), the country is perhaps more often noticed for its negative approach towards the EU and EU mobiles specifically—and especially in the course of 'Brexit'. Accordingly, its 2016 EU referendum vote triggered the first formal process of a member state exiting the bloc. The country's subsequent journey has been anything but smooth. Indeed, the Brexit vote paved the way for a series of political 'firsts' in the UK—and by a group of citizens whose natural disposition has been to refrain from any 'revolutionary' acts (English 2019).

Bottom-up, pro- and anti-EU campaigns and debates in on- and offline spaces absorbed large sections of society (Mindus 2017). For example, the anti-Brexit campaign has cumulated in the country's largest ever peaceful protest, calling for a second EU referendum, a so-called People's Vote. Despite these extensive pro-EU and anti-Brexit mobilisations however, the most recent 'snap' elections delivered two pro-Brexit Conservative governments, confirming continued English support for leaving rather than remaining in the EU, with the process set to be completed by the end of 2020 (BBC 2019). Although the impending changes to the UK's relationship with the EU have repeatedly caught commentators by surprise, from a historical perspective these developments may seem quite predictable.

A sceptical and often misinformed British public has ensured that the UK sat as a self-proclaimed 'outlier' in Europe after World War II and even after its 'formal' accession to the EU block in 1973 (Todd 2016). Any subsequent pro-EU position by its political elite was articulated in terms of the economic benefits of the country's EU membership and was coupled with relentless demands for EU reforms (Hertner and Keith 2017). These characteristics have also shaped the official 'Remain' campaign (Siklodi 2019a). While some softening in public reactions to the inflow of EU mobiles became perceptible after the implications of the referendum had sunk in, everyday discourses remained largely antagonistic (Blinder and Richards 2018). Against this backdrop, the experiences of EU residents in Brexit Britain has been marred by hostility and racism (Duda-Mikulin 2019). Brexit developments have also been important for broader considerations of citizenship and migration politics in the EU (Siklodi 2019b). Specifically, they mark the first time 'the right to have rights' and the right to have membership in the EU's community have been formulated from the bottom up (Brändle et al. 2018). Besides, despite some fears of a domino effect emerging in the wake of the Brexit vote (e.g. Hix and Sitter 2018), no other EU state has expressed an interest in following suit.

Quite the opposite. Brexit was a 'non-issue' in the post-2016 general elections in other EU states (van Kessel 2017), bar Ireland, for obvious reasons. Even more to the point, "love" for the EU appears to dominate public and even some populist discourses in other EU countries (Heath 2018), and support for the EU project has hit a 35-year high (European Parliament 2018). EU and national models of citizenship are thus likely be the reality rather than a phase in the vast majority of European citizens' lives outside the UK, at least.

Nonetheless, the EU public has, for years, been concerned about the political direction European integration has taken elsewhere too and, more recently, have become especially preoccupied about the socio-economic and political costs of heightened immigration and intra-EU mobility flows (European Commission 2018: 4). EU-led attempts to reduce public concern with these issues have mostly failed (Kramer et al. 2018; Eder 2019). This of course explains why some national responses have taken a markedly populist turn.

Perhaps the only area that has not really been affected by the resulting contradictory dynamics of today's European politics is intra-EU learning mobility.

Despite the fact that member states continue to retain competency in educational policies, the EU has dominated broader political discourses and, ultimately, shaped educational policies. The introduction of the Bologna process, especially, institutionalised the cycle system (from undergraduate to postgraduate transitions) and standardised quality assurance and recognition of qualifications across the member states of the European Higher Education Area (EHEA)—reaching beyond the EU's somewhat superficial borders (European Commission/EACEA/Eurydice 2018). Such structural changes have gone hand-in-hand with the EU's citizenship provisions. Together, these policies ensure that EU students wishing to complete a university degree in another EU country can do so on the same conditions as home students do (European Commission 2019b). In this context nearly 38% of all visiting students in the EU—1.7 million—came from another EU state during the 2017/18 academic year (Eurostat 2019b). The largest share, over 25.5%, studied in the UK. Of these numbers, approximately 143,000 were new EU students in 2017/18 (UKCISA 2019). The number of new EU students in Sweden for the same year stood at 11,400 (SCB 2019b).

Besides, a distinctive and much-celebrated programme of higher education student and institutional exchanges was also introduced under the umbrella of the European Community Action Scheme for the

Mobility of University Students (Erasmus) in 1987 (Keeling 2006). Facilitating the mobility of nearly four million students, the programme is showing no signs of slowing down (European Commission 2019a). Even more, as the EU's flagship higher education programme, the Erasmus budget has been doubled (from €15 to €30 billion) with the specific aim of tripling the current number of Erasmus students by 2027 (European Commission 2019a).

The anticipated returns of the EU's 'pedagogic approach' to citizenship, *enhancing* senses of EU citizenship, has also been articulated.

> European citizenship refers to a European identity, fuelled by a common history and common customs, and jointly constituting the European Union as a political entity... Erasmus wishes to further the underlying ideas of European citizenship... [since] [o]ne of the core strategic interests of mobility in Europe *is* the promotion of a European identity. (European Commission 2014: 33, 183, emphasis added)

There is some evidence to support the EU's 'pedagogic approach' to EU citizenship (Mitchell 2012; Mazzoni et al. 2018). However, there has also been plenty of evidence which questions the significant relationship between EU learning mobility—usually Erasmus—and EU citizenship (Sigalas 2010; Wilson 2011; Kuhn 2012; Van Mol 2014).

The resulting disparity between the expectations of EU citizens and national and EU actors makes addressing national and EU communities and models of citizenship as present in the context of intra-EU (learning) mobility urgent *and* timely. The next section introduces the conceptual framework with which the remainder of this book will investigate these issues.

1.2 A 'More Inclusive' Approach to National and EU Communities and Citizenships

Against the backdrop of recent developments, this book explores how contemporary political communities and citizenship are realised in the EU. Specifically, it focuses on young citizens' notions of national and EU communities and senses of national and EU citizenships in the context of intra-EU mobility and in the broader trends of European political integration. In order to provide a comprehensive assessment of senses of contemporary citizenship, the conceptual framework of this book draws upon the broader field of citizenship studies (Heater 2004; Magnette 2005; Isin and Turner 2007; Bellamy 2008; Bosniak 2008; Isin and Saward 2013; Isin and Nyers 2014; Mackert and Turner 2017).

According to scholars in this field, citizenship can be broadly defined as the dynamic bond between a sovereign political community and the individual and it has a key function in shaping community-building processes, including processes of differentiation and exclusion. The dichotomy of active/passive citizens has, traditionally, emerged from resulting considerations about how processes of differentiation affects popular attitudes and behaviour (Turner 1997). At the same time, the "other" of political communities is defined and reinforced in the course of processes of exclusion (Bauböck 1994: 23).

It is also generally accepted by scholars that models of citizenship entail three interlinked and collective dimensions—identity, rights and participation. These dimensions define the significance of each model. As such, they are anticipated to be central to contemporary models in the EU also.

Yet, they have hardly ever been addressed concurrently.

In fact, the extant literature on national and EU models of citizenship have mostly dealt with these models separately from one another (see section on 'Europes' in Isin and Nyers 2014: 407–486 as a typical example). The various normative, institutional and empirical frameworks of EU citizenship are also often examined in isolation—and usually from and EU studies and European integration perspective (Kostakopoulou 2001; Maas 2007; Bauböck 2019). In terms of the dimensions of citizenship, inclusive assessments are provided where national models are under scrutiny (e.g. by Mackert and Turner 2017). Yet, when the dimensions of EU citizenship are addressed, they are done so, once again, disjointedly (with Recchi [2015], Favell [2008, 2010], Sanders et al. [2012] notable exceptions). As a result, we have a fragmented and partial portrait about the concurrent significance of national and EU communities and models of citizenship.

By addressing national and EU models simultaneously and their dimensions concurrently, we can make significant contrition to the ongoing discussion initiated by the aforementioned scholars. To this end, I view EU citizenship as *another* model in the long list of citizenship models which have emerged across diverse historical and political contexts (Heater 2004 provides a useful review). This issue is expected to become especially apparent if and when the relevance of national and EU models

is accepted from the outset. After all, both models exist and are acknowledged and even practised by citizens in the EU on a daily basis—an issue
regularly documented by EU surveys.

A central argument of this book is that by applying the conceptual
framework of citizenship as derived from the field of citizenship studies
(shown in Table 1.1) to the case of the EU, a more comprehensive study
of contemporary community building processes and models of citizenship can be achieved. In this vein, academics, national politicians and
EU officials may wish to pay more attention to how the models of
national and EU citizenship *and* their dimensions manifest together in
their attempts to really address some of the recent tensions in European politics—be it in response to the economic and migration crises,
the slowing down of European political integration in the face of Brexit
and broader globalisation challenges such as the climate emergency.

1.3   Methodological Considerations

In order to contribute to the ongoing discussion on contemporary
community building and citizenship in Europe, this book adopts a mixed-
method approach to research (Bryman 2016: 643–652) and complements
its secondary analysis of recent EU-wide survey data (EB 89.1 2018) with
original focus group evidence from Sweden and the UK. The survey analysis depicts the likely changes in the interlinked dimensions of national
and EU models of citizenship, respectively, and related changes following
the introduction of intra-EU mobility and individual socio-economic
factors, especially age and educational level. These findings are explored
in more detail with the use of original focus group evidence, investigating novel community building processes and senses of national and
EU models of citizenship among the young and highly educated—and
actually mobile—citizens in more depth. To this end, I moderated ten
focus groups, eight with EU mobiles and two with stayers, in Sweden
and the UK between May 2012 and March 2013—at the height of the
economic crisis (a research note about methods is included in Appendix
1 at the end of the book).

Since the focus groups are exploratory and qualitative in character
(Morgan 1998), they have a somewhat limited scope to making gener-
alisations about broader senses of citizenship in the EU or specifically
about the intra-EU learning mobility-citizenship nexus. Considering that
public attitudes towards mobility and migration in the EU are still,

largely, studied from the perspective of EU stayers (with Recchi and Favell [2009] as notable exceptions), a qualitative interrogation is considered timely and important. Indeed, they are expected to shed new light on the likely impact intra-EU mobility has on the segment of EU nationals who are most susceptible to changes in their citizenship perceptions. The focus groups also allow for contradictory evidence to emerge—EU mobiles at Swedish and UK universities may exhibit a range of pro-nationalist and non-cosmopolitan or anti-EU citizenship attitudes and behavioural tendencies which survey data is, simply, not equipped to capture. Contemporary processes of community building are one such example.

This book seeks to complement the ongoing conversation in citizenship and EU studies and to develop a politically embedded, concurrent approach to contemporary citizenship—national and EU models—in the EU. Although existing qualitative research on young citizens' senses of EU citizenship recognises the importance of EU mobility, they have only investigated the perceptions of EU mobiles *or* stayers so far (Bruter 2005; Favell 2008; Ross 2015, 2019). While others made an attempt to draw on different types of data to reflect upon the perception of stayers and mobiles (Favell and Recchi 2011; Van Mol 2014; Recchi 2015), they largely followed an EU studies approach.

To compliment these works, this book offers novel empirical insights into how intra-EU learning mobility shapes mobiles and stayers' senses of community belonging and notions of citizenship. Examining the perceptions of young and highly educated segment of EU nationals, the supposed 'ideal' EU citizens, the book offers new evidence about the internal characteristics of what the Pangloss 'global community' *ought to*, though probably do not look like. Nonetheless, it cannot reach any conclusions about whether and how senses of national and EU models of citizenship change for those citizens who were originally targeted by the EU—the intra-EU *labour* mobiles (Maas 2007). Since young citizens determine what the future of national and EU models of citizenship hold, their perceptions warrant dedicated academic investigation.

1.4   OUTLINE OF THE BOOK

This book is organised around five substantive chapters, using a mix of quantitative and qualitative data in order to explore individual senses of national and EU communities and models of citizenship in the context of intra-EU (learning) mobility.

The book is structured as follows.

Chapter 2 sets the scene for concurrently addressing national and EU models of contemporary citizenship. First, to re-embed the study of national and EU citizenship following the agenda set by scholars working in the broader field of citizenship studies, the chapter draws attention to debates, which played out across diverse historical and political contexts, and the extent to which these debates accord with current institutional frameworks and norms in Sweden, the UK and the EU comparatively. Second, considering the structural dependence of EU citizenship on intra-EU mobility, the chapter underscores that there are important distinctions emerging in senses of citizenship along the mobile/stayer divide in the EU. It argues that the longevity of this divide is ensured by the EU's ever-expanding learning programmes. The chapter then provides an indication of how the dimensions of citizenship—identity, rights and participation—can be analysed in empirical terms.

Chapter 3 is a first attempt made in this book to genuinely re-embed the study of contemporary models of citizenship in the EU in the broader field of citizenship studies using empirical evidence. Secondary analysis of Eurobarometer data (EB 89.1 2018) demonstrates current national and EU attitudes along the key dimensions of citizenship. The chapter draws out the similarities and differences in senses of identity, awareness of EU rights and citizens' self-described 'voice' in national and EU politics that are apparent across the EU. Controls for migration experiences and attitudes as well as socio-economic factors, especially age and education level, are then used to explain some of the emerging disparities.

Chapter 4 addresses more closely one of the key topics of the book—community building processes in the EU, including processes of differentiation between EU nationals and processes of exclusion affecting member states' and the EU's "other". Each process is investigated in the light of their apparent impact on the dimensions of citizenship. The chapter accentuates changes in contemporary community building processes, along the mobile/stayer distinctions. Further divisions also appear to emerge on the basis of *perceived* cultural and religious and generational divides, as well as the East/West and South/North divides. The latter was especially highlighted by the then ongoing economic crisis. By comparison, processes of exclusion were often found to be blurred in the context of the EU's own, globalised higher education arena. These processes were nonetheless also deemed to be relevant, but along structural lines defined by national and EU laws. Yet, by prescribing the dimensions of their own citizenship in view of mobility experiences, the evidence presented in this chapter makes a strong case for redefining the active/passive national *and* EU citizen categories along the mobile/stayer dichotomy.

In order to illustrate the resulting effects of EU mobility on senses of national and EU citizenship among mobiles/stayers, Chapters 5 and 6 explore the dimensions of these models specifically.

First, Chapter 5 emphasises that EU mobility can and does transform the perceptions of young citizens about their national citizenship. Most importantly, it reinforces the significance of the national frames for the understanding of citizenship, broadly, and, especially, for citizenship as rights, senses of identity and engagement in politics for EU mobiles. Even more, their everyday practices, ranging from access to welfare provisions (e.g. university registration schemes and health provisions) to more basic and even mundane issues (e.g. opening a bank account or shopping online) were found to be shaped national structures. An EU-initiated policy agenda was only ever expected to emerge when some of the structural inequalities of the EU's 'market structures' are tackled. By comparison, stayers took it for granted that local and national policies dominated their daily lives, transposing this knowledge to make sense of EU politics in the one-off cases it was deemed as relevant—only when pressed about their abstention from EU participation.

Chapter 6 provides a close empirical study of senses of EU citizenship. It illustrates that the majority of EU mobiles who participated in the focus groups assumed that they share a bond with the EU as members of its *small* mobile elite. EU mobiles are presented as more likely to "feel European" than stayers. Indeed, for the latter any EU affiliation from senses of identity, to EU rights and participation were *always* seen as inferior to national and even local attachments. This is largely because EU mobility was identified as the basis on which a model of EU citizenship *might* materialise.

However, all groups, including EU mobiles and stayers framed the current EU model as inherently exclusive, fragmented and temporary. EU citizenship is only anticipated to be relevant to a small group of potential citizens who can already afford to move. Even then, it is only expected to prevail *whilst* they were on the move and lose its significance once they settled in the host country or returned home. Furthermore, mobility either within the heart of the EU's 'most integrated' region *or* towards particularly Eurosceptic national contexts were seen as further precondi-tions for EU citizenship to truly transpire. In all other cases, intra-EU mobility was found to accentuate the continued relevance of national distinctions, while extra EU migration emphasised *European* affinities. Hence, a fully developed model of EU citizenship does not exist—at least not yet. While participants in Sweden were slightly more hopeful about the potential of EU citizenship as "something for the future", UK participants dismissed the likelihood of it ever existing.

Chapter 7 provides an overall assessment of contemporary politics of mobile citizenship in Europe. It pays particular attention to some of the more nuanced findings of the study presented in this book. Specifically, it reinforces the benefits of adopting a citizenship studies approach to addressing contemporary practices in the EU, and its implications for genuinely reflecting upon the active/passive citizen dichotomy along the stayer/mobile distinctions. Furthermore, the chapter argues that there are some important lessons for policymakers and scholars who might wish to 'keep up' with the developments in citizenship and migration politics in an 'age of globalisation.'

For transnational actors, it might be beneficial to support mobility programmes for educational purposes and stress novel community-building processes on the basis of mobility status and personal attributes, such as education and nationality. By the same token, the pressure on nation state democracies is bound to grow. After all, it is the affluent segment of younger generations—the well-off and highly skilled—who tend to be the most encouraged and most likely to move. Such oppor-tunities are likely to turn the members of this group into "passive" national citizens, uprooted from national communities. Both develop-ments, in turn, provide exciting new research opportunities for interested academics.

NOTES

1. EU-15 member states are Austria, Belgium, Denmark, Finland, France, Germany, Greece, Ireland, Italy, Luxembourg, The Netherlands, Portugal, Spain, Sweden and the UK—that is until the end of January 2020. Malta and Cyprus became full EU members in 2004. CEE member states joined the EU in 2004. They include EU8 countries: Czech Republic, Estonia, Hungary, Latvia, Lithuania, Slovakia, Slovenia and Poland. The so-called

EU2 states, Bulgaria and Romania, joined in 2007. Finally, Croatia joined in 2013.
2. The Citizens' Initiative (CI) was introduced in Article 24 of TFEU in 2009. However, its impact has been marginal at best (cf. Conrad et al. 2016).
3. As a point of comparative reference, the number of TCNs residing in the EU stood at 22.3 million at the start of 2018—marking an increase of around one per cent overall for the 15-year period analysed in Table 1.1 (Eurostat 2019a). However, the concentration of TCNs in the big five EU-15 countries would have been much more noticeable than that of EU mobiles. Accordingly, Germany has had nearly 5.5 million, Italy 3.6 million, France 3.1 million, Spain 2.6 million and the UK 2.4 million TCNs in their territory in 2018. Added together, nearly as many TCNs were hosted by these five countries as the entirety of the EU's own mobile citizenry.
4. The EU rights of students are not restricted by transitional measures. However, students can only really enjoy the same rights as stayers once any restriction on their residence is also lifted (e.g. access to employment and health care).

REFERENCES

Bauböck, R. (1994). *Transnational Citizenship: Membership and Rights in International Migration*. Cheltenham: Edward Elgar Publishing.
Bauböck, R. (Ed.). (2019). *Debating European Citizenship*. Cham Switzerland: Springer Open.
BBC. (2019). *UK Elections 2019*. https://www.google.com/search?q=bbc+uk+election&rlz=1C5CHFA_enNO866NO866&oq=bbc+uk+election&aqs=chrome.0.0l8.4249j0j4&sourceid=chrome&ie=UTF-8.
Bellamy, R. (2008). *Citizenship: A Very Short Introduction*. Oxford: Oxford University Press.
Blinder, S. (2015). Imagined immigration: The impact of different meanings of 'Immigrants' in public opinion and policy debates in Britain. *Political Studies, 63*(1), 80–100.
Blinder, S., & Richards, L. (2018). UK public opinion toward immigration: Overall attitudes and level of concern. *Migration Observatory*. https://migrationobservatory.ox.ac.uk/resources/briefings/uk-public-opinion-toward-immigration-overall-attitudes-and-level-of-concern/#kp1.
Bosniak, L. (2008). *The citizen and the Alien: Dilemmas of Contemporary Membership*. Princeton: Princeton University Press.
Brändle, V. K., Galpin, C., & Trenz, H. J. (2018). Marching for Europe? Enacting European citizenship as justice during Brexit. *Citizenship Studies, 22*(8), 810–828. https://doi.org/10.1080/13621025.2018.1531825.

Brown, S. (2018). Sweden's election results: The view from across Europe. *LSE Europp: European politics and policy blog*. https://blogs.lse.ac.uk/europp blog/2018/09/10/swedens-election-results-the-view-from-across-europe/# Author.

Bruter, M. (2005). *Citizens of Europe? The Emergence of a Mass European Identity*. London: Palgrave Macmillan.

Bryman, A. (2016). *Social Research Methods* (5th ed.). Oxford: Oxford University Press.

Castles, S. (2005). Hierarchical citizenship in a world of unequal nation-states. *PS: Political Science & Politics, 38*(4), 689–692.

Castles, S., & Davidson, A. (2000). *Citizenship and Migration: Globalization and the Politics of Belonging*. Abingdon, UK: Routledge.

Checkel, J. T., & Katzenstein, P. (Eds.). (2009). *European Identity*. Cambridge, UK: Cambridge University Press.

Clarke, H. D., Goodwin, M., & Whiteley, P. (2017). *Brexit: Why Britain Voted to Leave the European Union*. Cambridge, UK: Cambridge University Press.

Conrad, M., Knaut, A., & Böttger, K. (Eds.). (2016). *Bridging the gap? Opportunities and Constraints of the European Citizens' Initiative*. Baden-Baden: Nomos Verlagsgesellschaft.

Crouch, D. (2015). Sweden slams shut its open-door policy towards refugees. *The Guardian*. https://www.theguardian.com/world/2015/nov/24/sweden-asylum-seekers-refugees-policy-reversal.

De Vreese, C. H., Azrout, R., & Boomgaarden, H. G. (2019). One size fits all? Testing the dimensional structure of EU attitudes in 21 countries. *International Journal of Public Opinion Research, 31*(2), 195–219. https://doi.org/10.1093/ijpor/edy003.

Duchesne, S., Frazer, E., Haegel, F., & Van Ingelgom, V. (Eds.). (2013). *Citizens' Reactions to European Integration Compared: Overlooking Europe*. London: Palgrave.

Duda-Mikulin, E. A. (2019). *EU Migrant Workers, Brexit and Precarity: Polish Women's Perspectives from Inside the UK*. London: Policy Press.

Eder, F. (2019). POLITICO Brussels Playbook: Parliament is closed—RIP asylum reforms—How to fight the Red Elephant. *Politico.eu*. https://www.politico.eu/newsletter/brussels-playbook/politico-brussels-playbook-parliament-says-no-asylum-reforms-are-dead/.

Elgenius, G., & Rydgren, J. (2017). The Sweden democrats and the ethno-nationalist rhetoric of decay and betrayal. *Sociologisk Forskning, 54*(4), 353–358.

English, O. (2019). How Brexit will save Britain. *Politico.EU*. https://www.politico.eu/article/brexit-uk-eu-referendum-just-what-britain-needs/.

Ericsson, M. (2018). "Sweden has been naïve": Nationalism, protectionism and securitisation in response to the refugee crisis of 2015. *Social Inclusion, 6*(4), 95–102. http://dx.doi.org/10.17645/si.v6i4.1512.

European Commission. (2011, April). *Special Eurobarometer, 346: New Europeans*.

European Commission. (2014). The European union support for student and staff exchanges and university cooperation in 2012–2013. *Erasmus Facts, Figures and Trends*. http://ec.europa.eu/education/library/statistics/ay-12-13/facts-figures_en.pdf.

European Commission. (2018, Spring). *Standard Eurobarometer 89: Public Opinion in the European Union*.

European Commission. (2019a). *Erasmus+: Another record year in 2017*. http://europa.eu/rapid/press-release_IP-19–601_en.htm.

European Commission. (2019b). *The Bologna process and the European higher education area*. https://ec.europa.eu/education/policies/higher-education/bologna-process-and-european-higher-education-area_en.

European Parliament. (2018). *Eurobarometer survey shows highest support for the EU in 35 years*. http://www.europarl.europa.eu/news/en/headlines/eu-affairs/20180522STO04020/eurobarometer-survey-highest-support-for-the-eu-in-35-years.

Eurostat. (2019a). *Migration and migrant population statistics*. https://ec.eur opa.eu/eurostat/statistics-explained/index.php/Migration_and_migrant_p opulation_statistics.

Eurostat. (2019b). *Learning mobility statistics*. https://ec.europa.eu/eurostat/statistics-explained/index.php/Learning_mobility_statistics#Number_and_share_of_students_from_abroad.

Favell, A. (2008). *Eurostars and Eurocities: Free Movement and Mobility in an Integrating Europe*. Oxford: Blackwell.

Favell, A. (2010). European identity and European citizenship in three "Eurocities": A sociological approach to the European Union. *Politique Européenne, 30*, 187–224.

Favell, A., & Recchi, E. (2011). Social mobility and spatial mobility. In A. Favell & V. Guiraudon (Eds.), *Sociology of the European Union* (pp. 50–75). London: Palgrave Macmillan.

Guild, E., Rotaeche, C. G., & Kostakopoulou, D. (Eds.). (2014). *The reconceptualization of European union citizenship*. Nijhoff: Brill. https://doi.org/10.1163/9789004251526.

Halikiopoulou, D. (2018). A right-wing populist momentum? A review of 2017 elections across Europe. *Journal of Common Market Studies, 56*(S1), 63–73. https://doi.org/10.1111/jcms.12769.

Hansen, P., & Hager, S. B. (2010). *The Politics of European Citizenship: Deepening Contradictions in Social Rights and Migration Policy*. New York: Berghahn Books.

Heater, D. (2004). *Citizenship: The Civic Ideal in World History, Politics and Education*. Manchester: Manchester University Press.

Heath, A., Davidov, E., Ford, R., Green, E. G., Ramos, A., & Schmidt, P. (2019). Contested terrain: Explaining divergent patterns of public opinion towards immigration within Europe. *Journal of Ethnic and Migration Studies*. https://doi.org/10.1080/1369183X.2019.1550145.

Heath, R. (2018). Europeans love the EU (and populists too): Levels of support for the EU have gone up in 26 of the bloc's 28 member countries, new survey finds. *Politico.EU*. https://www.politico.eu/article/europe ans-love-the-eu-and-populists-too/.

Hertner, I., & Keith, D. (2017). Europhiles or eurosceptics? Comparing the European policies of the labour party and the liberal democrats. *British Politics, 12*(1), 63–89.

Hix, S., & Sitter, N. (2018). Svexit or Huxit? How another country could follow the UK out of the EU. *LSE Brexit Blog*. https://blogs.lse.ac.uk/bre xit/2018/01/30/svexit-or-huxit-how-another-country-could-follow-the-uk-out-of-the-eu/.

Hooghe, L., & Marks, G. (2009). A postfunctionalist theory of European integration: From permissive consensus to constraining dissensus. *British Journal of Political Science, 39*(1), 1–23.

Isin, E. F., & Turner, B. S. (2007). Investigating citizenship: An agenda for citizenship studies. *Citizenship Studies, 11*(1), 5–17.

Isin, E. F. (2009). Citizenship in flux: The figure of the activist citizen. *Subjectivity, 29*(1), 367–388.

Isin, E. F., & Nyers, P. (Eds.). (2014). Introduction: Globalizing citizenship studies. In *Routledge Handbook of Global Citizenship Studies*. Abingdon: Routledge.

Isin, E. F., & Saward, M. (Eds.). (2013). *Enacting European Citizenship*. Cambridge, UK: Cambridge University Press.

Isin, E. F., & Nielsen, G. M. (Eds.). (2008). *Acts of Citizenship*. London: Zed Books.

Keeling, R. (2006). The Bologna process and the Lisbon research agenda: The European commission's expanding role in higher education discourse. *European Journal of Education, 41*(2), 203–223.

Kostakopoulou, D. (2001). *Citizenship, Identity, and Immigration in the European Union: Between Past and Future*. Manchester: Manchester University Press.

Kramer, D., Thierry, J. S., & van Hooren, F. (2018). Responding to free movement: Quarantining mobile union citizens in European welfare states. *Journal of European Public Policy, 25*(1), 1501–1521. https://doi.org/10.1080/135 01763.2018.1488882.

Kriesi, H. (2014). The populist challenge. *West European Politics, 37*(2), 361–378.

Kuhn, T. (2012). Why educational exchange programmes miss their mark: Cross-border mobility, education and European identity. *Journal of Common Market Studies, 50*(6), 994–1010.

Lewis, P., Clarke, S., Barr, C., Holder, J., & Kommenda, N. (2018). Revealed: one in four Europeans vote populist: Exclusive research shows how populists tripled their vote over the past two decades. *The Guardian.* https://www.theguardian.com/world/ng-interactive/2018/nov/20/revealed-one-in-four-europeans-vote-populist.

Lindberg, L. N., & Scheingold, S. A. (1970). *Europe's Would-Be Polity: Patterns of Change in the European Community.* Englewood Cliffs: Prentice-Hall.

Maas, W. (2007). *Creating European Citizens.* Lanham, MD: Rowman & Littlefield.

Maas, W. (2020). European citizenship and free movement after Brexit. In S. Greer & J. Laible (Eds.), *The European Union after Brexit.* Manchester: Manchester University Press.

Mackert, J., & Turner, B. S. (Eds.). (2017). *The Transformation of Citizenship: Boundaries of Inclusion and Exclusion.* Abingdon, UK: Routledge.

Magnette, P. (2005). *Citizenship: The History of an Idea.* Washington, DC: ECPR Press.

Mazzoni, D., Albanesi, C., Ferreira, P. D., Opermann, S., Pavlopoulos, V., & Cicognani, E. (2018). Cross-border mobility, European identity and participation among European adolescents and young adults. *European Journal of Developmental Psychology, 15*(3), 324–339. https://doi.org/10.1080/174 05629.2017.1378089.

McMahon, S. (2015). *Immigration and Citizenship in an Enlarged European Union: The Political Dynamics of Intra-EU Mobility.* London: Palgrave Macmillan.

Migration Watch UK. (2019). *Net migration statistics.* https://www.migration watchuk.org/statistics-net-migration-statistics.

Mindus, P. (2017). *European Citizenship after Brexit: Freedom of Movement and Rights of Residence.* London: Palgrave Macmillan.

Mitchell, K. (2012). Student mobility and European identity: Erasmus study as a civic experience? *Journal of Contemporary European Research, 8*(4), 490–518.

Moravcsik, A., & Vachudova, M. A. (2003). National interests, state power, and EU enlargement. *East European Politics and Societies, 17*(1), 42–57.

Morgan, D. L. (1998). *Planning Focus Groups.* Thousand Oaks, CA: Sage.

Motti-Stefanidi, F., & Cicognani, E. (2018). Bringing the European Union closer to its young citizens: Youth active citizenship in Europe and trust in EU institutions. *European Journal of Developmental Psychology, 15*(3), 243–249. https://doi.org/10.1080/17405629.2017.1423052.

Neuding, P. (2018). So long to Swedish political stability. *Politico.eu.* https://www.politico.eu/article/swedens-stability-comes-to-an-end/.

Norman, K. (2018). *Sweden's Dark Soul: The Unravelling of a Utopia.* London: C Hurst & Co Publishers.

O'Brien, C. (2016). Civics capitalist sum: Class as the new guiding principle of EU free movement rights. *Common Market Law Review, 53*(4), 937–977.

Olsen, E. D. H. (2012). *Transnational Citizenship in the European Union: Past, Present and Future.* London and New York: Continuum Books.

Recchi, E. (2015). *Mobile Europe: The Theory and Practice of Free Movement in the EU.* London: Palgrave Macmillan.

Recchi, E., & Favell, A. (Eds.). (2009). *Pioneers of European Integration: Citizenship and Mobility in the EU.* Cheltenham: Edward Elgar Publishing.

Ross, A. (2015). *Understanding the Constructions of Identities by Young New Europeans: Kaleidoscopic Selves.* Abingdon, UK: Routledge.

Ross, A. (2019). *Finding Political Identities: Young People in a Changing Europe.* London: Palgrave Macmillan.

Sanders, D., Magalhães, P., & Tóka, G. (Eds.). (2012). *Citizens and the European Polity: Mass Attitudes Towards the European and National Polities.* Oxford: Oxford University Press.

SCB. (2019a). *General elections, results.* https://www.scb.se/en/finding-statistics/statistics-by-subject-area/democracy/general-elections/general-elections-results/.

SCB. (2019b). *Higher education: International mobility in higher education from a Swedish perspective 2017/18.* https://www.scb.se/contentassets/593414d03 4e34644b3cee3adfe353ec5/uf0209_2017l18_sm_uf20sm1802.pdf.

Schierup, C.-U., & Ålund, A. (2011). The end of Swedish exceptionalism? Citizenship, neoliberalism and the politics of exclusion. *Race & Class, 53*(1), 45–64.

Schmidt, S. K., Blauberger, M., & Martinsen, D. S. (2018). Free movement and equal treatment in an unequal union. *Journal of European Public Policy, 25*(10), 1391–1402. https://doi.org/10.1080/13501763.2018.1488887.

Sloam, J., & Henn, M. (2019). *Youthquake 2017: The Rise of Young Cosmopolitans in Britain.* London: Palgrave Macmillan.

Sigalas, E. (2010). Cross-border mobility and European identity: The effectiveness of intergroup contact during the Erasmus year abroad. *European Union Politics, 11*(2), 241–265.

Siklodi, N. (2015). Active citizenship through mobility? Students' perceptions of identity, rights and participation in the EU. *Citizenship Studies, 19*(6–7), 820–835.

Siklodi, N. (2019a). Brexit: common ground between leave and remain activists that could help bridge divided Britain. *The Conversation*. https://theconver sation.com/brexit-common-ground-between-leave-and-remain-activists-that-could-help-bridge-divided-britain-115322.

Siklodi, N. (2019b). The brexit crisis: Potential implications for the EU and its citizens. In Europa Publications (Ed.). *European Union Encyclopedia and Directory 2020* (20th Ed.). Abingdon, UK: Routledge.

Todd, J. (2016). *The UK's Relationship with Europe: Struggling over Sovereignty*. London: Palgrave Macmillan.

Turner, B. S. (1997). Citizenship Studies: A general theory. *Citizenship Studies, 1*(1), 5–18.

Turner, B. S., & Khondker, H. H. (2010). *Globalization East and West*. Thousand Oaks, CA: Sage.

UKCISA. (2019). *International Student Statistics: UK Higher Education*. https://www.ukcisa.org.uk/Research–Policy/Statistics/International-stu dent-statistics-UK-higher-education.

Van Ingelgom, V. (2014). *Integrating Indifference: A Comparative, Qualitative and Quantitative Approach to the Legitimacy of European Integration*. Washington, DC: ECPR Press.

van Kessel, S. (2017). No domino effect: Brexit is close to constituting a non-issue in European politics. *LSE Brexit Blog*. https://blogs.lse.ac.uk/brexit/2017/10/11/no-domino-effect-brexit-is-close-to-constituting-a-non-issue-in-european-politics/.

Van Mol, C. (2014). *Intra-European Student Mobility in International Higher Education Circuits: Europe on the Move*. London: Palgrave Macmillan.

von der Leyen, U. (2019). *A Union that Strives for more: My Agenda for Europe*. https://ec.europa.eu/commission/sites/beta-political/files/politi cal-guidelines-next-commission_en.pdf.

Wilson, I. (2011). What should we expect of "Erasmus Generations"? *Journal of Common Market Studies, 49*(5), 1113–1140.

CHAPTER 2

Citizenship, Free Movement and the EU

Much has been written about how globalisation redefines the politics of citizenship from a global perspective. But the case of the European Union (EU)—and within it national and EU citizenships—as an exemplar of the internal dynamics of a 'global community' is too often overlooked, or only viewed from a specialist, EU studies viewpoint. This chapter makes a case for re-embedding the study of EU models in the field of citizenship studies and offers a conceptual framework on how this might be done.

With EU citizenship described as an experimental, *sui generis* case, that is neither recognisable or not *as yet* worthy of true 'citizenship' designation (Seubert 2017: 147), perhaps it is not so surprising that most studies have addressed this model separately from national examples. Similarly, the legal structures and the institutional, normative and empirical frameworks of EU citizenship are often addressed in isolation from one another and from their national counterparts. What we now have is a specific EU citizenship—perhaps even better termed as EU identity and EU participation—literature which has emerged in response to European integration developments. Accordingly, academic scrutiny of "the search for" EU identity or participation has not referred specifically to EU citizenship (Bruter 2005; White 2011; Duchesne et al. 2013; Van Mol 2014; Ross 2015, 2019) with *some* notable exceptions (Favell 2008, 2010; Recchi and Favell 2009; Recchi 2015).

© The Author(s) 2020
N. Siklodi, *The Politics of Mobile Citizenship in Europe*,
Politics of Citizenship and Migration,
https://doi.org/10.1007/978-3-030-49051-5_2

By comparison, studies of national citizenship in Europe have adopted a concurrent perspective, following the agenda set by the field of citizenship studies (Isin and Turner 2002; Isin and Nyers 2014; Mackert and Turner 2017). They have thus addressed the dimensions of national citizenship—and their interrelated character—simultaneously, though often in relation to one national context.

It is also notable that academic scrutiny of EU and national models is frequently detached from one another. In the handful of cases where a more inclusive approach to national and EU models of citizenship—and their dimensions—was adopted, more enthusiastic conclusions were then reached about their significance (especially Sanders et al. 2012). Indeed, in the majority of cases when EU citizenship is addressed from a comparative perspective, it is mostly done with reference to models present in 'other' federal communities, most notably in North America (Prügel and Thiel 2009; Maas 2013). So we know little about senses of EU and national citizenship from a *comparable* perspective.

Despite elite, public and media discourses taking an increasingly antagonistic view of the figure of the mobile EU citizen, the interdependence between member state and EU citizenships has been reinforced recently (van den Brink and Kochenov 2019). At the same time, the expansion of EU citizenship—specifically, to cosmopolitan or truly EU-level political aspirations—has been halted and the ongoing significance of national models accentuated (Bellamy and Castiglione 2019). Nonetheless, serious challenges, such as the refugee crisis and Brexit (Benli and Archiburgi 2017; Siklodi 2019), have not led to doubts about the endurance of EU citizenship. With national *and* EU models set to shape citizens' everyday lives, it is perhaps more timely than ever to develop a conceptual framework that can facilitate their *concurrent* study.

To this end, this chapter provides an overview of some of the key strands in the existing literature on contemporary citizenship in Europe.

The chapter is structured as follows. The first part of the chapter explores in detail some of the key tenets of the Swedish, British and EU models of citizenship in order to showcase the similarities between these models and makes a case for a more politically embedded study of EU citizenship, along with national examples, in a mobile Europe. The benefits of the proposed conceptual framework are then illustrated by showcasing how mobility transforms senses of citizenship in the context of intra-EU learning mobility specifically. The resulting distinctions are set out by revisiting the findings of some of the recent and essential empirical studies on citizenship and mobility in the EU, namely Bruter (2005), Favell (2008), Van Mol (2014), Recchi (2015), and Ross (2015, 2019). The chapter ends with a conceptual framework of the dimensions of citizenship, which will serve as empirical indicators for the remainder of this book.

2.1 RE-EMBEDDING THE STUDY OF CONTEMPORARY CITIZENSHIP IN THE EU IN THE FIELD OF CITIZENSHIP STUDIES

Broadly speaking, citizenship can be defined as a dynamic and direct bond between a sovereign political community and the individuals within it (Isin and Turner 2002; Mackert and Turner 2017). Given the lack of an "elaborate" citizenship theory (Turner 1993: viii), scholars in the field of citizenship studies have been concerned with "producing analytical and theoretical tools" which *aid* the comparability of different models (Isin and Turner 2002: 4; Heater 2004a: 288; Bellamy 2004: 3).

Specifically, they tend to draw attention to a number of recurring debates:

(1) how different models of citizenship emerge, transform and are consolidated over time;
(2) what resulting community building processes tell us about the scope of each model (exploring processes of differentiation and exclusion);
(3) and how they then can be described and compared to one another (studying the dimensions of citizenship, namely identity, rights and participation).

Their relevance is illustrated in this section with references to contemporary British, Swedish and EU citizenships.

First, while it is true that a definition of citizenship must have a "broader and deeper meaning" (Heater 2004a: 293), citizenship studies scholars have warned us not to stretch this concept too far either. In other words, we should not try and define citizenship differently from one context to the next. Such a claim may sound simplistic, but it does respond to a tendency in the vast literature to observe *any* new phenomenon as novel (Magnette 2005: 8). However, simply recognising that each political community has its own citizenship, should not challenge the "heuristic advantage" of adopting an inclusive approach to studying this issue, nor lead to further diversity in the broader field of citizenship studies (Magnette 2005: 2).

Indeed, it *should be* common sense to recognise that contemporary national models of citizenship vary from one state to the next and even within state boundaries—in space and over time. For example, British citizenship has had an "extraordinarily confused history" (Dummett 2006: 554). At the outset, it signalled a liberal bond between residents, the Empire and the Crown (Heater 2004a: 298). More recently, we can see a slow but gradual shift towards a territorially defined status (Dummett 2006: 560–561). In reality however, there is still no clear definition of what British citizenship really entails (Mycock 2009).

This is no exception.

Sweden is very similar in this respect and even more radical in others. The Swedish 'Citizenship Act' defines *medborgarskap* as a legal status. With the phrase 'citizenship' missing from Swedish vocabulary however, *medborgarskap* refers *only* to the acquisition or loss of a legal residency status. It is quite distinct from the subjective status present in British legislation to put it mildly.

Indeed, the sociopolitical aspects of citizenship are largely missing from Swedish legal discourses or even everyday vocabulary (Midtbøen et al. 2018: 19). By comparison, perhaps one of the most well-known, certainly most cited, assessments of citizenship by Marshall (1950) traced the development of legal, social and political aspects of citizenship rights in the UK. It would however be erroneous to conclude that Sweden has had no diverging models of citizenship.

In fact, in Sweden too we can trace a recent shift towards a more liberal model of citizenship—manifested in the relative ease with which citizenship can be acquired (Howard 2009: 77), the opening up of the Swedish labour market (Anxo and Ericcson 2015: 27) and peoples' social and professional openness towards migrant workers (Ferrera and Pellegata 2018: 1471). Despite the negative media surrounding the migration crisis in Sweden (Abdelhady 2019), openness still characterises Swedish legal citizenship. No official citizenship or language test has been introduced, and the cost of *medborgarskap* application at 1500SEK (circa £135) remains relatively affordable.

This is especially so when compared to the UK where the average citizenship application costs around £2000. The associated processes are also rather burdensome, making the British passport "the most expensive thing" owned by a number of naturalised British citizens (Stewart and Mulvey 2011: 52; Prabhat 2018: 77–108). This grants a somewhat 'elitist' character to British citizenship—an issue that has, at least recently, penetrated would-be citizens' attitudes towards acquiring British citizenship (Duda-Mikulin 2019).

Despite some decline in the overall number of citizenship applications in both countries, mainly to do with the migration crisis and Brexit, respectively, they are still in the top five of EU countries granting nationality in recent years (Eurostat 2019a). Even though national citizenship has had different meanings in different states—including the acquisition of citizenship as shown earlier—it is only EU citizenship that has been observed as distinctive and *sui generis*. As such, it has been deemed *in*comparable to national models (Cheneval and Ferrin 2018: 2–5).

True, the connotation between EU citizenship and the legacy of the market citizen—specifically, reliance on intra-EU mobility—is as relevant today as it was in the early days of its introduction (Meehan 1993; Siklodi 2014; O'Brien 2016). Besides, there is not a single EU citizenship acquisition process akin to national practices (van den Brink and Kochenov 2019). EU citizenship is not a status any individual can acquire *directly* or hold on to *without* member state citizenship (*Janko Rottmann v. Freistaat Bayern, 2010*). We have been told, time and again, that a loss of member state nationality results in the loss of EU citizenship (recently in *Tjebbes and Others v Minister van Buitenlandse Zaken*). If Brexit has taught us anything, it reinforced the inherently indirect character of EU citizenship. Hence, even if, in principle, EU citizenship serves as the fundamental status of member state nationals, it is the status of the nationals of member states *only*. A country losing (or giving up) its EU membership results in the collective loss of EU citizenship for its nationals (Austin-Greenall and Lipinska 2017). While this indirect loss of status on a large scale is certainly unusual, it merely emphasises the 'influx' character of citizenship politics (Isin 2009).

Second, debates about the general definition of citizenship are usually accompanied by references to its function in shaping community building processes. Both national and EU models of citizenship share this function at the national and EU levels, respectively (Bosniak 2008; Checkel and Katzenstein 2009). However, with debates on "what the nature of the beast is" (Risse-Kappen 1995) continuing—attempting to settle whether the EU is a political, economic or a regulatory community—its citizenship policies and associated developments have been bound to follow suit, shifting from economic, political and social models and back again (Seubert 2017). Scholars tracing changes in the EU's discourse on and the institutional framework of EU citizenship have certainly suggested the same (especially Maas 2007; Olsen 2012; Pukallus 2016).

Two types of community building processes have been particularly highlighted by the extant citizenship literature, both of which underscore the inherently contested character of citizenship. First, processes of differentiation are required to unpack the nuances in citizens' role *within* political communities and how this role, in turn, affects citizens' perceptions of one another and the redistribution of socio-economic benefits among them (Bosniak 2008: 19–25; Isin 2008). Processes of exclusion, by comparison, draw attention to the distinctions and inequalities apparent between the members and non-members of political communities (Isin and Nielson 2008; Isin and Saward 2013). They emphasise the range of preconditions non- or to-be citizens *must* meet in order to gain access to "rooted" political communities and the related changes in attitudes among the members and non-members of communities (Miller 1995: 96; Ramos et al. 2019).

The political engagement perspective—focusing on citizens' participation in traditional (voting or party membership) or, more recently, alternative forms of engagement (protesting or volunteering)—dominated the bulk of the literature for a long time, establishing not only the active/passive citizen dichotomy (Hoskins and Mascherini 2009) but also the contours of good, or bad, citizenship ideals (for Europe see, for example, Van Deth et al. 2007). However, a consideration of this issue alone may not be enough to fully understand contemporary models, after all they all place emphasis on a slightly different issue. For instance, given the central role of the welfare state in Sweden, the extent to which citizens are able to exercise "control" over the providers of public provisions emerges as the most fitting indicator of the success and failure of its active citizenship (Sivesind et al. 2017: 10).

While slightly more embedded in political participation, the UK model has also seen considerable changes in its 'good citizenship' notion (*empirically* addressed by Pattie et al. 2004; Tam 2019). Following the decline in citizens' sense of public duty and levels of political participation (internationally, as outlined by Franklin 2004), citizens have had unequal opportunities to influence British politics (Sloam and Henn 2019). This issue has been further exaggerated by the sudden increase in citizen participation in online spaces and at the cost of their electoral turnout—among *some* groups, the young and well educated. But this shift offers no guarantees for equal access, representation or input to the UK's policy decisions (Dennis 2019). These distinctions have already polarised the British electorate (to take the 2017 and 2019 UK elections as examples, see McDonnell and Curtis 2019) and are expected to have a longer-term defining role in the UK's novel 'global' (citizenship) politics post-Brexit (Duffy et al. 2019).

Considered in this light, it is perhaps less surprising that the institutional framework of EU citizenship has set out the active/passive categories of citizens on the basis of their intra-EU mobility experience rather than their political participation (European Commission 1993). In reality, EU treaties require citizens to move first in order to activate their EU status (Maas 2007). There is now evidence show casing that this expectation has had considerable impact on the sense of national *and* EU citizenship among stayers (Heath et al. 2019). There are also important differences at the aggregate level between national and EU attitudes and political dispositions, generally along the South/East and North/West, or, more to the point, the sending/host country fault lines (Heath and Richards 2019). If anything, these findings hint at the effect intra-EU mobility is likely to have not only in distinguishing between mobiles and stayers as active/passive EU citizens but also as active/passive national citizens.

In the context of nation states, nationality and citizenship become interchangeable—making processes of exclusion a central feature of *national* community building processes (Bauböck 1994: 23). While such processes often rely on the perceived homogeneity of its citizens along ethnic, religious or cultural factors, the reality could not be further from the truth. If we take perhaps the most basic sign of heterogeneous communities as our measure, we find that the percentage of the population described as foreign born has increased across the EU. By 2011, Britain counted over 7.5 million people in its 'foreign born' population (just under 15% of the total), of which over 50% came from a non-white ethnic background (ONS 2015). While the comparative numbers are much smaller in Sweden, the share of foreign population is higher here than in the UK, reaching nearly 20% (or two million) by 2018.[1]

Despite the inevitable presence of 'others' in the EU, processes of exclusion have enjoyed a boost in recent years, facilitating the gradual securitisation of national citizenships (Nyers 2009). The EU model has been no exception. Anti-immigration sentiment towards non-EU nationals defines the institutional framework of EU citizenship (Hansen and Hager 2010: 7–8), challenging any cosmopolitan promise it was once meant to deliver (Soysal 1994). In response to such practices, there has been an increase in 'acts of citizenship'—the making of citizenship claims by formally non-recognised EU citizens with particular professional or ethnic backgrounds, such as mobile sex workers, EU Roma citizens or TCNs (especially Isin and Nielsen 2008; Aradau et al. 2010; Isin and Saward 2013). Members of these groups make important attempts to redefine the institutional and normative frameworks of national and EU citizenship 'from the margins' (Ataç et al. 2016; Juverdeanu 2019).

Third, the similarities and variations in models of contemporary citizenship are also replicated when their collective and interrelated dimensions—namely identity, rights and participation (Balibar 1988: 724; Isin and Turner 2002: 1–10; Heater 2004a: 166; Joppke 2010: 28)—are observed. Perhaps due to its role in categorisation processes, the identity dimension has become particularly dominant with national citizenships. From the outset, states begin to reconfigure citizens' senses of belonging by adding geographically and culturally distinct layers to their pre-existing social identities (Miller 1995). The resulting national identity of citizens has become infused with exclusionary, ethnic and culturist ideals (Fukuyama 2018) and continues to nourish group struggles for recognition (Balibar 2009).

There is much variation in senses of identity from one state to the next—offering a wide array of policy developments in response. For instance, there has been an impetus for promoting ethnic, British identity-fuelled migration and citizenship policies in order to reduce hostility towards migrants and support for hard Brexit (Kaufmann 2019). In Sweden however, the increasing presence of EU—read CEE—beggars seemed to have only elevated appreciation for *civic* citizenship virtues, once again in relation to welfare state provisions (Hansson and Jansson 2019). At the same time, there has also been a surge in supporting Sweden's idealised exceptionalism (Schierup and Ålund 2011) and 'neutral' (instead of ethnic nationalism) stance in citizenship politics (Agius 2006).

By comparison, EU citizenship does not—on the surface—appear to have a similar impact on its citizens' senses of identity. Instead of setting out to promote *a* collective sense of EU identity, it appears to fuel *dual* senses of identities—that is national *and* EU identities together (European Commission 1993: 2). However, in order to promote EU identity specifically, increasing efforts have gone into applying a range of identity technologies—similar to those prevalent in nation states (see, for example, Billig 1995)—through top-down and bottom-up processes (for an overview, see Karolewski 2009: 62–68). Top-down processes have relied on the visibility of EU symbols (European day, flag, hymn and the Euro) (Risse 2003: 487–505), values (democracy and peace) (Della Sala 2010) and the EU's normative, cosmopolitan and civilian images (Lavenex 2001: 851–874). Bottom-up processes have required citizens' actual involvement in the EU's polity, by exercising their intra-EU mobility and political rights or using the Euro, shopping across state borders and so on (Bruter 2005).

These processes have had varying results—some enhancing the exclusive aspect of citizens' national identity, and so by extension creating multiple European *internal* 'others' (Risse 2010: 50–55). There have also been important distinctions between their long-term effects. While top-down processes appear to have enhanced cognitive affiliations, bottom-up processes seem to have boosted the affective feature in citizens' senses of EU identity (Kaina and Karolewski 2013). Although the readings of EU identity have been largely underwhelming, initial interpretations of EU rights were perhaps overly optimistic, fuelling anticipations of EU citizenship as the first supra- and post-national model of citizenship with global and cosmopolitan potentials (Soysal 1994; Habermas 2003; Kostakopoulou 2008).

More often than not EU rights have faced criticism for their limited scope vis-à-vis national rights (Shaw 1998). Most importantly, there is an ongoing debate about the extent to which the 'legacy of market citizenship' (Meehan 1993) can be abolished when EU citizenship remains largely dependent on a chiefly economic model and the social exclusion of TCNs (O'Brien 2016; Seubert 2017).

How this affects the EU's lack of democratic credentials remains anyone's guess (and there have been quite some guesses—mostly negative, even by European Parliament [2017]).

There are, nevertheless, similarities between the rights offered by national and EU citizenships, starting with the "ontological priority of the individual" (Karolewski 2010: 11). This requires the guarantee of equal status for *every* citizen *within* a given territory (Poggi 2003: 42). Yet, neither the British, Swedish nor the EU models have managed to fully implement this requirement. In the UK, there are unresolved residency queries going back to the dissolution of the British Empire (Sawyer and Wary 2014). They have recently made headlines in relation to the forced removal of members of the Windrush generation (Taylor 2018).

In a similar vein, a general lack of awareness about the residency requirements of Swedish citizenship (Bernitz 2012) has resulted in some high-profile *Kompetensutvisning* [deportation] of highly skilled migrant workers—the type of migrants the country actually needs (Lindsay 2018). While we may see some resolution to these country-specific issues, the EU's free movement provisions add another potential problem by challenging the territorial principles of national models coming from the member states.

EU citizenship is also under considerable internal strain. The EU's constantly changing borders as well as some of the overlapping yet contradictory free movement opportunities provided to non-EU citizens have proven difficult to manage (European Commission 2017). Besides, some states hold opt-outs from some of EU citizenship's rights provisions— such as the Polish (and until recently British) opt-out from the Charter of Fundamental Rights. Others introduced limitations on how EU citizens coming from another state *can* exercise their EU rights, for example, through transitional measures or residency requirements (Guild et al. 2019).

While a coordinated response from EU citizens could, theoretically at least, challenge such practices, pro-EU mobilisation or indeed EU participation is a rarity—most recently making headlines in response to Brexit (Brändle et al. 2018). But more often than not, these events too have had a state-orientated parameter (Siklodi 2019).

It is precisely this issue, the participation dimension, without which national models of citizenship have been deemed as "meaningless" (Dalton and Klingemann 2007: 1–3). While EU citizenship appears to lack the institutional structures to enhance *sufficient* citizen input, national citizenship is marred by a widespread decline in citizens' political participation (Dassonneville and Hooghe 2018). It is yet to be seen whether such developments signal a broader crisis for national models (as suggested by Putnam 2001; Barber 2007: 291–339) or are simply an upshot of broader processes, notably the personalisation of politics (Bennett 2012).

We are left with considerable variation in the types and levels of citizens participation from one state to the next. For example, the electoral turnout at the 2018 Swedish parliamentary elections peaked at over 87%—one of the highest ever recorded in the country's history (SCB 2019). The 67% turnout in the 2019 UK election—a respectable 10% surge in the course of ten years (BBC 2019)—may seem poor by comparison. While alternative forms of engagement have increased in both countries and, especially, among younger generations (Kaun 2015; Dennis 2019), their actual contribution towards policy input or even 'awareness raising' has likely been overblown. If anything, these developments suggest that national citizenship 'as we know it' has been 'interrupted' (Bennett and Segerberg 2013: 200).

The lack of direct citizen input into EU politics seems to be so overwhelming for some scholars, that they have gone as far as to identifying this issue as *the* most serious challenge not only to the significance of EU citizenship (Favell 2010) but also to the democratic legitimacy of the Union as a whole (Schmidt 2013). The only direct input citizens have in EU politics is through the European Parliament (EP) elections. But the candidates come from national lists and national parties. Upon the completion of Brexit, we may see the arrival of the first *truly* transnational list of EP candidates (Verger 2018). However, such a development is likely to bring with it its own challenges, if the historically low level of public recognition of European politicians is anything to go by (Hix 2004). Considered in this light, it may be tempting to dismiss the significance of EU citizenship all together and ask, "how can one be a citizen of a *non-state?*" (Shore 2004: 32, emphasis in original).

Finally, while scholars tend to recognise the multidimensional character of European national citizenship, they also increasingly accept the interrelated feature of these dimensions (Tilly 2003: 611; Isin and Turner 2007; Bellamy 2010: xvi). This signals an important shift away from the main theoretical traditions of citizenship (and have been considered by more recent studies, such as Isin and Nyers 2014 and Mackert and Turner 2017 for example).

Specifically, republican, liberal and communitarian approaches have idealised the political, legal *or* social dimensions of Greek, Roman and national models of citizenship, respectively (Marshall 1950; Etzioni 1995; Dagger 2002). The cosmopolitan, multicultural and feminist approaches by comparison set out to highlight the universality of citizenship as rights (e.g. Yuval-Davis 2007; Delanty 2009; Vertovec and Wessendorf 2010). However distinct, these approaches have one important feature in common. They have a clear preference for addressing the issue of citizenship through *one* dimension, and in doing so end up idealising one 'absolute' model of citizenship. As such, they can only grant a somewhat stagnant explanation of contemporary practices.

In reality, the interaction between the dimensions of citizenship is much more complex and far-reaching. While making headlines in the context of Brexit, there have been long-running concerns about the weakening bond between the British state and some of its citizens as well as the tension between the civic and ethnic components of British national identity and, subsequently, citizens' low levels of political participation (Whiteley 2012). The Swedish case seems to be almost the opposite in this respect. The promotion of 'Swedish exceptionalism' has been effective in enhancing a sense of Swedish civic identity and in mobilising citizens' participation in politics (Borevi 2012: 70–73). While the intensity of the dimensions of EU citizenship may be lagging behind by comparison, there is already some evidence to suggest similar dynamics in this model also.

In one of the few pieces of empirical research carried out on EU and national models of citizenship, Sanders and his colleagues (Sanders et al. 2012; Sanders et al. 2012) demonstrate that rational cost–benefit calculations direct citizens' senses of EU citizenship. This is not surprising given the free movement and liberal market driven model that has been put in place. However, they suggest that senses of EU citizenship could be enhanced by better facilitating citizens EU political participation. They end up proposing that "the glass of EU citizenship is perhaps best regarded as half full rather than half empty" and that "a sense of EU citizenship among European mass publics is *extensive*", faring well against comparable national standards (Sanders et al. 2012: 222, 231, emphasis added).

Despite EU treaties positioning free movement at the heart of EU citizenship, this issue was not addressed by these authors. In fact, we still seem to have very little information about how the relationship between EU citizenship and EU mobility actually shapes our understanding of the issue of citizenship (Brändle 2018). In an attempt to complement the existing literature from citizenship studies and start conversing with the EU studies' angle on contemporary citizenship in Europe, the next section explores further how citizenship in the EU was expected to emerge and has been revised in the context of intra-EU learning mobility—with a special focus on policies attempting to 'groom' young and educated citizens into 'ideal', 'good' and active EU *and* national citizens.

2.2 INTRA-EU LEARNING MOBILITY AND EU CITIZENSHIP

To study how the EU has become "the classic historical counter-example to the political and social ontology of the nation state" (Beck and Grande 2007: 2), two developments require our attention—the abolition of state borders and growing opportunities for intra-EU mobility. Their impact for national models of citizenship is crucial, especially considering the opportunities (or lack thereof) they may provide for 'breaking' the link between political participation and *nation* states (Follesdal 2001: 313).

While these issues are important and timely, not least because of Brexit developments, there has been much less attention paid to them by citizenship scholars. Indeed, they hardly ever accept that EU mobility *can* serve as the basis for developing citizens' *collective* senses of EU citizenship, or EU identity, or EU participation for that matter (recently in Bellamy and Castiglione 2019). They have, instead, time and again questioned whether any development in EU citizenship law, such as the promise of non-discrimination on the basis of nationality, can be sufficient in offsetting the limitations of an inherently individualistic practice (Bellamy et al. 2006: 10). This is why most of the focus has been on how EU developments *might* affect national models of citizenship (Bellamy et al. 2004, 2006; Bellamy and Castiglione 2019). Those who have looked at the issue of EU mobility vis-à-vis EU citizenship more explicitly—with the notable exception of Isin and Saward (2013), who studied processes of differentiation and exclusion—fall outside traditional citizenship studies.

This section makes an attempt to reconcile these seemingly contradictory conceptual assumptions emerging from EU and citizenship studies with a special focus on intra-EU learning mobility.

EU studies scholars have placed their study of EU citizenship—usually only dimensions—ideals and practices within transactionalist (Deutsch et al. 1968) and neofunctionalist (Haas 1958) approaches to European integration. As such, they observe citizens' EU mobility as the counterpart to, or natural succession of, broader economic integration in Europe. Indeed, both approaches have predicted citizens' intra-EU mobility as one of the basic principles of the EU's social and political integration.

They anticipated two related outcomes.[2]

First, heightened flows of intra-EU mobility are supposed to boost the general sense of EU identity among citizens, creating a separate, truly EU-level society. Second, and as a consequence of the first, intra-EU mobility is expected to legitimise community building processes at the EU level. Subsequent empirical studies investigated the senses of EU and national identities and levels of sociopolitical awareness of EU nationals in an ever more integrated and highly mobile Europe.

More often than not, they have found that citizens' EU affiliation is "driven by material interests" (Fligstein 2008: 139). This may explain why, for example, EU-15 stayers with strong senses of national identity and low human capital have consistently been found to oppose the free movement of other EU nationals, while CEE stayers and stayers from member states with lower economic clout support it (Davidov et al. 2019; Vasilopoulou and Talving 2019).

These discrepancies have compelled national politicians to treat EU residents differently (Ford and Mellon 2019), which in turn has lessened stayers' willingness to interact with them (Green et al. 2019). We also know that the perceived—consistently overestimated rather than the genuine—size of EU mobile populations is mostly relied upon when stayers form their opposition to EU politics (Gorodzeisky and Semyonov 2019). Hence, as long as EU integration remains infused with intra-EU mobility, it seems inevitable for daily politics and elections to be dictated by anti-immigrant and populist parties in the EU and its member states (Halikiopoulou 2018).

Yet, it is precisely the political component of EU citizenship which has most often been omitted from empirical studies on free movement (especially notable for the purposes of this book are Bruter 2005; Ross 2015, 2019; Van Mol 2014). To be fair, in the few cases where EU participation was investigated, it was deemed to be largely irrelevant (Muxel 2009; Favell 2010; Recchi 2015). In the same vein, while we have plenty of information about and can even trace the impact of heightened mobility flows on stayers' attitudes and political behaviour, studies of EU mobiles' attitudes have been a rarity.

To date, there is no readily available EU-wide data set, or even sample data, facilitating the investigation of the behaviour and attitudes of EU mobiles.

Most studies have thus had to be spearheaded by individual researchers. Perhaps the most well-known in this respect are the Pioneur (2003–2006) and Moveact (2011–2013) projects, led by Recchi, Favell and colleagues. They show quite clearly that EU mobility enhances senses of belonging towards both the EU and the host country, regardless of where EU mobiles come from (EU-15 or CEE countries) (Recchi 2015: 143). At the same time, pro-EU and welcoming attitudes in the host country have been found to make it *less* likely for EU mobiles to form a substantive EU attachment (Rother and Nebe 2009). As mentioned before, EU mobility seems to have little impact on citizens' propensity to participate in the politics of the host country (Muxel 2009). In fact, strong senses of attachment to the EU and longer-term residency in the host country have recently been established as prerequisites for EU mobiles' EU participation (Recchi 2015: 118).

Despite these somewhat muddled—and often underwhelming—findings, if any aspect of EU legislation has seen a gradual boost in its remit, it is the interlink between EU free movement and EU citizenship (Olsen 2015). This has been the case even with the slowdown of European integration (Guiraudon et al. 2015)—or, according to some, the start of the EU's disintegration process (Rosamond 2016). Yes, more and more obstacles are introduced to limit EU mobiles' access to welfare provisions by member states, almost on a daily basis (Schmidt et al. 2018). And, naturally, these obstacles are transposed from one state to the next (Bruzelius 2019). This was especially the case at the height of the migration crisis and continues to dominate leading Brexit discourses. These obstacles thus prevent EU citizens from practising their EU citizenship and free movement rights fully.

However, no comparable obstacles have been introduced to deter the free movement of young member state nationals, especially those in university education. For example, even during the back-and-forth of the Brexit negotiations EU students were guaranteed access to British universities—on equal terms with home students. The UK's subsequent withdrawal from the EU's Erasmus programme has been met with much criticism and demand for alternative resolutions (BBC 2020).

This is interesting considering that the democratic quality of any political community rests on the educational attainment of citizens (Heater 2004b: vii). Indeed, levels of education have been found to bolster senses of national identity (Zajda et al. 2009), support for cosmopolitan and civic values as well as human rights (Dilworth 2008) and, importantly for the EU context, political literacy and propensity to engage in politics (Almond and Verba 1963: 315–316).

For quite a while, citizenship scholars have conveyed the same message about the relationship between levels of education and 'good/bad' citizenship specifically. Simply put, "[t]he educated citizen is attentive, knowledgeable, and participatory, and the uneducated citizen is not" (Converse 1972: 324). Students with higher education qualifications are seen as more politically engaged than those who leave education early (Hoskins et al. 2008: 397). On this basis, it has been quite common for nation states to use education as a tool for creating politically active citizens (Heater 2004b: 26–64).

The same can be said of the EU.

A "pedagogic approach" to EU citizenship quickly followed its formal introduction, identifying the young and highly educated—mobile—citizens to be the most prone to realise—and so by extension redefine—the transnational economic and political objectives of 'active citizenship' in the EU. The intermittent omission of 'EU', 'Union' or even 'national' to clarify the affected model of citizenship seems important—and likely to allude to the interdependent character of national and EU citizenships.

> Learning for active citizenship includes access to the skills and competencies that young people will need for effective economic participation under conditions of technological modernisation, economic globalisation, and, very concretely, transnational European labour markets. (European Commission 2001: 12)

Hence, mobility was quietly expected to affect both national and EU models.

Nonetheless, since "[i]t is as *EU* citizens that students – and their families – have the right to move and reside anywhere in the Union" (European Commission 2010: 6, emphasis added), "a Europe of knowledge" was recognised as an "indispensable component" of the EU's political and democratic aspirations. More specifically, it was hoped to

> consolidate and enrich the [idea of] European citizenship, capable of giving its citizens the necessary competences to face the challenges of the new millennium, together with an awareness of shared values and belonging to a common social and cultural space. (EHEA 1999: 1)

Although education was formally recognised as an EU competence in the 1993 Maastricht Treaty (at the same time as EU citizenship), it was the introduction of the European Community Action Scheme for the Mobility of University Students (Erasmus) in 1987 that truly started the development of a European higher education arena (Corbett 2012: 48). Success in this field has been particularly elevated when compared to other policy fields, resulting in the conformation of higher education curricula and university degree structures, as well as the increased recognition of educational qualifications across the EU in a mere 30-year period (European Commission/EACEA/Eurydice 2018).

These developments have granted a dual economic and political role for universities too. The constant emphasis on enhancing students' skills and employability (Walkenhorst 2008: 576; Van Mol 2014: 10) and the pressure on universities to support the privatisation and commercialisation of scientific research turned them into the EU's very own 'marketised institutions' (Lock and Martins 2009). Nonetheless, by providing young EU citizens with "the necessary competences to face the challenges of the new millennium" (EHEA 1999: 1) universities have been expected to demonstrate the EU's 'cultural unity' as well as its 'common values' to young and future active citizens (European Commission 1985: 355).

It is the anticipated economic and political returns which serve as the rationale for the extensive financial support the EU has given to the intra-EU learning mobility of university students (European Commission 2010). Today, this takes up the largest share of the EU's educational budget, eating up on two-thirds of the €14.4 billion figure (European Commission 2019). Such spending seems to have paid off if the persistent praise and the number of students participating—a total of 4.4. million—in these programmes are anything to go by (European Commission 2019).

EU mobile student numbers have also seen year-on-year growth, jumping a hundred-fold from just 3244 students in its first year in 1987 to 312,300 by 2017 (European Commission/EACEA/Eurydice 2018: 19). Of these numbers, the UK received 31,243 students—the third highest only beaten by Spain and Germany—while Sweden had 10,340 Erasmus students in 2017. It is also notable that the current seven-year period aims to facilitate the mobility of two million students—nearly half of the total number of Erasmus students up to now (European Commission 2019).

While Erasmus+ opportunities are not, strictly speaking, available for EU students only, the attachment of the non-discrimination principle to EU citizenship does suggest that we are entering a territory of a specialised EU geographical area, where the learning mobility of young member state nationals *is* sustained first and foremost. After all, Erasmus is not the only aspect whereby the EU's 'educational' leadership has manifested.

Explicitly relying on the EU's non-discriminatory and citizenship provisions, full- and part-time EU students wishing to complete their degree in another member state have been guaranteed the same tuition fees and residence rights as home students (European Commission 2019). This type of intra-EU learning mobility interferes with national educational and citizenship practices to a much greater extent than Erasmus ever could and also comes at much higher financial costs and longer-term commitment from EU students.

Yet, its number has also been growing gradually, reaching commendable levels, especially compared to Erasmus student numbers (Eurostat 2019b). Hence, from a potential pool of 19.6 million students, around 3% are likely to be an EU student studying in another member state on a semi-permanent basis (Eurostat 2019c). The UK has been a particularly popular choice among EU students, with 139,000 new students starting their degree in the country in 2018. This was four times as many as the number of arriving Erasmus students (Parliament.uk 2019). The number of EU students in Sweden has been more modest, recently reaching 11,362 (ÜKA 2019: 41). The differences in these numbers are understandable, given the more demanding cost of living and the language requirements the completion of a full Swedish versus full British degree is likely to require. The international reputation of British universities has also boosted their EU student recruitment (King 2003).

By comparison, Erasmus is likely to offset some of these costs, for instance by ensuring that visiting EU students can gather the sufficient amount of credits for free and in a language familiar to them. They also require spending a much shorter time abroad—up to a year at most. The completion of a basic degree in the EU can take anything between three to five years, with the length of master's degrees also varying between one and two years.

There is *some* empirical evidence to support the EU's 'pedagogic approach' to young peoples' EU citizenship (European Commission 2017). For example, university degree completion appears to make it more likely for students to use their mobility rights later in life (Fligstein

2008: 25), echoing the EU's mantra in this respect (European commission 2010). Learning mobility has also been deemed particularly effective in enhancing young citizens senses of EU identity (King 2003; Petit 2007; Mitchell 2012, 2014), while also improving their awareness of EU-level status and rights (Fernández 2005: 60). However, there have also been some indications which contradict the optimism of these findings. These have warned us that intra-EU learning mobility experiences do not, *necessarily*, have a significant and positive impact on students' senses of EU identity (Sigalas 2009, 2010a, b; Wilson 2011; Kuhn 2012; Van Mol 2014). They also often underscore that learning mobility is likely to have an elitist character from the outset, imitating broader intra-EU labour mobility practices.

Furthermore, just as is the case with free movement, the flow of EU students has been uneven across the EU (for an overview and evaluation, see Curaj et al. 2012). EU students are likely to find the opportunity to study in English a strong incentive. This issue is, in fact, one of the key factors influencing their choice of country (Mitchell 2012, 2014). Hence, a large number of EU students have chosen degree programmes which are delivered at least partially in English. By the same token, students from English-speaking countries have been less likely to study abroad because there is a reduced incentive for them to do so.

Besides, considerably different economic resources are required if a student from CEE or Southern states attempts to move to EU-15 or northern member states. Even in the context of the Erasmus programme, the financial contribution students might have to make can be substantial due to the variation in living costs (that *should* be reflected in the EU's financial assistance provided). These issues have been found to deter a large number of students from participating in study exchanges altogether (Souto-Otero et al. 2013: 70).

The question is then whether and to what extent the intra-EU learning mobility can deliver "attentive, knowledgeable, and participatory" citizens (Converse 1972: 324). "[T]he articulate citizens that Europe needs to create jobs, economic growth and prosperity" (European Commission 2011: 2). Against this backdrop, recent qualitative inquiries provide us with some novel and crucial insights into how perceptions and behaviour are likely to change as a result of intra-EU mobility and/or greater exposure to mobility (Bruter 2005; Favell 2008; Ross 2015, 2019; Van Mol 2014; Recchi 2015).

This book seeks to complement their work specifically, which is why the below section recounts their research and main findings in more depth.

Aiming "to understand how EU citizens *feel*", Bruter (2005: 6 emphasis in original) demonstrated the key role political institutions have in developing "a mass European identity" (Bruter 2005: 123–133). In his assessment, EU identity "continues to grow and has already achieved high enough levels not to be ignored by academic commentators and politicians" (Bruter 2005: 166). Most importantly for the purposes of this book, Bruter (2004: 26) draws attention to two central components which *should* be present in citizens' EU/European *political* identity—a cultural and a civic component.

He finds that citizens' cultural European—rather than EU—identity is likely to emerge from a 'shared baggage' related to a number of historical, cultural and social features of the continent on the whole (Bruter 2005: 85). By comparison, the civic component facilitates citizens' identification with the EU and the EU as a central source of their mobility rights and cosmopolitan identity (Bruter 2004: 34–35). Overall, his findings underscore the "predominantly positive" EU/European identity of citizens (Bruter 2004: 36) that is only really challenged by the EU's changing borders (Bruter 2005: 159).

In a similarly positive tone, Alistair Ross (2015, 2019) investigated how nearly 2000 young citizens (aged 11–19) construct their identity across 'Europe'. To start with, Ross underscores that no longer do young citizens identify with national "fixed tribes". They are, instead, "comfortably constructing flexible and multiple political identities... with a range of political locations, from the local to the global... [and] drawing on comparatively recent (and sometimes local) events to support their narratives" (Ross 2019: 2, 279). Ross (2015: 183) finds that young citizens often use "a palette of materials" to construct a range of *kaleidoscopic* identities, whereby reflections about personal socio-economic backgrounds, age, nationality and ethnicity are fused with emerging senses of political identity.

As a result, young peoples' political identity is best characterised as "momentary, situational [and] observer-dependent" (Ross 2015: 184). By repeatedly distinguishing themselves from older generations, young citizens alluded to the presence of national 'internal others'. The resulting distinctions were presumed to offer young citizens with a sense of distinct inclusive national and EU identity (Ross 2019: 171–182). Furthermore, young citizens seemed concerned with the prevailing inequalities across

European societies and presented a united and ready-to-act front to ratify these problems—with an expressed preference of doing so *within* the EU's structures (Ross 2019: 69–82).

While both Bruter and Ross explored young stayers' senses of EU identity, Van Mol (2014) assessed senses of identity in the context of Erasmus specifically. The reflective evidence of three groups of students, including the not-yet-mobile, ex-mobile and immobile students, underscored the "located nature of identity and identification processes" (Van Mol 2014: 118). This finding implies that only 'favourable' EU contexts can ever be beneficial for enhancing young Erasmus students' senses of EU identity.

Importantly, Van Mol's (2014: 152–157) study also begins to illustrate some of the contours of EU community building processes along the intra-EU learning mobility nexus. This too is found to be characterised by differentiation and exclusivity—mediating the control effects higher educational institutions supposed to offer (Van Mol 2014: 5–8). Van Mol warns (2014: 80–89) that limited interactions between Erasmus and home students are likely to occur—and this issue is attributed to students' language considerations and the perceived difficulties of 'breaking into' local, gated communities (Van Mol 2014: 80–89).

Considered in this light, Erasmus students were found to go through the 'full migration experience', even though their Erasmus mobility takes place in a largely organised setting. Van Mol (2014: 40–65) thus makes a strong case for considering Erasmus mobility less distinctively as an EU-specific experience and, instead, as another example of international student migration.

Moving away from 'younger' EU citizens but still focusing on citizens on the move, Favell's (2008) seminal ethnographic research about 'Eurostars'—the highly skilled EU-15 mobiles—in three 'Eurocities' (Amsterdam, Brussels and London) remains the only in-depth qualitative study, which explored how EU mobiles realise the dimensions of *EU* citizenship to date. In particular, Favell inquired about *who* EU mobiles are and *what* the social and political contours of their EU citizenship resemble. Although he seeks to compare the experiences of EU mobiles and stayers, the latter group was not actually included in his project—and so cannot corroborate or challenge his main findings.

Specifically, Favell (2008: x, 222) finds that "[t]he real boundaries [of the EU] lie only at the edge of the nation [state]". The inconsistencies in national provisions on social welfare especially were observed to benefit stayers *only*. As long as stayers make up the majority of the

EU population, 'Eurostars' did not experience nor expected to see "the replacement of the stabilized national structures for a fully massified and thereby Europeanized system" (Favell 2008: 96).

Favell thus ends up drawing attention to the ongoing significance of the national framework, which seems to be the key factor shaping EU mobiles experiences—even in ideal 'Europeanised' contexts. After all, each city Favell studies was selected for its 'de-nationalised' setting and marked cosmopolitan tendencies. Besides, Favell only studied EU-15 movers. These movers make up a select group, *never* in danger of being affected by transitional measures and *less* targeted by negative stereotypes (De Giorgi and Pellizari 2009).

A similarly gloomy portrait emerged when the political participation of 'Eurostars' was brought to the centre stage of Favell's (2010) analysis. 'Eurostars' hardly expressed the kind of *political* citizenship EU actors (European Commission 2012) and other researchers with a clear pro-EU stance appear to have vouched for (some detailed earlier). Although 'Eurostars' seem to be more interested in politics than stayers and they are presented with ample opportunities to influencing the host city's political landscape, the actual level of their participation, particularly via traditional forms of engagement, was found to be negligible at best (Favell 2010: 203–212).

Nevertheless, Favell also presents *some* evidence supporting *some* aspects of the EU mobility—EU citizenship linkage. For example, the emerging EU identity of 'Eurostars' seems to assist a few of them in their attempts at juggling between and feeling comfortable with their otherwise incompatible national and regional identities. Favell (2008: 3–11) also met with 'de-nationalised' 'Eurostars', whose original reasons to move was to be freed from national frameworks. These findings indicate that distinctions between the identities and lifestyles of EU mobiles and privileged *mobiles* in the EU, especially considering their senses of 'freedom', are a reality.

The European *movers* thus open up dimensions in their life, perceived as inaccessible to the national *stayers*: the people back home whose lives are immersed and contained in their own national culture. Move even once, and it has consequences; it changes you. You can never really go back. The liberating feeling can even get to be quite addictive. You might keep chasing it. It could even hold the key to the deepest freedom of all: freedom from your *self.* (Favell 2008: 11, emphasis in original)

More recent studies on EU mobiles' senses of EU citizenship reached a similarly lukewarm conclusion. Accordingly, "those Europeans who decide to profit from their citizenship by going to live in another EU member state are not particularly inclined to activate such citizenship in the public sphere" (Recchi 2015: 143). At the same time, there is much indication that, in terms of EU identity, "cross-national mobility [still] makes Europe 'blossom' within Europeans" (Recchi 2015: 143).

Although these scholars have offered somewhat diverging conclusions about the likely returns of intra-EU (learning) mobility, prioritising policies which assist mobility remains a popular choice—supported by citizens, national and EU politicians alike (European Commission 2018). Even the Brexit fiasco has not stopped internal UK policy reports from underscoring the difficulties the country is likely to face in its attempt to try and replicate their successes after withdrawal, including their economic and financial benefits (House of Lords 2019). These developments strongly suggest that the EU's educational and learning mobility provisions are here to stay for the foreseeable future (European Commission 2020). The contradictory findings about their effects on senses of EU citizenship and the lack of a comprehensive study about their implications for both senses of national and EU citizenship mean that there is an urgent requirement for an in-depth study of these issues—a contribution this book seeks to make to the ongoing conversation about these issues in EU and citizenship studies.

The next section clarifies the empirical indicators used for investigating the effects of intra-EU learning mobility on senses of national and EU citizenship in the later chapters.

2.3   Conceptualising the Key Dimensions of Citizenship

So far, this chapter has shown that once we have a general definition of citizenship and recognise its function in community building processes, the dimensions of citizenship determine how models of citizenship are realised in practice. Since this book will mainly explore how young and educated citizens realise national and EU models of citizenship in the context of intra-EU mobility, these dimensions are placed at the centre

Table 2.1 Analytical framework to studying contemporary citizenship

The dimensions of citizenship	Empirical indicators		
Identity	A sense of belonging to the political community	Shared identity among citizens (a sense of "we")	Recognition of the "other" (the non-citizens)
Rights	Awareness of citizenship rights	Access to civil, social and political rights	Membership in the political community
Participation	Who participates (Socio-economic background)	Reasons for participation (Models of participation)	Forms of engagement (Traditional v alternative forms)

of the succeeding chapters. In order to provide an operational definition of each of these dimensions, they are broken down into their constituent elements—as summarised in Table 2.1. The rest of this chapter defines these elements in some depth.

2.3.1   Citizenship as Identity

Although most scholars acknowledge the significance of identity for citizenship considerations (for example Tilly 1995; Heater 2004a: 187–197), there is disagreement about the *genuine* meaning of, and the most appropriate methods for addressing this issue. Scholars tend to disagree about, for example, the importance of individual and collective identities for citizenship (Smith 1992; Bellamy 2004: 10–15) and find the concept largely ambiguous due to the ever-expanding list of multidisciplinary approaches (Kaina 2013). In some cases, identity has even been deemed meaningless for the purposes of social research (Brubaker and Cooper 2000: 2).

In response, more and more scholars now separate the concept of identity—in relation to citizenship—into constituent elements, namely a sense of belonging to a sovereign political community, shared identity with fellow citizens (a "we" feeling) and recognition of the non-citizens (the "other") (Kanter 2006; Duchesne 2008; Risse 2010: 22–28; Karolewski 2011: 37–57).

This book follows their approach.

First, a sense of belonging to the community is expected to legitimise the workings of the community, including the regulation of citizens' lives

(Bellamy 2010: xvii). This element places an emphasis on *how* citizens identify with the community and *whether* the community accepts them as one of its members (Smith 1992: 59f; Bruter 2005: 8). The collective self-image of citizens assists in recognising the community as a group from within *and* from the outside (Díez Medrano and Gutiérrez 2001: 754). Even if citizens only hold a single citizenship status, they can often *feel* a sense of belonging to a number of political communities—in the case of the EU this could be both national and EU communities.

However, these feelings are not necessarily placed in order or clash with one another (Risse 2004: 249). More and more studies point out that most EU citizens feel a sense of belonging to continental Europe, the EU and their nation states *simultaneously* (Kuhn 2015). Hence, citizens' senses of belonging are not necessarily exclusive in practice. In this context, top-down processes can be particularly fruitful in enhancing citizens' sense of belonging (see, for example, Risse's [2003] assessment about the constructive effects of the Euro). Top-down processes may include the establishment of definite geographical boundaries, common symbols (e.g. a hymn, a flag or a common currency) and shared values (e.g. democracy and peace), as well as promoting a positive self-image of the community (e.g. democracy abroad) (Billig 1995; Leddy-Owen 2019).

By comparison, bottom-up processes emphasise what citizens *do*, including the exercising of rights, use of certain gestures and language, and how these practices then consolidate the effects of top-down processes (Risse 2010: 30–33). If we are interested in exploring how citizens realise their citizenship, the focus becomes, clearly, on their responses to top-down processes and their participation in bottom-up processes of identity formation, especially the exercising of their rights—traditionally political participation (Bellamy 2010: xvii).

Second, a shared identity among citizens affects their ability to realise citizenship and live their lives on an equal basis as 'legitimate members' of a political community (Kofman 1995: 130). In particular, it requires that citizens *collectively* recognise one another as full members of the community. Even though the importance of a shared identity is disputed by some scholars (Bellamy 2010: xvii), a "fellow-feeling" is expected to produce a sense of social trust and obligations among citizens, both of which are necessary preconditions for democratic decision-making (Miller 1995).

A shared identity can arise from a common purpose, history, language and culture (Gellner 1983: 7; Kanter 2006: 507–508; Risse 2010: 25–26).[3] It can then be enhanced by citizens' interactions with one another, which may lead to mutual recognitions of a common fate and purpose (Smith 1992: 58; Fuss and Grosser 2006: 212–213; Citrin and Sears 2009: 151–152). Nonetheless, a shared identity is expected to be "both inherently limited and sovereign" (Anderson 1983: 6) because not every citizen of a community knows each other. As a result, it is built on a collective understanding among citizens that their fellows share in their sense of identity. They thus define an 'imagined community' (Anderson 1983)—a sense of "we" compared to the "other", the non-citizens.

Third, and stemming from the last point, for citizenship as identity to emerge, a clear definition of the "other" is required (Castano et al. 2002: 319). Similarly to senses of a shared identity, the "other" can only be meaningful if it is recognised collectively by citizens. 'Codes of distinctions' (Eisenstadt and Giesen 1995: 74) may facilitate this recognition, particularly definitive geographical, political, economic and cultural self-images (Herrmann and Brewer 2004: 6). These codes reinforce the actual boundaries of the political community, making an initially 'imagined community' *real* in the minds of citizens (Castano et al. 2003: 450–452; Risse 2010: 23).

This issue then points to identity and, by association, citizenship as a form of 'categorisation' (Karolewski 2010: 26). While recognition of the "other" is often regarded as one of the most significant components of citizenship as identity (Citrin and Sears 2009: 146; Risse 2010: 26), it also underscores the increasingly controversial and exclusive character of contemporary citizenship models (illustrated excellently in the English context by Leddy-Owen 2019). So, for example, resulting processes of exclusion have enhanced negative attitudes (and often negative feelings) towards the "other" (Brewer 2001: 119). This is because when citizenship as identity becomes increasingly conventional and accepted by citizens, their rejection of the "other" is also taken as ordinarily recognised (Neumann 1996: 150–154).

Furthermore, citizens' senses of identity is anticipated to be multiple and multi-layered in practice (Citrin and Sides 2004). As mentioned earlier, citizens can belong to a number of political communities and social groups simultaneously. In fact, citizens' socio-individual relationships in each of these communities and groups may result in separate, nested, cross-cutting or multi-layered identities (Herrmann and Brewer

2004: 8–10).[4] Their identity is also likely to be influenced by a number of intersecting social factors, including gender, race, class and social standing (Yuval-Davis 2007: 562–563). However, even if multiple in number, citizens' identities do not (necessarily) clash, with some layers comprising others, for instance (Taylor 1989: 25). This holds particularly true for youth citizenship as identity (Ross 2019).

It is quite normal for citizens to negotiate between the contrasting senses of their identities on a daily basis (related to gender and religion, for example) and according to the egalitarian principles of citizenship. The latter emphasises the virtue in conciliating clashing identities and taming disruptive behaviours (Hobsbawm 1996: 39). Thus, citizens tend to negotiate between the different layers of their identities and often use them according to the specific context (Kofman 1995: 130). These contexts can then promote the endorsement of different social identities and sustain certain elements of citizenship as identity, while neglecting others.

Finally, the depth of citizenship identities depends on whether it seems to be positioned at the cognitive (awareness of citizenship), affective (evaluation of and feelings about citizenship) or behavioural levels (collective motivations) (Abdelal et al. 2009: 27–31). While the cognitive level is expected to denote a weak identification, the behavioural level is indicative of strong senses of national and EU citizenships.

2.3.2   Citizenship as Rights

Citizenship as rights refers to the "resources provided by social institutions which protects and legitimises the existence, the needs and interests, or the actions of the *bearer* of the right" (Bauböck 1994: 209, emphasis added). Due to the legitimising role of rights, scholars tend to regard it as *the* principal dimension of citizenship (Marshall 1950; Isin and Turner 2002: 1). They define the legal structure of citizenship and provide an indication of the attitude of a particular community towards its citizens (Bauböck 1994: 211). Rights can thus shed light on what the community expects citizenship to look like in reality.

However, there is an inherent tension in the idea of citizenship as rights, because the former is expected to have a collective character, but rights are, by default, individually orientated (Karolewski 2010: 11). Moreover, rights are the only institutionalised dimensions of citizenship.

In other words, the contours of this dimension are not defined by citizens' practices on an everyday basis—as is the case with the other two dimensions of citizenship—but by the political elite. Since citizens do not directly define these rights, at least not to start with, we must first try and shed light on the extent to which they are aware of their rights and can recognise the junctures in which they tend to exercise them. We can then move on to exploring two elements of citizenship as rights—membership in a sovereign political community and access to political rights, and civil, social and economic entitlements (Vink and Bauböck 2013: 5–9).

The first element, membership, refers to the formal rules individuals must follow in order to gain access to the political community and, subsequently, to citizenship as a status. This element reinforces the idea that citizenship is exclusive (Bauböck 1994: 23). Contemporary models of citizenship use territorial principles to separate citizens from non-citizens (most notably state borders) (Brubaker 1992: 21) and also offer access to citizenship upon non-citizens' fulfilment of certain criteria, from visa to residential and, often, language requirements (Prabhat 2018). Although these criteria are wide-ranging, there is some convergence in the EU context, due to the degree of European integration (Joppke 2007). While this development may, on the surface at least, suggest that member state citizenships are bound to become less exclusive, paving the way for new citizens' access to the EU's transnational community for example (Soysal 1994: 195–206), the actual, formal rules of access have, in reality, been defined by ever more exclusive and nationalistic legislation (Hansen 2009). The basic idea of membership in the EU's various political communities remains "a conceptually clear [and] legally consequential ... distinction between citizens and foreigners" (Brubaker 1992: 21).

The second element of rights refers to the ability of citizens to access political rights, and civil, social and economic entitlements on an equal basis (Marshall 1950).[5] Citizens' access to political rights is, perhaps, the most important for their citizenship because it allows them to "decide what rights they should have and ...[to] influence the character of the community to which they belong" (Bellamy et al. 2006: 7). Hence, their equal access to political rights opens up the opportunity for realising, among others, a democratic form of citizenship. In comparison, citizens' equal access to civil, social and economic entitlements is perhaps best described as a *virtue* of their citizenship status (Bellamy 2006: 163–170).

It cannot shape the legal structure of their citizenship in the same way as political rights do.

This issue may explain why, broadly speaking, longer-term residents tend to gain access to civil and social entitlements but not to political rights. It is also the reason why EU mobiles have not yet secured access to national level voting rights in the host countries. Therefore, the differences in the access of residents and citizens to political rights and socio-economic entitlements are likely to reinforce the inclusive/exclusive character of contemporary models (Karolewski 2010: 3).

2.3.3   Citizenship as Participation

This chapter has already established the fundamental role participation has had in activating various models of citizenship (see, for example, Bosniak 2008). Political participation can be broken down into three elements, underscoring who (socio-economic background), why (models of participation) and how (forms of participation) participates.

First, there is plenty of evidence to suggest that there is a gap in the participation of younger and older citizens, most notably in their approaches to and preferences for how they make their voices heard in politics today.

The reasons for this are many fold and include generational, life cycle and period-effect factors (Norris 2003). Furthermore, young people have been found to participate when political issues have a clear, personal relevance to them (Sloam 2014a). In addition to age, studies have often demonstrated the positive effects education and gender have had on citizens' propensity to participate in politics (Torney-Purta et al. 2008). Thus, for example, women have been found to participate more frequently than men (Torney-Purta and Amadeo 2011).

A number of theoretical models of participation—from the voting behaviour literature—have been proposed to explain the reasons for citizens' decision to participate in politics. The continuous application of these models suggests that more than one may be relevant at any given time (for an overview see Smets and van Ham 2013).

The rational choice model suggests that a cost–benefit analysis and, also, citizens' senses of civic duty are important determinants of participation (Blais 2000). The resource model suggests that the most important factors are related to individual resources (i.e. money, time and civic skills) (Verba and Nie 1963). So, the well-off, highly educated and politically knowledgeable citizens are expected to be the most likely to participate. The mobilisation model argues that we "must move beyond the worlds of individuals to include [the effects of] family, friends, neighbours, and co-workers, plus politicians, parties, activists, and interest groups" in order to really understand why citizens participate (Rosenstone and Hansen 1993: 23). Psychological models focus on the role of attitudes and psychological predispositions such as political interests (Mattila 2003), while socio-logical models explore the effects of socialisation, education and habit formation (Plutzer 2002) on decisions about participation.

Finally, political and institutional contexts, e.g. the electoral systems or propensity of the political elite to allow and listen to public demonstra-tions, are the focus of the political institutional model (Jackman 1987). However, recognising the decline in citizens' participation in traditional forms of engagement (voting, standing for public office, party member-ship and so on as outlined by Franklin 2004), in order to explore how citizens realise their citizenship today, we must take a broader approach to participation and allow *them* to tell us about *their preferred* forms of engagement and their reasons for doing so (Sloam 2014b). Accordingly, a growing number of citizens participate in individualised and alternative forms of engagement, including public demonstrations, volunteering, acts of civil disobedience (such as riots), consumerism and online petitions (Dennis 2019: 71–95). Such changes in forms of participation are bound to redefine contemporary models of citizenship and the contours of their political community.

2.4   SUMMARY

This chapter laid down the conceptual foundations of the issue of citi-zenship—the main theme of this book—and shed light on why it has been difficult to apply to the case of the EU. In particular, the chapter drew parallels between EU and citizenship studies approaches to current models of national and EU citizenship. It has argued that, in order to develop a more nuanced understanding of these models, it is impor-tant to apply the citizenship studies framework to the EU and national contexts systematically, studying the broad significance of each model, related processes of community building and the dimensions of citi-zenship together, while also recognising their *collective* and *interlinked* character. Subsequently, the chapter considered how EU citizenship is likely to be enhanced by its institutional framework—which places a particular emphasis on citizens' intra-EU learning mobility. The final part of this chapter then proposed a conceptual framework for addressing the dimensions of citizenship—which have, so far, been either addressed separately from one another or only within the EU and national realms. This is an important oversight, in my view, given that these dimensions account for *how* citizenship is practised in real terms.

The remainder of this book applies this framework to provide an in-depth, empirical examination of national and EU models of citizenship in the context of mobility, using EU-wide survey data and original focus group evidence. In so doing, the rest of this book endeavours to compliment the ongoing conversation in EU and citizenship studies on the politics of contemporary mobile citizenship in Europe with novel empirical insights.

NOTES

1. Sweden does not provide statistical information about the ethnic composition of its population. This is my estimate calculated from data provided by SCB (2020).
2. Neofunctionalist and transactionalist approaches interpret European integration from different angles. While neofunctionalists focus on the 'spill-over' effects of an elite-led process (Haas 1958: 292), transactionalists consider citizens' cross-border mobility as one of the most important drivers of integration (Deutsch et al. 1968: 170).
3. The literature refers to these issues as "the *contents* of identity". They are anticipated to be shaped by citizens as well as the political elite (Abdelal et al. 2009: 27).
4. Multiple identities have a number of opportunities to fit together, including separate, nested, cross-cutting and multi-layered or marble cake identities. Their likely configurations in the EU context have been usefully summarised by Herrmann and Brewer (2004: 8–10).
5. Civil, political and social rights are the three strands of rights defined by Marshall (1950). Nonetheless, the actual list of citizenship rights "is open ended and varies with particular political traditions, social structures and cultural understandings" (Bauböck 1994: 211). An investigation of this list thus provides an indication of how the political community approaches and sets out to treat its citizens.

REFERENCES

Abdelal, R., Herrera, Y. M., Johnston, A. I., & McDermott, R. (Eds.). (2009). Identity as a variable. In *Measuring Identity: A Guide for Social Scientists* (pp. 17–33). Cambridge: Cambridge University Press.

Abdelhady, D. (2019). Framing the Syrian refugee: Divergent discourses in three national contexts. In M. R. Menjivar & E. Ness (Eds.), *The Oxford Handbook of Migration Crisis*. Oxford University Press. https://doi.org/10.1093/oxfordhb/9780190856908.013.16.

Agius, C. (2006). *The Social Construction of Swedish Neutrality: Challenges to Swedish Identity and Sovereignty*. Manchester: Manchester University Press.

Almond, G., & Verba, S. (1963). *The Civic Culture: Political Attitudes and Democracy in Five Nations*. Princeton: Princeton University Press.

Anderson, B. (1983). *Imagined Communities: Reflections on the Origins and Spread of Nationalism*. London: Verso.

Anxo, D., & Ericson, T. (2015). Labour market measures in Sweden 2008–13: The crisis and beyond. *International Labour Office*. https://www.ilo.org/wcmsp5/groups/public/—dgreports/—inst/documents/publication/wcms_449934.pdf.

Aradau, C., Huysmans, J., & Squire, V. (2010). Acts of European citizenship: A political sociology of mobility. *Journal of Common Market Studies, 48*(4), 945–965.

Ataç, I., Rygiel, K., & Stierl, M. (2016). Introduction: The contentious politics of refugee and migrant protest and solidarity movements: Remaking citizenship from the margins. *Citizenship Studies, 20*(5), 527–544.

Austin-Greenall, G., & Lipinska, S. (2017). Brexit and loss of EU citizenship: Cases, options, perceptions. *ECAS: Citizens Brexit Observatory*. http://ecas.org/wp-content/uploads/2017/12/Brexit-and-Loss-of-EU-Citizenship-1.pdf.

Balibar, E. (1988). Propositions on citizenship. *Ethics, 98*, 723–730.

Balibar, E. (2009). *We, the People of Europe?: Reflections on Transnational Citizenship*. Princeton: Princeton University Press.

Barber, B. (2007). *Consumed: How Markets Corrupt Children, Infantilize Adults, and Swallow Citizens Whole*. New York: W. W. Norton and Company.

Bauböck, R. (1994). *Transnational Citizenship*. Aldershot: Edward Elgar.

BBC. (2019). *Election results 2019: Analysis in maps and charts*. https://www.bbc.com/news/election-2019-50770798.

BBC. (2020). *Erasmus: What could happen to scheme after Brexit?* https://www.bbc.co.uk/news/education-47293927.

Beck, U., & Grande, E. (2007). *Cosmopolitan Europe*. Cambridge: Polity.

Bellamy, R. (2004). Introduction: The making of modern citizenship. In R. Bellamy, D. Castiglione, & E. Santoro (Eds.), *Lineages of European Citizenship: Rights, Belonging and Participation in Eleven Nation States* (pp. 1–21). Basingstoke: Palgrave.

Bellamy, R. (2006). *Rethinking Liberalism.* London: Continuum International Publishing.

Bellamy, R. (2010). Introduction: The importance and nature of citizenship. In R. Bellamy & A. Palumbo (Eds.), *Citizenship* (pp. 6–25). Farnham: Ashgate.

Bellamy, R., & Castiglione, D. (2019). *From Maastricht to Brexit: Democracy, Constitutionalism and Citizenship in the EU.* London: Rowman & Littlefield International.

Bellamy, R., Castiglione, D., & Santoro, E. (Eds.). (2004). *Lineages of European Citizenship: Rights, Belonging and Participation in Eleven Nation States.* Basingstoke: Palgrave.

Bellamy, R., Castiglione, D., & Shaw, J. (Eds.). (2006). *Making European Citizens: Civic Inclusion in a Transnational Context: Civic Inclusion in Transnational Context.* Basingstoke: Palgrave Macmillan.

Benli, A. E., & Archibugi, D. (2017). *Claiming Citizenship Rights in Europe: Emerging Challenges and Political Agents.* London: Routledge.

Bennett, W. L. (2012). The personalization of politics: Political identity, social media, and changing patterns of participation. *The ANNALS of the American Academy of Political and Social Science, 644*(20), 20–39.

Bennett, W. L., & Segerberg, A. (2013). *The Logic of Connective Action: Digital Media and the Personalization of Contentious Politics.* Cambridge: Cambridge University Press.

Bernitz, H. (2012). *Country Report: Sweden.* Florence: EUDO Citizenship Observatory.

Billig, M. (1995). *Banal Nationalism.* London: Sage.

Blais, A. (2000). *To Vote or Not to Vote? The Merits and Limits of Rational Choice Theory.* Pittsburgh: University of Pittsburgh Press.

Borevi, K. (2012). Sweden: The flagship of multiculturalism. In G. Brochmann, A. Hagelund, K. Borevi, & H. V. Jønsson, & K. Petersen (Eds.), *Immigration Policy and the Scandinavian Welfare State 1945–2010* (pp. 25–96). Basingstoke: Palgrave Macmillan.

Bosniak, L. (2008). *The Citizen and the Alien: Dilemmas of Contemporary Membership.* Princeton: Princeton University Press.

Brändle, V. K. (2018). Reality bites: EU mobiles' experiences of citizenship on the local level. *Journal of Ethnic and Migration Studies,* 1–18. https://doi.org/10.1080/1369183X.2018.1524750.

Brändle, V. K., Galpin, C., & Trenz, H. J. (2018). Marching for Europe? Enacting European citizenship as justice during Brexit. *Citizenship Studies, 22*(8), 810–828.

Brewer, P. R. (2001). Value words and lizard brains: Do citizens deliberate about appeals to their core values? *Political Psychology, 22,* 45–64.

Brubaker, R. (1992). *Citizenship and Nationhood in France and Germany.* Cambridge: Harvard University Press.

Brubaker, R., & Cooper, F. (2000). Beyond identity. *Theory and Society, 29*(1), 1–47.

Bruter, M. (2004). On what citizens mean by feeling 'European': Perceptions of news, symbols and borderless-ness. *Journal of Ethnic and Migration Studies, 30*(1), 21–39.

Bruter, M. (2005). *Citizens of Europe? The Emergence of a Mass European Identity.* Basingstoke: Palgrave Macmillan.

Bruzelius, C. (2019). Freedom of movement, social rights and residence-based conditionality in the European Union. *Journal of European Social Policy, 29*(1), 70–83.

Castano, E., Paladino, M. P., Coull, A., & Yzerbyt, V. Y. (2002). Protecting the ingroup stereotype: Ingroup identification and the management of deviant ingroup members. *British Journal of Social Psychology, 41*(3), 365–385.

Castano, E., Yzerbyt, V., & Bourguignon, D. (2003). We are one and I like it: The impact of ingroup entitativity on ingroup identification. *European Journal of Social Psychology, 33,* 735–754.

Checkel, J. T., & Katzenstein, P. (Eds.). (2009). *European Identity.* Cambridge: Cambridge University Press.

Cheneval, F., & Ferrín, M. (Eds.). (2018). *Citizenship in Segmented Societies: Lessons for the EU.* Cheltenham: Edward Elgar.

Citrin, J., & Sears, D. O. (2009). Balancing national and ethnic identities: The psychology of E Pluribus Unum. In R. Abdelal, Y. M. Herrera, A. I. Johnston, & R. McDermott (Eds.), *Measuring Identity: A Guide for Social Scientists* (pp. 145–175). Cambridge: Cambridge University Press.

Citrin, J., & Sides, J. (2004). More than nationals: How identity choice matters in the new Europe. In R. K. Herrmann, T. Risse, & M. B. Brewer (Eds.), *Transnational Identities: Becoming European in the EU* (pp. 161–185). Lanham: Rowman & Littlefield Publishers.

Commission, E. (2012). *The Citizen's Effect: 25 Features About the Europe for Citizens Programme.* Luxembourg: Publications Office of the European Union.

Converse, P. E. (1972). Change in the American Electorate. In A. Campbell & P. E. Converse (Eds.), *The Human Meaning of Social Change* (pp. 263–337). New York: Russell Sage.

Corbett, A. (2012). Principles, problems, politics: What does the historical record of EU cooperation in higher education tell the EHEA generation? In A. Curaj, P. Scott, L. Vlasceanu, & L. Wilson (Eds.), *European Higher Education at the*

Cross-Roads: Between the Bologna Process and National Reforms (pp. 39–58). Dordrecht: Springer.

Curaj, A., Scott, P., Vlasceanu, L., & Wilson, L. (Eds.). (2012). *European Higher Education at the Crossroads: Between the Bologna Process and National Reforms*. Netherlands: Springer.

Dagger, R. (2002). Republican citizenship. In E. F. Isin & B. S. Turner (Eds.), *Handbook of Citizenship Studies* (pp. 145–158). London: Sage.

Dalton, R. J., & Klingemann, H. D. (Eds.). (2007). *Oxford Handbook of Political Behaviour*. Oxford: Oxford Handbooks.

Dassonneville, R., & Hooghe, M. (2018). Indifference and alienation: Diverging dimensions of electoral dealignment in Europe. *Acta Politica, 53*(1), 1–23.

Davidov, E., Seddig, D., Gorodzeisky, A., Raijman, R., Schmidt, P., & Semyonov, M. (2019). Direct and indirect predictors of opposition to immigration in Europe: Individual values, cultural values, and symbolic threat. *Journal of Ethnic and Migration Studies*. https://doi.org/10.1080/1369183X.2018.1550152.

De Giorgi, G., & Pellizzari, M. (2009). Welfare migration in Europe. *Labour Economics, 16*(4), 353–363.

Delanty, G. (2009). *The Cosmopolitan Imagination: The Renewal of Critical Social Theory*. Cambridge: Cambridge University Press.

Della Sala, V. (2010). Political Myth, Mythology and the European Union. *JCMS: Journal of Common Market Studies, 48*, 1–19. https://doi.org/10.1111/j.1468-5965.2009.02039.

Dennis, J. (2019). *Beyond Slacktivism: Political Participation on Social Media*. Basingstoke: Palgrave Macmillan.

Deutsch, K. W., Burrel, S. A., Kann, R. A., Lee, M. Jr., Lichterman, M., Lindgren, R. E., et al. (1968). *Political Community and the North Atlantic Area*. Princeton: Princeton University Press.

Díez Medrano, J., & Gutiérrez, P. (2001). Nested identities: National and European identity in Spain. *Ethnic and Racial Studies, 24*(5), 753–778.

Dilworth, P. P. (2008). Multicultural citizenship education. In J. Arthur, I. Davies, & C. Hahn (Eds.), *The Sage Handbook for Education and Citizenship and Democracy* (pp.424–437). London: Sage.

Duchesne, S. (2008). Waiting for a European identity … Reflections on the process of identification with Europe. *Perspectives on European Politics and Society, 9*(4), 397–410.

Duchesne, S., Frazer, E., Haegel, F., & Van Ingelgom, V. (Eds.). (2013). *Citizens' Reactions to European Integration Compared: Overlooking Europe*. Basingstoke: Palgrave.

Duda-Mikulin, E. A. (2019). *EU Migrant Workers, Brexit and Precarity: Polish Women's Perspectives from Inside the UK*. Bristol: Policy Press.

Duffy, B., Hewlett, M. J., & Hall, J. (2019). *Divided Britain? Polarisation and Fragmentation Trends in the UK*. The Policy Institute: King's College London. https://www.kcl.ac.uk/policy-institute/assets/divided-britain.pdf.

Dummett, A. (2006). United Kingdom. In R. Bauböck, E. Ersbøll, K. Groenendijk, & H. Waldrauch (Eds.), *Acquisition and Loss of Nationality Policies and Trends in 15 European States Volume 2: Country Analyses* (pp. 551–587). Amsterdam: Amsterdam University Press.

EHEA. (1999, June 19). *The Bologna Declaration: Joint declaration of the European Ministers of Education Convened*. Bologna.

Eisenstadt, S. N., & Giesen, B. (1995). The construction of collective identity. *European Journal of Sociology, 26*(1), 72–102.

Etzioni, A. (1995). *The Spirit of Community*. London: Fontana.

European Commission. (1985, July 9). *Proposal for a council: Directive on a general system for the recognition of higher education diplomas, COM(85) 355 final*. Brussels.

European Commission. (1993, December 21). *First report on citizenship of the Unio, COM(93) 702 final*. Brussels.

European Commission. (2001, November 21). *Making a European area of lifelong learning a reality, COM/2001/0678 final*. Brussels.

European Commission. (2010, September 15). *Youth on the move: A guide to the rights of mobile students in the European Union, COM(2010) 477 final*. Brussels.

European Commission. (2011, September 20). *Supporting growth and jobs—An agenda for the modernisation of Europe's higher education systems, COM (2011) 567 final*. Brussels.

European Commission. (2017). *The Erasmus impact study*. https://op.europa.eu/en/publication-detail/-/publication/13031399-9fd4-11e5-8781-01aa75ed71a1.

European Parliament. (2017). *Report on EU Citizenship Report 2017: Strengthening Citizens' Rights in a Union of Democratic Change, (2017/2069(INI))*.

European Commission. (2018). *Erasmus+ annual report 2017*. https://op.europa.eu/en/publication-detail/-/publication/4e5c3e1c-1f0b-11e9-8d04-01aa75ed71a1.

European Commission. (2019). *Erasmus+*. https://ec.europa.eu/programmes/erasmus-plus/node_en.

European Commission. (2020). *Erasmus+ programme guide 2020*. https://ec.europa.eu/programmes/erasmus-plus/resources/documents/erasmus-programme-guide-2020_en.

European Commission/EACEA/Eurydice. (2018). *The European Higher Education Area in 2018: Bologna Process Implementation Report*. Luxembourg: Publications Office of the European Union.

Eurostat. (2019a). *Acquisition of citizenship statistics.* https://ec.europa.eu/eur ostat/statistics-explained/index.php/Acquisition_of_citizenship_statistics.

Eurostat. (2019b). *Learning mobility statistics.* https://ec.europa.eu/eurostat/statistics-explained/index.php/Learning_mobility_statistics#Number_and_share_of_students_from_abroad.

Eurostat. (2019c). *Tertiary education statistics.* https://ec.europa.eu/eurostat/statistics-explained/index.php/Tertiary_education_statistics.

Favell, A. (2008). *Eurostars and Eurocities: Free Movement and Mobility in an Integrating Europe.* Oxford: Blackwell.

Favell, A. (2010). European identity and European citizenship in three "Eurocities": A sociological approach to the European Union. *Politique Européenne, 30,* 187–224.

Fernández, Ó. (2005). Towards European citizenship through higher education? *European Journal of Education, 40*(1), 59–68.

Ferrera, M., & Pellegata, A. (2018). Worker mobility under attack? Explaining labour market chauvinism in the EU. *Journal of European Public Policy, 25*(10), 1461–1480.

Fligstein, N. (2008). *Euroclash: The EU, European Identity and the Future of Europe.* Oxford: Oxford University Press.

Follesdal, A. (2001). Union citizenship: Unpacking the beast of burden. *Law and Philosophy, 20*(3), 313–343.

Ford, R., & Mellon, J. (2019). The skills premium and the ethnic premium: A cross-national experiment on European attitudes to immigrants. *Journal of Ethnic and Migration Studies.* https://doi.org/10.1080/1369183X.2018.1550148.

Franklin, M. N. (2004). *Voter Turnout and the Dynamics of Electoral Competition in Established Democracies Since 1945.* Cambridge: Cambridge University Press.

Fukuyama, F. (2018). *Identity: Contemporary Identity Politics and the Struggle for Recognition.* London: Profile Books.

Fuss, D., & Grosser, M. A. (2006). What makes young Europeans feel European? Results from a cross-cultural research project. In I. P. Karolewski & V. Kaina (Eds.), *European Identity: Theoretical Perspectives and Empirical Insights* (pp. 209–242). Berlin: LIT Verlag.

Gellner, E. (1983). *Nations and Nationalism.* Oxford: Basil Blackwell.

Gorodzeisky, A., & Semyonov, M. (2019). Perceptions and misperceptions: Actual size, perceived size and opposition to immigration in European societies. *Journal of Ethnic and Migration Studies.* https://doi.org/10.1080/1369183X.2018.1550158.

Green, E. G. T., Visintin, E. P., Sarrasin, O., & Hewstone, M. (2019). When integration policies shape the impact of intergroup contact on threat perceptions: A multilevel study across 20 European countries. *Journal of Ethnic and Migration Studies.* https://doi.org/10.1080/1369183X.2018.1550159.

Guild, E., Peers, S., & Tomkin, J. (2019). *The EU Citizenship Directive: A Commentary.* Oxford: Oxford University Press.

Guiraudon, V., Ruzza, C., & Trenz, H. J. (Eds.). (2015). *Europe's Prolonged Crisis: The Making or the Unmaking of a Political Union.* Basingstoke: Palgrave Macmillan.

Haas, E. B. (1958). *The Uniting of Europe: Political, Social and Economic Forces 1950–1957.* Stanford: Stanford University Press.

Habermas, J. (2003). Towards a cosmopolitan Europe. *Journal of Democracy, 14*(4), 86–100.

Halikiopoulou, D. (2018). A right-wing populist momentum? A review of 2017 elections across Europe. *Journal of Common Market Studies, 56*(S1), 63–73.

Hansen, R. (2009). The poverty of postnationalism: Citizenship, immigration, and the new Europe. *Theory and Society, 38*(1), 1–24.

Hansen, P., & Hager, S. B. (2010). *The Politics of European Citizenship: Deepening Contradictions in Social Rights and Migration Policy.* New York: Berghahn Books.

Hansson, E., & Jansson, D. (2019). Who's afraid of the 'beggar'? A psychoanalytic interpretation of the crises triggered by the begging of 'EU migrants' in Sweden. *Social and Cultural Geography, 7*, 1–18.

Heater, D. (2004a). *Citizenship: The Civic Ideal in World History, Politics and Education.* Manchester: Manchester University Press.

Heater, D. (2004b). *A History of Education for Citizenship.* London: Routledge Falmer.

Heath, A. F., Davidov, E., Ford, R., Green, E. G., Ramos, A., & Schmidt, P. (2019). Contested terrain: Explaining divergent patterns of public opinion towards immigration within Europe. *Journal of Ethnic and Migration Studies.* https://doi.org/10.1080/1369183X.2019.1550145.

Heath, A. F., & Richards, L. (2019). Contested boundaries: Consensus and dissensus in European attitudes to immigration. *Journal of Ethnic and Migration Studies.* https://doi.org/10.1080/1369183X.2018.1550146.

Herrmann, R., & Brewer, M. B. (2004). Identities and institutions: Becoming European in the EU. In R. K. Herrmann, T. Risse, & B. M. Brewer (Eds.), *Transnational Identities: Becoming European in the EU* (pp. 1–22). Oxford: Rowman & Littlefield.

Hix, S. (2004). Electoral institutions and legislative behavior: Explaining voting defection in the European Parliament. *World Politics, 56*(2), 194–223.

Hobsbawm, E. (1996). Identity politics and the left. *New Left Review, 217,* 38–47.

Hoskins, B., D'Hombres, B., & Campbell, J. (2008). Does formal education have an impact on active citizenship behaviour? *European Educational Research Journal, 7*(3), 386–402.

Hoskins, B. L., & Mascherini, M. (2009). Measuring active citizenship through the development of a composite indicator. *Social Indicators Research, 90*(3), 459–488.

House of Lords. (2019). *Brexit: the Erasmus and Horizon programmes.* https://publications.parliament.uk/pa/ld201719/ldselect/ldeucom/283/283.pdf.

Howard, M. M. (2009). *The Politics of Citizenship in Europe.* Cambridge: Cambridge University Press.

Isin, E. F. (2008). Theorizing acts of citizenship. In E. F. Isin & G. M. Nielsen (Eds.), *Acts of Citizenship* (pp. 15–43). Basingstoke: Palgrave Macmillan.

Isin, E. F. (2009). Citizenship in flux: The figure of the activist citizen. *Subjectivity, 29*(1), 367–388.

Isin, E. F., & Nielsen, G. M. (Eds.). (2008). *Acts of Citizenship.* London and New York: Zed Books Limited.

Isin, E. F., & Nyers, P. (Eds.). (2014). Introduction: Globalizing citizenship studies. In *Routledge Handbook of Global Citizenship Studies* (pp. 1–11). London: Routledge.

Isin, E. F., & Saward, M. (Eds.). (2013). *Enacting European Citizenship.* Cambridge: Cambridge University Press.

Isin, E. F., & Turner, B. S. (Eds.). (2002). *Handbook of Citizenship Studies.* London: Sage.

Isin, E. F., & Turner, B. S. (2007). Investigating citizenship: An agenda for citizenship studies. *Citizenship Studies, 11*(1), 5–17.

Jackman, R. (1987). Political institutions and voter turnout in industrial democracies. *American Political Science Review, 81,* 405–423.

Joppke, C. (2007). Transformation of citizenship: Status, rights, identity. *Citizenship Studies, 11*(1), 37–48.

Joppke, C. (2010). The inevitable lightening of citizenship. *European Journal of Sociology/Archives Européennes de Sociologie, 51*(1), 9–32.

Juverdeanu, C. (2019). The different gears of EU citizenship. *Journal of Ethnic and Migration Studies.* https://doi.org/10.1080/1369183X.2019.1632697.

Kaina, V. (2013). How to reduce disorder in European identity research? *European Political Science, 12,* 184–196.

Kaina, V., & Karolewski, I. P. (2013). EU governance and European identity. *Living Reviews in European Governance, 8*(1), 1–41.

Kanter, C. (2006). Collective identity as shared ethical self-understanding: The case of the emerging European identity. *European Journal of Social Theory, 9*(4), 501–523.

Karolewski, I. P. (2010). *Citizenship and Collective Identity in Europe.* London: Routledge.

Karolewski, I. P. (2009). European nationalism and European identity. In I. P. Karolewski & A. Suszycki (Eds.), *Multiplicity of Nationalism in Contemporary Europe* (pp. 59–80). Plymouth: Rowman & Littlefield.

Karolewski, I. P. (2011). *The Nation and Nationalism: An Introduction.* Edinburgh: Edinburgh University Press.

Kaufmann, E. (2019). Can narratives of white identity reduce opposition to immigration and support for hard Brexit? A survey experiment. *Political Studies, 67*(1), 31–46.

Kaun, A. (2015). When narratives travel: The occupy movement in Latvia and Sweden. In J. Uldam & A. Vestergaard (Eds.), *Civic Engagement and Social Media: Political Participation Beyond Protest* (pp. 111–130). Basingstoke: Palgrave Macmillan.

King, R. (2003). International student migration and the European 'Year Abroad': Effects on European identity and subsequent migration behaviour. In J. Doomernik & H. Knippenberg (Eds.), *Migration and Immigrants: Between Policy and Reality* (pp. 155–179). Amsterdam: Aksant Academic Publishers.

Kofman, E. (1995). Citizenship for some but not for others: Spaces of citizenship in contemporary Europe. *Political Geography, 14*(2), 121–138.

Kostakopoulou, T. (2001). *Citizenship, Identity and Immigration in the European Union: Between Past and Future.* Manchester: Manchester University Press.

Kostakopoulou, D. (2008). *The Future Governance of Citizenship.* Cambridge: Cambridge University Press.

Kuhn, T. (2012). Why educational exchange programmes miss their mark: Cross-border mobility, education and European identity. *Journal of Common Market Studies, 50*(6), 994–1010.

Kuhn, T. (2015). *Experiencing European Integration: Transnational Lives and European Identity.* Oxford: Oxford University Press.

Lavenex, S. (2001). Migration and the EU's new eastern border: Between realism and liberalism. *Journal of European Public Policy, 8*(1), 24–42.

Leddy-Owen, C. (2019). *Nationalism, Inequality and England's Political Predicament.* London: Routledge.

Lindsay, F. (2018). Why Sweden is deporting high-skilled labor migrants. *Forbes.* https://www.forbes.com/sites/freylindsay/2019/02/13/why-sweden-is-deporting-high-skilled-labor-migrants/#123a1f7f4510.

Lock, G., & Martins, H. (2009). The European universities, citizenship and its limits: What won't solve the problems of our time. *European Educational Research Journal, 8*(2), 159–174.

Mackert, J., & Turner, B. S. (Eds.). (2017). *The Transformation of Citizenship: Boundaries of Inclusion and Exclusion.* London: Routledge.

Maas, W. (2007). *Creating European Citizens.* Lanham: Rowman & Littlefield.

Maas, W. (2013). Free movement and discrimination: Evidence from Europe, the United States, and Canada. *European Journal of Migration and Law, 15*(1), 91–110.

Magnette, P. (2005). *Citizenship: The History of an Idea.* Colchester: ECPR Press.

Marshall, T. H. (1950). *Citizenship and Social Class and Other Essays.* Cambridge: Cambridge University Press.

McDonnell, A., & Curtis, C. (2019). How Britain voted in the 2019 general election. *YouGov.* https://yougov.co.uk/topics/politics/articles-reports/2019/12/17/how-britain-voted-2019-general-election.

Mattila, M. (2003). Why bother? Determinants of turnout in the European elections. *Electoral Studies, 22*(3), 449–468.

Meehan, E. (1993). *Citizenship and the European Community.* London: Sage.

Midtbøen, A. H., Birkvad, S. R., & Erdal, M. B. (2018). *Citizenship in the Nordic Countries: Past, Present, Future.* Rosendals.

Miller, D. (1995). Reflections on British national identity. *Journal of Ethnic and Migration Studies, 21*(2), 153–166. https://doi.org/10.1080/1369183X.1995.9976481.

Mitchell, K. (2012). Student mobility and European identity: Erasmus study as a civic experience? *Journal of Contemporary European Research, 8*(4), 490–518.

Mitchell, K. (2014). Rethinking the 'Erasmus Effect' on European identity. *JCMS: Journal of Common Market Studies.* https://doi.org/10.1111/jcms.12152.

Muxel, A. (2009). EU movers and politics: Towards a fully-fledged European citizenship? In E. Recchi & A. Favell (Eds.), *Pioneers of European Integration* (pp. 156–178). Cheltenham: Edward Elgar.

Mycock, A. (2009). British citizenship and the legacy of empires. *Parliamentary Affairs, 63*(2), 339–355.

Neumann, I. B. (1996). Self and other in international relations. *European Journal of International Relations, 2*(2), 139–174.

Norris, P. (2003). Young people and political activism: From the politics of loyalties to the politics of choice? *Report Presented for the Council of Europe Symposium.* Strasbourg, France.

Nyers, P. (Ed.). (2009). *Securitizations of Citizenship.* London: Routledge.

O'Brien, C. (2016). Civis capitalist sum: Class as the new guiding principle of EU free movement rights. *Common Market Law Review, 53*(4), 937–977.

Olsen, E. D. H. (2012). *Transnational Citizenship in the European Union: Past, Present and Future.* London and New York: Continuum Books.

Olsen, E. D. H. (2015). Eurocrisis and EU citizenship. In V. Guiraudon, C. Ruzza, & H. J. Trenz (Eds.), *Europe's Prolonged Crisis: The Making or the Unmaking of a Political Union* (pp. 85–103). Basingstoke: Palgrave Macmillan.

ONS. (2015). *2011 Census analysis*. https://www.ons.gov.uk/peoplepopulatio nandcommunity/culturalidentity/ethnicity/articles/2011censusanalysisethnic ityandreligionofthenonukbornpopulationinenglandandwales/2015-06-18.

Parliament.uk. (2019). *International and EU students in higher education in the UK FAQs*. https://researchbriefings.parliament.uk/ResearchBriefing/ Summary/CBP-7976#fullreport.

Pattie, C., Seyd, P., & Whiteley, P. (2004). *Citizenship in Britain: Values, Participation and Democracy*. Cambridge: Cambridge University Press.

Petit, I. (2007). Mimicking history: The European Commission and its education policy. *World Political Science, 3*(1), 1–24.

Plutzer, E. (2002). Becoming a habitual voter: Inertia, resources, and growth in young adulthood. *American Political Science Review, 96*, 41–56.

Poggi, G. (2003). Citizens and the state: Retrospect and prospect. In B. Stråth & Q. Skinner (Eds.), *States and Citizens: History, Theory Prospects*. Cambridge: Cambridge University Press.

Prabhat, D. (2018). *Britishness, Belonging and Citizenship: Experiencing Nationality Law*. Bristol: Policy Press.

Prüge, E., & Thiel, M. (Eds.). (2009). *Diversity in the European Union*. New York: Palgrave Macmillan.

Pukallus, S. (2016). *Representations of European Citizenship Since 1951*. Basingstoke: Palgrave Macmillan.

Putnam, R. D. (2001). *Bowling Alone: The Collapse and Revival of American Community*. New York: Simon & Schuster.

Ramos, A., Pereira, C. R., & Vala, J. (2019). The impact of biological and cultural racisms on attitudes towards immigrants and immigration public policies. *Journal of Ethnic and Migration Studies*. https://doi.org/10.1080/136 9183X.2018.1550153.

Recchi, E. (2015). *Mobile Europe: The Theory and Practice of Free Movement in the EU*. Basingstoke: Palgrave Macmillan.

Recchi, E., & Favell, A. (Eds.). (2009). *Pioneers of European Integration: Citizenship and Mobility in the EU*. Cheltenham: Edward Elgar Publishing.

Risse, T. (2003). The Euro between national and European identity. *Journal of European Public Policy, 10*(4), 487–505.

Risse, T. (2004). European institutions and identity change: what have we learned? In R. K. Herrmann, T. Risse, & M. B. Brewer (Eds.), *Transnational Identities: Becoming European in the EU* (pp. 247–271). Lanham: Rowman & Littlefield.

Risse, T. (2010). *A Community of Europeans? Transnational Identities and Public Spheres*. Ithaca: Cornell University Press.

Risse-Kappen, T. (1995). Exploring the nature of the beast: International relations theory and comparative policy analysis meets the European Union. *Journal of Common Market Studies, 34*(1), 54–80.

Rosamond, B. (2016). Brexit and the problem of European disintegration. *Journal of Contemporary European Research, 12*(4), 864–871.

Rosenstone, S. J., & Hansen, J. M. (1993). *Mobilization, Participation, and Democracy in America.* New York: MacMillan.

Ross, A. (2015). *Understanding the Constructions of Identities by Young New Europeans: Kaleidoscopic Selves.* London: Routledge.

Ross, A. (2019). *Finding Political Identities: Young People in a Changing Europe.* Basingstoke: Palgrave Macmillan.

Rother, N., & Nebe, T. M. (2009). More mobile, more European? Free movement and EU identity. In E. Recchi & A. Favell (Eds.), *Pioneers of European Integration* (pp. 120–155). Cheltenham: Edward Elgar.

Sanders, D., Belluci, P., Tóka, G., & Torcal, N. (Eds.). (2012). *The Europeanization of National Polities? Citizenship and Support in a Post-Enlargement Union.* Oxford: Oxford University Press.

Sanders, D., Magalhães, P., & Tóka, G. (Eds.). (2012). *Citizens and the European Polity: Mass Attitudes Towards the European and National Polities.*Oxford: Oxford University Press.

Sawyer, C., & Wary, H. (2014). Country report: UK. *EUDO Citizenship Observatory.* https://cadmus.eui.eu/bitstream/handle/1814/33839/EUDO-CIT_2014_01_UK.pdf.

SCB. (2019). *Analysis of voter turnout in the 2018 general elections.* https://www.scb.se/en/finding-statistics/statistics-by-subject-area/democracy/general-elections/general-elections-participation-survey/pong/statistical-news/general-elections-electoral-participation-survey-2018/.

SCB. (2020). *Population by country of birth, age and sex. Year 2000–2018.* http://www.statistikdatabasen.scb.se/pxweb/en/ssd/START__BE__BE0101__BE0101E/FodelselandArK/.

Schierup, C.-U., & Ålund, A. (2011). The end of Swedish exceptionalism? Citizenship, neoliberalism and the politics of exclusion. *Race and Class, 53*(1), 45–64.

Schmidt, V. A. (2013). Democracy and legitimacy in the European Union revisited: Input, output and 'throughput'. *Political Studies, 61*(1), 2–22.

Schmidt, S. K., Blauberger, M., & Martinsen, D. S. (2018). Free movement and equal treatment in an unequal union. *Journal of European Public Policy, 25*(10), 1391–1402. https://doi.org/10.1080/13501763.2018.1488887.

Seubert, S. (2017). Antinomies of European citizenship: On the conflictual passage of a transnational membership regime. In J. Mackert & B. S. Turner (Eds.), *The Transformation of Citizenship: Boundaries of Inclusion and Exclusion* (pp. 135–151). London: Routledge.

Shaw, J. (1998). Citizenship of the Union: Towards post-national membership? *Collected Courses of the Academy of European Law, VI*(1), 237–347 (Kluwer).

Shore, C. (2004). Whither European citizenship? Eros and civilization revisited. *European Journal of Social Theory, 7*(1), 27–44.

Sigalas, E. (2009). Does ERASMUS Student Mobility promote a European Identity? *Webpapers on Constitutionalism and Governance beyond the State*, 2009/2.

Sigalas, E. (2010a). Cross-border mobility and European identity: The effectiveness of intergroup contact during the ERASMUS year abroad. *European Union Politics, 11*(2), 241–265.

Sigalas, E. (2010b). The role of personal benefits in public support for the EU: Learning from the Erasmus students. *West European Politics, 33*(6), 1341–1361.

Siklodi, N. (2014). Multi-level citizenship: Labour migration and the transformation of identity in the EU. In C. Rumford & D. Buhari-Gulmez (Eds.), *European Multiplicity* (pp. 129–146). Newcastle upon Tyne: Cambridge Scholars Publishing.

Siklodi, N. (2019). The Brexit crisis: Potential implications for the EU and its citizens. In Europa Publications (Ed.). *European Union Encyclopedia and Directory 2020* (20th Ed.). Abingdon, UK: Routledge.

Sivesind, K. H., Trætteberg, H. S., & Saglie, J. (2017). The future of the Scandinavian welfare model: User choice, parallel governance systems, and active citizenship. In K. Sivesind, J. Saglie, & I. Kh (Eds.), *Promoting Active Citizenship. Markets and Choice in Scandinavian Welfare* (pp. 285–310). Oslo: Palgrave Macmillan.

Sloam, J. (2014a). New voice, less equal: The civic and political engagement of young people in the United States and Europe. *Comparative Political Studies, 47*(5), 663–688.

Sloam, J. (2014b). "The outraged young": Young Europeans, civic engagement and the new media in a time of crisis. *Information, Communication and Society, 17*(2), 217–231.

Sloam, J., & Henn, M. (2019). *Youthquake 2017: The Rise of Young Cosmopolitans in Britain*. Basingstoke: Palgrave Macmillan.

Smets, K., & Van Ham, C. (2013). The embarrassment of riches? A meta-analysis of individual-level research on voter turnout. *Electoral Studies, 32*(2), 344–359.

Smith, A. D. (1992). National identity and the idea of European Identity. *International Affairs, 68*(1), 55–76.

Souto-Otero, M., Huisman, J., Beerkens, M., de Wit, H., & Vujić, S. (2013). Barriers to international student mobility: Evidence from the Erasmus program. *Educational Researcher*, 42(2), 70–77. https://doi.org/10.3102%2F0013189X12466696.

Soysal, Y. N. (1994). *Limits of Citizenship: Migrants and Postnational Membership in Europe*. Chicago: University of Chicago Press.

Stewart, E., & Mulvey, G. (2011). Becoming British citizens?: Experiences and opinions of refugees living in Scotland. *Scottish Refugee Council.* http://www.scottishrefugeecouncil.org.uk/assets/0000/1460/Citizenship_report_Feb11.pdf.

Tam, H. (Ed.). (2019). *Whose Government Is It? The Renewal of State-Citizen Cooperation.* Bristol: Policy Press.

Taylor, C. (1989). *Sources of the Self: The Making of Modern Identity.* Cambridge: Harvard University Press.

Taylor, D. (2018). UK removed legal protection for Windrush immigrants in 2014. *The Guardian.* https://www.theguardian.com/uk-news/2018/apr/16/immigration-law-key-clause-protecting-windrush-immigrants-removed-in-2014.

Tilly, C. (1995). Citizenship, Identity and Social History. *International Review of Social History, 40,* 1–17.

Tilly, C. (2003). Political identities in changing polities. *Social Research,70,* 605–620.

Torney-Purta, J., & Amadeo, J. A. (2011). Participatory niches for emergent citizenship in early adolescence: An international perspective. *The ANNALS of the American Academy of Political and Social Science, 633,* 180–200.

Torney-Purta, J., Barber, C., Wilkenfield, B., & Homana, G. (2008). Profiles of civic life skills among adolescents: Indicators for researchers, policymakers, and the public. *Child Indicators Research, 1,* 86–106.

Turner, B. S. (Ed.). (1993). *Citizenship and Social Theory.* London: Sage.

ÜKA. (2019). *Higher Education Institutions in Sweden 2019.* https://english.uka.se/download/18.672af1d416b8ffabaa9e33e/1565767111266/report-2019-08-14-higher-education-institutions-in%20sweden-status-report.pdf.

Van Den Brink, M., & Kochenov, D. (2019). Against Associate EU Citizenship. *JCMS: Journal of Common Market Studies.* https://doi.org/10.1111/jcms.12898.

Van Deth, J. W., Montero, J. R., & Westholm, A. (Eds.). (2007). *Citizenship and Involvement in European Democracies: A Comparative Analysis.* London: Routledge.

Van Mol, C. (2014). *Intra-European Student Mobility in International Higher Education Circuits: Europe on the Move.* Basingstoke: Palgrave Macmillan.

Vasilopoulou, S., & Talving, L. (2019). Opportunity or threat? Public attitudes towards EU freedom of movement. *Journal of European Public Policy.* https://doi.org/10.1080/13501763.2018.1497075.

Verba, S., & Nie, N. H. (1963). *Participation in America: Political Democracy and Social Equality.* New York: Harper and Row.

Verger, C. (2018). Transnational lists–A political opportunity for Europe with obstacles to overcome. *Policy Paper, 216(7).* https://institutdelors.eu/wp-content/uploads/2018/02/Transnationallists-Verger-Feb18.pdf.

Vertovec, S., & Wessendorf, S. (Eds.). (2010). *Multiculturalism Backlash: European Discourses, Policies and Practices*. London: Routledge.

Vink, M. P., & Bauböck, R. (2013). Citizenship configurations: Analyzing the multiple purposes of citizenship regimes in Europe. *Comparative European Politics, 11*, 621–648.

Walkenhorst, H. (2008). Explaining change in EU education policy. *Journal of European Public Policy, 15*(4), 567–587.

White, J. (2011). *Political Allegiance after European Integration*. Basingstoke: Palgrave Macmillan.

Whiteley, P. (2012). *Political Participation in Britain: The Decline and Revival of Civic Culture*. Basingstoke: Palgrave Macmillan.

Wilson, I. (2011). What should we expect of "Erasmus Generations"? *Journal of Common Market Studies, 49*(5), 1113–1140.

Yuval-Davis, N. (2007). Intersectionality, citizenship and contemporary politics of belonging. *Critical Review of International Social and Political Philosophy, 10*(4), 561–574.

Zajda, J., Daun, H., & Saha, L. (Eds.). (2009). *Nation-Building, Identity and Citizenship Education: Cross-Cultural Perspectives*. New York: Springer Science+Business Media.

CHAPTER 3

A Snapshot of Mobile Citizenship in the EU

European studies scholars have provided empirically rich evidence of how senses of European citizenship change across the European Union (EU), within its member states and over time. Rather than breaking new ground in quantitative evaluation, this chapter complements their work by introducing a more political reading of contemporary trends in senses of national and European citizenship (as set out by Chapter 2), along the mobile/stayer distinctions.

For instance, EU studies have repeatedly shown us that European *and* national identities are permanent fixtures in citizens' lives, offering critical insights into the interaction between national *and* European affiliations (McLaren 2006; Risse 2010; Kuhn 2015). In 'searching for a *collective* European identity', they raised reservations about the contradictory effects of individual socio-economic factors and national frames on European identity (for an overview, see Duchesne 2008). They also warned about the likely implications which rational cost-benefit calculations and the lack of EU political participation have for the EU's democratic legitimacy (Hooghe and Marks 2004; Kuhn 2019).

Instead of soothing these concerns, the introduction of EU citizenship seems to have made them worse.

Contributing to the arrival of a 'constraining dissensus'—more popular engagement with but less support for further European integration (Hooghe and Marks 2009)—the apparent failure of the EU to 'win the

© The Author(s) 2020
N. Siklodi, *The Politics of Mobile Citizenship in Europe*,
Politics of Citizenship and Migration,
https://doi.org/10.1007/978-3-030-49051-5_3

hearts' of citizens (Duchesne and Frognier 1994, 2008) began to shape approaches to politics. Hence, more and more decisions to vote and select candidates were found to have been affected by EU political considerations (Hobolt et al. 2009; Shackel 2018). Accordingly, the consistently low turnout levels at the European Parliament (EP) elections—with an average of 51.93% between 1979 and 2019—are a sign of popular dissatisfaction with EU politics (Matilla 2003; Hix and Marsh 2011; Stockemer 2012; Fiorino et al. 2019).

The implications of these findings for broader political developments are startling.

The increased support enjoyed by Eurosceptic and populist politicians serves as an incentive for member state governments 'to blame Europe' for domestic political failures (Hobolt and Tilley 2014; De Vries 2018). They fragment the EP considerably, which in turn affects its significance relative to other European and national actors (Laffan 2019) and the quality of democracy at the highest levels of the EU (Hobolt 2012). The intrinsic relationship between European and national politics has also meant that changes in one political system affect the other—as apparent in United Kingdom (UK) developments during Brexit (Diamond et al. 2018).

In addition, EU studies have emphasised and repeatedly tested the bi-level structure of national and EU citizenship. Their findings cast some doubt on the reservations of citizenship studies scholars—most notably the supposed incompatibility of national and EU models (e.g. Bellamy 2008).

By relying on secondary data, often funded by the Union, EU studies have also had to make some necessary conceptual and analytical concessions. Recognising the relationship between identity politics and political behaviour, they have had to limit the scope of their analyses to one or other issue (e.g. in Kuhn 2019), inevitably leading to a fragmented understanding about the dimensions of citizenship in Europe.

Sanders and colleagues are notable exceptions (Sanders et al. 2012a, 2012b), providing the first, and so far only, comprehensive and systematic assessment of the dimensions of national and European citizenship. They show the inherent connections *and* tensions apparent in these affiliations but emphasise reasons to applaud rather than critique the direction EU citizenship is taking. What is, nonetheless, missing from their study is a consideration of how experiences of free movement and mobility affect senses of citizenship.

In fact, empirical assessment of this issue only became a 'trendy' topic after the mid-2000s—with the surge in EU mobility flows (Table 1.1). Dissecting how emerging trends of transnationalism and European identity are affected by cross-border interactions, student mobility and stayers' perceptions of free movement has, however, led to conflicting conclusions (compare, for instance, King and Ruiz-Gelices 2003; Wilson 2011; Kuhn 2012a, 2012b; Mitchell 2012, 2014).

Despite the assertion of legally minded scholars and EU actors, empirical evaluation of EU mobility as *the* stimulus for EU citizenship remains sparse (Brändle 2018). Assessment of the broader contours of *mobile* citizenship in Europe is nearly exclusively studied by Recchi and colleagues (especially Recchi and Favell 2009; Recchi 2015).

This chapter seeks to complement their work by bringing together the rich insights EU data can provide (EB 89.1, 2018), and the more inclusive conceptual approach advocated by citizenship studies. Given the complexity of these issues, the chapter paves the ground for a closer inspection of contemporary citizenship via in-depth, qualitative interrogation.

The chapter is structured as follows.

The first part provides an EU-wide and cross-country (Swedish and UK) longitudinal snapshot of multiple senses of citizenship as well as attitudes towards migrants. The second draws attention to the relevance of mobility for contemporary notions of citizenship. The third part provides a multivariate analysis of individual senses of European citizenship in the light of mobility and the relevant dimensions of citizenship as well as key sociological indicators.

3.1   MULTIPLE SENSES OF CITIZENSHIP AND MIGRANT ATTITUDES IN EUROPE

The vast research done by EU studies underscores that an empirical snapshot of national and European senses of citizenship refutes the long-standing assumptions about the incompatibility of these models.

To support this, Table 3.1 provides an indication of overtime and cross-country trends in senses of national and European citizenship in the EU-28 and, specifically, in Sweden and the UK (from where the focus group evidence used in the later chapters was collected).

Table 3.1 indicates that the majority of citizens hold dual senses of national and European citizenship across the EU-28. Starting at an average of 56% in 2015, we can observe a general increase in these associations over time, reaching 63% by 2018.

The table also underscores that differences in senses of citizenship are apparent between member states *and* within them. The Swedish example shows a similarly positive but perhaps a slightly more consistent trend in senses of European citizenship. It even overtakes the EU average recorded in the middle of the examined 2015–2018 period—after the Brexit vote and at the height of the migration crisis debate.

Although the UK is the only region in the table where senses of European citizenship were not asserted by a majority in 2018, it recorded the largest increase in European affiliations over time. There is a near 20% increase from 2016 to 2017 and, for the whole period, a 10% positive change. If anything, the growing trend in senses of European citizenship is likely to provide some support to the assumption that the significance of the EU—and so EU citizenship—is likely to be enhanced by presumptions of threat (Patrikios and Cram 2015).

Before giving too much weight to this issue however, it is important to recognise that the share of 'exclusive' European citizenship is by far

Table 3.1 Senses of national and European citizenship in the EU, Sweden and the UK (2015–2018)

Year/Sense of citizenship	Sweden				United Kingdom				EU-28			
	2015	2016	2017	2018	2015	2016	2017	2018	2015	2016	2017	2018
Nationality only	37	37	34	37	66	62	45	51	41	39	35	35
Nationality and European	56	57	58	56	29	31	45	41	51	51	54	55
European and Nationality	4	4	5	4	3	3	7	6	5	6	7	6
European only	1	1	2	1	1	1	2	1	1	2	2	2
Total European	61	62	65	61	33	35	54	48	57	59	63	63

Source European Commission (2016); European Commission (2017); EB89.1 (2018) Sweden N=1005, UK N=1337, EU-28 N=27,988

the smallest recorded in the Table 3.1. The maximum of 2% claiming to hold such attachment at any given time and in any given region is even more striking compared to the highs (66% in the UK in 2015) and lows of 'exclusive' nationality especially (35% in the EU-28 in 2018).

Continued importance of national affiliations is clearly shown in the data (Fligstein 2008; Khun 2015; Recchi 2015). In all three regions, exclusive 'nationality only' and more inclusive 'nationality and European' categories, together, counted for approximately 90% of public attitudes. Perhaps counter-intuitively, the UK was the only region to record any noticeable decline in national attachments over time—a solid 15% in 'exclusive' nationality.

Finally, Table 3.1 shows how important the 'ordering' of national and European dual attachments is for citizens. Indeed, 'national first' attachments outnumber 'European first' attachments by nearly 10 times for the time period considered. Even after 25 years of EU citizenship, there are only a handful of people who are likely to describe themselves as Europeans first.

The apparent complexity in senses of citizenship is likely to be further increased by how community building processes are revised by different forms of migration (as proposed in Chapter 2.1), including EU nationals' internal mobility and third country nationals' (TCNs') immigration.

To illustrate related trends, Fig. 3.1 charts public attitudes towards different migrant groups, including EU mobiles and TCNs across Sweden, the UK and the EU in 2018 (Source: EB 89.1, 2018).

At first, it seems as if 'fairly positive' attitudes characterise feelings towards migrants in the EU broadly speaking. However, a closer inspection reveals a marked decline in positive, and marked increase in negative, attitudes where distinctions are made between types of migrants.

Certainly, in the context of the unrelenting refugee crisis these attitudes translated into unequivocal processes of exclusion of TCNs—either in the form of institutionalised, antagonistic policies (proposed following elite claims for the need to 'securitise' the Swedish immigration system [Ericson 2018]) or emerged more organically in the form of a hostile social and political milieu (in news reporting on the UK government's 'catastrophic' settled status scheme for EU residents suggest [Carlo 2019]). Interestingly, both Sweden and the UK appear to hold a more

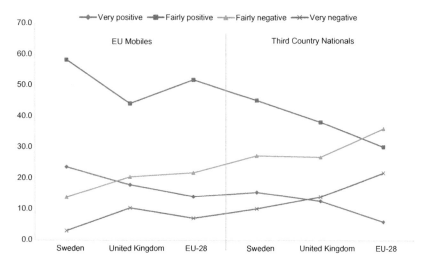

Fig. 3.1 Attitudes towards migrant groups in Sweden, the UK and the EU-28 in 2018

positive view of TCNs than the EU-28 average, where most survey respondents record a 'fairly negative' position.

Figure 3.1 also illustrates that most positive attitudes towards migrants are directed at EU mobiles across all three regions. Over 80% of Swedes hold positive attitudes towards EU mobiles—one of the highest across the EU. In fact, positive views of EU mobiles and migrants have persisted in Sweden for quite a number of years, despite some long-standing popular reservations about the extent to which migrants can integrate into the Swedish society given language restrictions for instance (GMF 2013). The positive Swedish attitude can also be interpreted in the light of the high senses of European citizenship recorded in the country (Table 3.1) and the observation of free movement as *the* most positive EU benefit by nearly 75% of Swedes (European Commission 2018: 21).

A slightly different picture emerges about UK attitudes towards EU mobiles from Fig. 3.1. 'Fairly positive' attitudes still account for the largest group in the country at around 44%. However, this number is smaller than the same recorded for the EU-28. In fact, the UK average of all positive and all negative attitudes towards EU mobiles is smaller and higher, respectively, than that of the EU-28 average. In the light of the

UK's much talked about 'outlier' position in the EU (Todd 2016) and the increased adversity towards EU mobiles, especially from Central and Eastern Europe (CEE) in the course of Brexit (Duda-Mikulin 2019), the large negative and the small positive sentiments towards EU mobiles are not surprising.

3.2 Citizenship and Migration Attitudes in the Context of Mobility

Given the complexities in, often, dual senses of national and European citizenship and approaches to migrant groups, this section examines these issues in more depth and by introducing the mobility factor in order to explore its relevance in shaping some of these trends in the EU-28—as set out in Chapter 1.

To this end, survey participants who 'benefitted' from the opportunity to undertake semi-permanent EU mobility, including studying, living and working in another member state, were grouped together in the 'EU mobile' category (N = 8237), and those who did not were grouped as 'Stayers' (N = 19,751) (Source: EB 89.1, 2018).

Figure 3.2 demonstrates differences between self-described senses of dual national and European citizenship along mobility experiences.

It indicates that nearly 70% of EU mobiles are likely to hold some senses of EU affiliations, compared to around 55% of stayers and 60% of the EU-28. A similar gap is also apparent in 'exclusive' national affiliations—with stayers outnumbering EU mobiles and the EU-28 average. Similarly, EU mobiles recorded senses of citizenship with a European dimension in larger numbers than stayers or the EU-28 average did. Hence, some of the broader EU trends on dual senses of national and European affiliations, including exclusive nationality might be fuelled by the prevailing differences in the attitudes of EU mobiles and stayers as expected by EU actors (e.g. European Commission 2016).

At the same time however, there is quite a high percentage of EU mobiles holding onto their exclusive nationality. Indeed their share is much higher than the number apparently holding European affiliations first. So, the impact of mobility on an individual's sense of European citizenship might actually be less than expected or indeed previously reported (Rother and Nebe 2009).

Figures 3.3 and 3.4 show some of the key differences in attitudes towards groups of migrants among stayers and mobiles. They show clearly

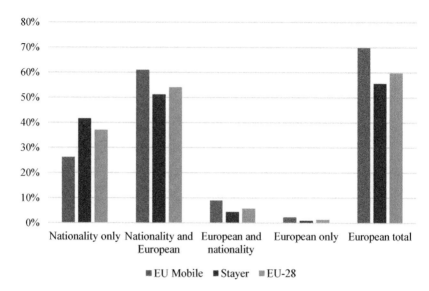

Fig. 3.2 Mobile/stayer senses of European citizenship

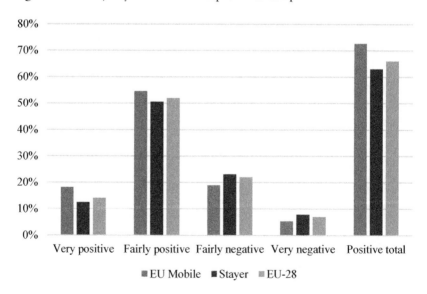

Fig. 3.3 Mobile/stayer attitudes towards EU mobiles

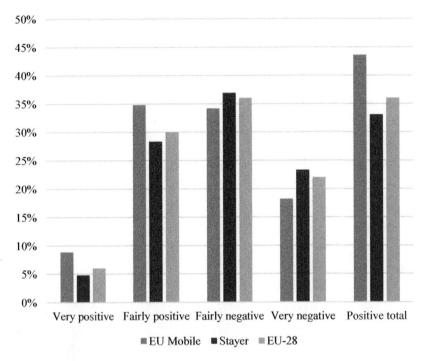

Fig. 3.4 Mobile/stayer attitudes towards TCNs

that more EU mobiles hold more positive attitudes towards migrant groups than stayers. The EU average recorded more positive score than that of stayers in this respect. By comparison, over 90% of stayers across the EU and around 75% of mobiles record negative attitudes towards migrants generally speaking. These differences indicate some shift in citizens' attitudes based on their mobility experiences (Roeder 2011; Sojka 2019).

Nonetheless, the data shows considerable differences in preferences between groups of migrants by both EU mobiles and stayers. For instance, 73% of EU mobiles hold absolute positive attitudes towards their fellow EU mobiles and only 44% feel similarly friendly towards TCNs. The same numbers are approximately 10% less for stayers at 63% and 33%, respectively. Hence, EU mobility may not be able to offset some of the broader, chiefly antagonistic trends apparent in European public attitudes towards migration (European Commission 2018).

Turning more specifically to the two dimensions of citizenship which this chapter has not looked at so far—rights and participation—Figs. 3.5 and 3.6 show levels of stated familiarity with EU rights specifically (no comparable measures for national rights are present in the data) and differences in how citizens' assumptions about whether or not their 'voice' counts in national and EU politics.

Three issues are apparent from the outset.

First, while EU mobility seems to play a role in boosting familiarity with EU rights, it is not relevant to how citizens see their perceived influence on national and European politics. Accordingly, there is a near 20% difference in claimed familiarity with EU rights and a mere 1% in their perceived overall influence in politics between EU mobiles and stayers. Even though only a few EU studies have looked at this issue, they have repeatedly found little to no evidence that mobility increases interest and

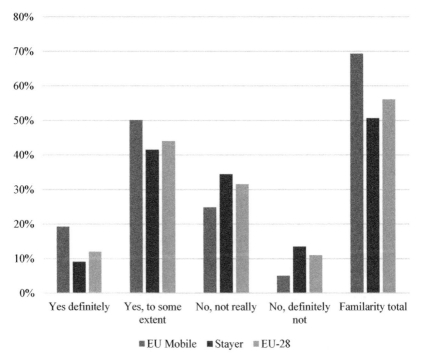

Fig. 3.5 Mobile/stayer familiarity with EU rights

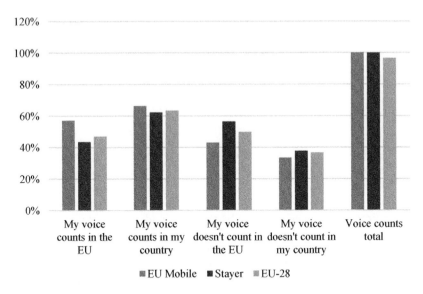

Fig. 3.6   Mobile/stayer views on 'voice counts' in politics

actual engagement in political participation (Muxel 2009; Recchi 2015: 105–121).

Second, stayers seem to be evenly split between knowing and not knowing about their EU rights. Hence, the considerably higher, positive record in EU mobiles' familiarity with their EU rights could be responsible for skewing the score for the EU-28. After all, we also know that many citizens claim to know most about and also largely support their *own* EU free movement rights (European Commission 2016, 2017).

Third, the data shows that citizens were equally (un)convinced about how their voices are heard in national and EU politics. There is no difference between the two levels, actually. This issue may suggest that the oft-cited gap between EU citizens and EU politics is closing (Muxel 2009). Or, to the contrary, that citizens observe a growing gap between their own preferences and those pursued by member state governments (Hobolt and Tilly 2014; De Vries 2018). If the latter issue is the case, it may propel citizens to turn to non-institutionalised forms of participation in larger numbers in the future, and so we should see more and more citizens taking part in protests or signing online petitions in order to make their voices *actually* heard (Hoskins and Mascherini 2009). Whatever the reason, this finding maybe the most 'encouraging' message about individual perceptions of EU participation that emerges from the survey data.

3.3   THE CONTOURS OF MOBILE CITIZENSHIP IN EUROPE

The previous section showed that there is a relationship between mobility and senses of citizenship in the EU. This section examines what this relationship looks like using a multivariate regression analysis.

Given the differences in the number of stayers and mobiles in the survey, it was necessary to 'simplify' the independent variable at this stage. Hence, exclusive national citizenship is compared with all instances where senses of European citizenship are mentioned. Given the slightly crude independent variable that emerges from this simplification, the multivariate analysis presented in this section is just a rough examination of the contours of mobile citizenship in the EU.[1]

In addition to the various aspects of citizenship which were found to be relevant earlier—and so this means the obligatory exclusion of the issue of participation—I also control for sociological factors, specifically education, social class, gender and age, which have been found to influence senses of European citizenship elsewhere (Citrin and Sides 2004; Risse 2010).

Table 3.2 presents two models, with and without EU mobility, on the binary dependent variable about self-prescribed senses of national and European citizenship.

From *Model 2* it is apparent that controlling for all other variables, mobility enhances quite considerably our understanding of the inconsistencies present in senses of European citizenship—we get a higher variance score and a smaller value of standard error in Model 2 than in Model 1.

Semi-permanent mobility thus emerges as a strong, significant predictor, increasing the likelihood of citizens holding European affiliations by about 44%. Mobility experiences also appear to mitigate the odds of all other predictors included in the model bar one—'still studying'. There is thus a strong indication from the data that mobility increases senses of European citizenship significantly (Rother and Nebe 2009; Recchi 2015).

Table 3.2 Determinants of senses of European citizenship in 2018: Binary logistic regression

	Model 1	Model 2 with EU mobility
Reference category: National Only with European		
EU mobility (ref Stayer)		1.441***
Attitudes towards EU mobiles (ref Negative)	2.070***	2.066***
Attitudes towards immigrants (ref Negative)	1.318***	1.303***
Familiarity with EU rights (ref Less)	2.260***	2.186***
Education level by age (ref No education)		
>15	1.543	1.532
Still in education	2.093***	2.098***
>19	1.942***	1.912***
20+	2.587***	2.536***
Social class (ref Lower class)		
Middle class	1.556***	1.531***
Upper class	2.292***	2.212***
Gender (ref Men)	0.898***	0.907**
Age	0.989***	0.990***

Source EB89.1 (2018) N=25,831. Model 1 df=11, Chi square=3576.152, Nagelkerke R^2=0.193
Model 2 df=12, Chi square=3798.154 Nagelkerke R^2=0.199
Notes **$p < 0.01$, ***$p < 0.001$. Coefficients are odd ratios

Across both models, higher levels of education are also associated with higher predictor values. Accordingly, education beyond the tertiary levels emerges as *the* strongest predictor for senses of European citizenship in Table 3.2. Indeed, the highly educated citizens in this group are 2.5 times more likely to hold senses of European citizenship than the others. While this may be further compounded by mobility experiences—if 'the still studying' group is to be relied upon (King and Ruiz-Gelices 2003; Mitchell 2012, 2014). However, we should also remain mindful that students with existing European affiliations are likely to choose to participate in student mobility programmes (Kuhn 2012a; Van Mol 2019).

Considering the various aspects of citizenship discussed earlier in the chapter, all retain their role as significant positive predictors in the multivariate analysis. The most relevant issue is positive attitudes towards EU mobiles, corresponding with some of the EU discourses and literature on how constructive popular readings about free movement can boost European and transnational ties (Fligstein 2008; European Commission 2018). Familiarity with EU rights (Fernandez 2005: 60) and positive attitudes towards TCNs (Sojka 2019) also remain significant predictors even after experiences of mobility are controlled for.

From the other sociological factors, social class emerges as a particularly relevant feature. Indeed, citizens who describe themselves in upper-class categories, including upper middle and upper class, are over twice as likely to develop senses of European citizenship .

However, if we considered the odd ratio scores for high levels of education and higher social class together, the models seem to echo the likely 'elitist' character of European affiliations (Fligstein 2008, 2009).

By comparison, gender emerges as relevant with a negative coefficient score, suggesting that men are more likely to hold European attachments than women (Nelson and Gruth 2000). Nevertheless, gender loses some of its significance once mobility is introduced into the analysis.

3.4   Summary

This chapter provided a secondary analysis of broad senses of national and European citizenship through the lens of citizenship studies. An overview of how citizenship attitudes and approaches towards migrants differ across the EU and between member states—with a specific focus on the UK and Sweden—made a case for comparative analyses of these issues. Furthermore, the examination of citizenship and migration attitudes along with the dimensions of national and European models underscored the relevance of intra-EU mobility especially. The subsequent explanatory analysis of dual senses of European citizenship further corroborated these findings, showing that the identity dimension and attitudes to EU rights remain significant even when we control for key sociological factors—most importantly education.

Overall, then the chapter is indicative of the complexity present in contemporary senses of citizenship in the EU. Yet, survey examination of these issues along the mobile/stayer dichotomy remains somewhat challenging and requires the simplification of measures. This is likely to be the key reason for the contradictory findings we have about EU citizenship from the EU studies research. At the same time, simplified measures are bound to play down some of the complexities in citizenship attitudes which are prevalent in more in-depth interrogations (Duchesne 2008).

Given that even these quantitative analyses are affected by subtle differences in citizenship affiliations, there is clearly a case for more in-depth interrogation using qualitative evidence in order to clearly delineate these contradictions. The next three chapters of this book will accordingly examine senses of national and European citizenship using focus group evidence from Sweden and the UK with young and highly educated EU mobiles and stayers.

NOTE

1. However, it is a necessary step, given the lack of representative data about EU mobiles and stayers from other sources if we are to *broadly* examine the anticipation of European integration scholars and EU actors about the positive role mobility—and especially educational mobility—has in enhancing senses of European affiliations (European Commission 2017).

REFERENCES

Bellamy, R. (2008). Evaluating union citizenship: Belonging, rights and participation within the EU. *Citizenship Studies, 12*(6), 597–611.

Brändle, V. K. (2018). Reality bites: EU mobiles' experiences of citizenship on the local level. *Journal of Ethnic and Migration Studies*. https://doi.org/10. 1080/1369183X.2018.1524750.

Braun, M., & Arsene, C. (2009). The Demographics of Movers and Stayers in the European Union. In E. Recchi & A. Favell (Eds.), *Pioneers of European Integration: Citizenship and Mobility in the EU*. Cheltenham: Elgar.

Carlo, A. (2019). The government's settled status scheme isn't working—and the results will be catastrophic for EU migrants, *The Independent*, https://www.independent.co.uk/voices/theresa-may-hostile-environment-home-office-conservatives-settled-status-eu-migrants-a8781506.html.

Citrin, J., & Sides, J. (2004). More than nationals: How identity choice matters in the New Europe. In R. K. Herrmann, T. Risse & M. B. Brewer (Eds.), *Transnational Identities: Becoming European in the EU*. Oxford: Rowman & Littlefield.

De Vries, C. E. (2018). *Euroscepticism and the Future of European Integration*. Oxford: Oxford University Press.

Diamond, P., Nedergaard, P., & Rosamond, B. (Eds.) (2018). *Routledge Handbook of the Politics of Brexit*. Abingdon: Routledge.

Duchesne, S. (2008). Waiting for a European identity … Reflections on the process of identification with Europe. *Perspectives on European Politics and Society, 9*(4), 397–410.

Duchesne, S., & Frognier, A. P. (1994). Is there a European identity? In O. Niedermayer & R. Sinnott (Eds.), *Beliefs in Government: Vol. 4. Public Opinion and the International Governance* (pp. 193–226). Oxford: Oxford University Press.

Duchesne, S., & Frognier, A. P. (2008). National and European identifications: A dual relationship. *Comparative European Politics, 6*(2), 143–168.

Duda-Mikulin, E. A. (2019). *EU Migrant Workers, Brexit and Precarity: Polish Women's Perspectives from Inside the UK*. Cambridge, UK: Policy Press.

Ericson, M. (2018). "Sweden has been naïve": Nationalism, protectionism and securitisation in response to the refugee crisis of 2015. *Social Inclusion, 6*(4), 95–102. http://dx.doi.org/10.17645/si.v6i4.1512.

European Commission. (2016, Spring). *Standard Eurobarometer 85: Public Opinion in the European Union.*

European Commission. (2017, Autumn). *Standard Eurobarometer 88: Public Opinion in the European Union.*

European Commission. (2018, Spring). *Standard Eurobarometer 89, Public opinion in the European Union.*

Fernandez, O. (2005). Towards European citizenship through higher education? *European Journal of Education, 40*(1), 59–68.

Fiorino, N., Pontarollo, N., & Ricciuti, R. (2019). Supranational, national and local dimensions of voter turnout in European Parliament elections. *JCMS: Journal of Common Market Studies, 57*(4), 877–893.

Fligstein, N. (2008). *Euroclash: The EU, European Identity and the Future of Europe*. Oxford: Oxford University Press.

GMF. (2013). *Transnational Trends: Key Findings.* http://trends.gmfus.org/files/2013/09/TT-Key-Findings-Report.pdf.

Hix, S., & Marsh, M. (2011). Second-order effects plus pan-European political swings: An analysis of European Parliament elections across time. *Electoral Studies, 30*(1), 4–15.

Hobolt, S. B. (2012). Citizen satisfaction with democracy in the European Union. *Journal of Common Market Studies, 50*(S1), 88–105.

Hobolt, S. B., & Tilley, J. (2014). *Blaming Europe?: Responsibility Without Accountability in the European Union*. Oxford: Oxford University Press.

Hobolt, S. B., Spoon, J. J., & Tilley, J. (2009). A vote against Europe? Explaining defection at the 1999 and 2004 European Parliament elections. *British Journal of Political Science, 39*(1), 93–115.

Hooghe, L., & Marks, G. (2004). Does identity or economic rationality drive public opinion on European integration? *PS: Political Science and Politics, 37*(3), 415–420.

Hooghe, L., & Marks, G. (2009). A postfunctionalist theory of European integration: From permissive consensus to constraining dissensus. *British Journal of Political Science, 39*(1), 1–23.

Hoskins, B. L., & Mascherini, M. (2009). Measuring active citizenship through the development of a composite indicator. *Social Indicators Research, 90*(3), 459–488.

King, R., & Ruiz-Gelices, E. (2003). International student migration and the European 'year abroad': Effects on European identity and subsequent migration behaviour. *International Journal of Population Geography, 9*(3), 229–252.

Kuhn, T. (2012a). Why educational exchange programmes miss their mark: Cross-border mobility, education and European identity. *Journal of Common Market Studies, 50*(6), 994–1010.

Kuhn, T. (2012b). Europa ante portas: Border residence, transnational interaction and Euroscepticism in Germany and France. *European Union Politics, 13*(1), 94–117.

Kuhn, T. (2015). *Experiencing European Integration: Transnational Lives and European Identity*. Oxford: Oxford University Press.

Kuhn, T. (2019). Grand theories of European integration revisited: Does identity politics shape the course of European integration? *Journal of European Public Policy, 27*(7), 1–18.

Laffan, B. (2019). The European Parliament in turbulent political times: Concluding Reflections. *Journal of European Integration, 41*(3), 405–416.

Mattila, M. (2003). Why bother? Determinants of turnout in the European elections. *Electoral Studies, 22*(3), 449–468.

McLaren, L. M. (2006). *Identity, Interests and Attitudes to European Integration*. New York: Palgrave Macmillan.

Mitchell, K. (2012). Student mobility and European identity: Erasmus study as a civic experience? *Journal of Contemporary European Research, 8*(4), 490–518.

Mitchell, K. (2014). Rethinking the 'Erasmus Effect' on European identity. *Journal of Common Market Studies (JCMS)*. https://doi.org/10.1111/jcms.12152.

Muxel, A. (2009). EU movers and politics: Towards a fully-fledged European citizenship? In E. Recchi & A. Favell (Eds.), *Pioneers of European Integration* (pp. 156–178). Cheltenham: Edward Elgar Publishing.

Nelson, B., & Guth, J. (2000). Exploring the gender gap: Women, men and public attitudes toward European integration. *European Union Politics, 1*, 267–291.

Patrikios, S., & Cram, L. (2015). Better the devil you know: Threat effects and attachment to the European Union. *Comparative European Politics, 14*(6), 717–734.

Recchi, E. (2015). *Mobile Europe: The Theory and Practice of Free Movement in the EU*. New York: Palgrave Macmillan.

Recchi, E., & Favell, A. (Eds.) (2009). *Pioneers of European Integration: Citizenship and Mobility in the EU*. Cheltenham: Edward Elgar Publishing.

Risse, T. (2010). *A Community of Europeans? Transnational Identities and Public Spheres*. Ithaca and London: Cornell University Press.

Roeder, A. (2011). Does mobility matter for attitudes to Europe? A multi-level analysis of immigrants' attitudes to European unification. *Political Studies, 59*(2), 458–471.

Rother, N., & Nebe, T. M. (2009). More mobile, more European? Free movement and EU identity. In Recchi, E. & Favell, A. (Eds.), *Pioneers of European Integration* (pp. 120–155). Cheltenham: Edward Elgar Publishing.

Sanders, D., Belluci, P., Tóka, G., & Torcal, N. (Eds.) (2012a). *The Europeanization of National Polities? Citizenship and Support in a Post-Enlargement Union*. Oxford: Oxford University Press.

Sanders, D., Magalhães, P., & Tóka, G. (Eds.) (2012b). *Citizens and the European Polity: Mass Attitudes Towards the European and National Polities*. Oxford: Oxford University Press.

Schakel, A. H. (2018). Rethinking European Elections: The importance of regional spillover into the European Electoral Arena. *JCMS: Journal of Common Market Studies, 56*(3), 687–705.

Sojka, A. (2019). The limits of diversity in European unity: The effect of European identification on migration attitudes. Paper presented at 2019 CES conference, Madrid, July.

Stockemer, D. (2012). Citizen support for the European Union and participation in European Parliament elections. *European Union Politics, 13*(1), 26–46.

Todd, J. (2016). *The UK's Relationship with Europe: Struggling over Sovereignty*. New York: Palgrave Macmillan.

Van Mol, C. (2019). Intra-European student mobility and the different meanings of 'Europe'. *Acta Sociologica*. https://doi.org/10.1177/0001699319833135.

Wilson, I. (2011). What should we expect of "Erasmus Generations"? *Journal of Common Market Studies, 49*(5), 1113–1140.

CHAPTER 4

Community Building Processes and EU Mobility

One of most distinctively *political* functions of citizenship is its ability to shape community building processes (Bosniak 2008; Isin and Nielsen 2008). European actors accordingly set the bolstering of an 'ever closer union among the peoples of Europe' as one of the key objectives of European Union (EU) citizenship (European Commission 1993; Pukallus 2016). Yet, it is precisely this issue that we seem to know very little about. This chapter provides a politically embedded and in-depth qualitative interrogation of how mobile citizenship on Europe shapes contemporary community building processes, including processes of differentiation and exclusion.

So far, EU community building processes have been assessed with broader European integration debates in mind. Indeed, contrary to their concerns with the EU's legitimacy, most studies have applied a chiefly sociocultural lens to their assessment of collective identities (Recchi and Favell 2009; Risse 2010; Van Mol 2014; Khun 2015). In the exceptional case where a more comprehensive, politically embedded approach to European and national citizenship was adopted it followed the more traditional, political perspective approach—overlooking the issue of mobility entirely. Yet, its findings corroborate some of the reservations expressed by the aforementioned EU studies scholars—namely despite its potential for enhancing senses of a *collective* European identity among citizens, EU

© The Author(s) 2020
N. Siklodi, *The Politics of Mobile Citizenship in Europe*,
Politics of Citizenship and Migration,
https://doi.org/10.1007/978-3-030-49051-5_4

participation in its own right has failed to generate related community building processes (Sanders et al. 2012: 222).

This is an important limitation, after all, the so-called distinctions between active/passive—or indeed 'good' and 'bad'—citizens are most often assessed on the basis of their non-engagement or non-interest in politics (Turner 1997; Schwartz 2017). Of course, the gradual decline in traditional forms of engagement in advanced democracies (Franklin 2004) already suggests that some of these assumptions are likely to be outdated. But even if we reflect upon the enhanced position of alternative forms of engagement in Western Europe (Theocharis and van Deth 2018), we find little evidence of such trends affecting cross-EU practices (Brändle et al. 2018).

A different portrait of political community processes in Europe emerges when we view them in the context of EU mobility. Although "virtually synonymous" with EU citizenship (European Commission 2011: 1), citizenship studies scholars have only addressed processes of differentiation affecting EU minorities and processes of exclusion affecting third country nationals (TCNs) (especially in Isin and Saward 2013). Yet, it is precisely the intrinsic relationship between EU mobility and broader transnational interactions that have been found to enhance emerging senses of *collective* European affiliations by EU studies' scholars (Bruter 2005; Recchi 2015; Ross 2019).

While far from generating an all-encompassing sense of EU identity, the repeated strengthening of EU mobility via, for instance, the non-discrimination principle on the basis of nationality (Guild et al. 2019) and EU mobiles' participation opportunities in the host state (Bellamy 2019) have begun to alter community building processes which were previously specific to member states. These changes are most apparent in the diverse approaches policymakers and EU nationals have adopted towards different migrant groups, including EU mobiles and TCNs (Chapter 3.1; Fangen et al. 2016; Pries and Bekassow 2017; Ford and Mellon 2019). Empirical studies provide us with insight into the antagonism present in preoccupations towards EU mobiles and immigrants not only within the EU but also within national communities (McMahon 2015). In fact, preoccupation with migration has been found to be *the* leading public concern across Europe (European Commission 2018). While nourishing the EU's image as a top-down, gated community (Van Houtum and Pijpers 2007), these developments are evidence of the changing role of citizens within and across national and EU communities. They also signal a shift in the likely interactions between citizens and non-citizens, and how non-citizens are able to make 'claims' for citizenship rights—the so-called acts of citizenship (Isin and Nielsen 2008; Isin and Saward 2013).

Applying the citizenship studies framework to the case of mobile European citizenship, this chapter examines contemporary processes of differentiation and exclusion (as defined in Chapter 2.1). While important, it does not assess the formal structures within which European community processes are occurring in this context (for the likely contours of EU differentiation processes see O'Brien 2016, and for exclusion see Hansen and Hager 2010 or indeed Isin and Saward 2013). Instead, drawing on original focus group evidence with prototype EU and national citizens—highly educated, young (18–30 years old) EU and home students—in Sweden and the United Kingdom (UK) (more detailed methodology can be found in Appendix 1), this chapter illustrates processes of differentiation and exclusion as apparent across the dimensions of citizenship—identity, rights and participation.

Before turning to the focus group evidence, it is important to note that, if we expect young citizens to find it challenging to articulate their perceptions of contemporary citizenship (Duchesne et al. 2013), community building processes are likely to be even harder to express. This is because, essentially, we are required to find examples of 'contestation'—whereby established citizenship affiliations, rights and practices are disputed *and* redefined. Qualitative evidence fits this purpose perfectly. Hence, rather than challenging the legitimacy of a given community, community building processes are expected to enhance the community's distinctively political character—that is, citizenship.

The rest of the chapter is structured along the dimensions of citizenship (Chapter 2.3).

The first part examines community building processes within national and EU/European communities, pointing to the prevalence of internal and external "others". The second part elucidates how the resulting complexity and tension between citizens and non-citizens are enhanced in the realm of *chiefly* mobile citizenship rights—and are anchored in how people carry 'different values' in a mobile and immobile Europe. The third part shows how these novel community building processes are likely to be enhanced further by distinct approaches to political participation. Overall, the chapter argues that the active/passive citizen dichotomy and good citizenship ideals for contemporary national *and* EU citizenship are gradually redefined by EU mobility.[1]

4.1   COMMUNITY BUILDING PROCESSES AND SENSES OF IDENTITY IN THE EU: MULTIPLE "US" AND MULTIPLE "OTHERS"

Processes of differentiation between EU citizens and nationals were apparent throughout the focus group debates, but, especially, in participants' attempts at defining what a European or indeed *EU* community should look like. Every group attempted and later failed to agree on whether the EU itself is likely to signify an "economic union", a "political construct", a "community of Europeans", a "European federation" or, merely, a "congregation" of nation states. Their diverse definitions seemed to have emerged as a result of distinctive national framing of the EU by member states (Medrano 2003) as well as the EU's own inability to move beyond the economic legacy of its citizenship provisions (O'Brien 2016). In the light of the identity dimension of citizenship (defined in Chapter 2.3), the ensuing debates are perhaps best characterised as a 'hot bed' for multiple European/national "us" and "others" to emerge (Ross 2015, 2019). Hence, while failing to enhance a single collective sense of EU citizenship, the mere presence of these "others" already made it difficult for young citizens to separate the EU (civic) and European (cultural) spheres of their identity (Bruter 2005; Ross 2019).

To start with, the majority of participants seemed apprehensive about the idea of the EU as a single political union due to the historical differences between member states. While they accepted that the EU is different from the rest of Europe, participants often made sense of it as a prototype example of 'regionalisation', an important first step towards a transnational political community '*light*'—in which more established national communities would be sustained for the foreseeable future.

> *Lithuanian Male, EU Group 3, Sweden*: I think, [the] European Union and Europe are different. I would say... So you can be, like, from also Europe but not part of the European Union. So they would still refer to you as European.
> *German Female*: Yes, that's true!

Lithuanian Male: So, I think, it's a political construct, European Union citizenship. And [it] does not really work. Well, they are trying to [make it work], but I do not think it does, *at the moment*.

Hungarian Female: Yeah. It is a construction, as you said. And so, we are kind of in the European Union. And maybe in our heads it even goes further than that. But it isn't....

French Male: And then if we are going to become a European federation, I don't know, you will still identify yourself from your country or from your region, even if there is European citizenship....

Lithuanian Male: But, I think, "European" does not exist in general. I don't think "European identity" exists. It's just politically constructed. If you see, the countries *are* very different. Like, you have France and Portugal, Dutch and then English kind of civilisations.... It's very different approaches, not alike.

French Male: But, look at the nations as well! Like, France, Italy, Germany—[they] were [first] nothing ... but politically and economically constructed a few hundred years ago. And then the [national] identity was founded after that.

Lithuanian Male: Yeah, sure.... In general, Europe is changing... [It used to be a place for] nationalism-construction. So now, national states will fade away and become, like, more institutionalised organisations, like kind of [the] European Union. And then Latin America tries to do UNASUR [Union of South American Nations]—maybe a similar thing? I do not know... I think, it's [a] new creation, regionalisation!

Not all participants were as enthusiastic about impending closer EU integration, however

Turning to the issue of *shared* identities, quite a few were quick to underscore the emerging distinctions between citizens' senses of 'us' along the mobile/stayer divides as well as important regional fault lines. Accordingly, all groups underlined that EU mobiles were more inclined to "stick together" than to socialise with stayers. Their perception of an ever-mobile EU community was then seen an excellent backdrop for EU mobiles to meet one another (Van Mol 2014). Similarly, opportunities for learning mobility were identified as "a place to meet with fellow visiting students".

By comparison, exchanges with stayers in the host country were described both as less common and less desirable. "[The EU is] not so much a place where British [residents] and foreigners encounter" (German Male, EU Group 1, UK). This issue may be the result of antagonistic national contexts—which were claimed to have been explicitly present in both Sweden and the UK. Once the idea of a "mobile EU family"—made up of 'active EU citizens—was introduced, more and more EU mobiles seemed at ease to share their experiences *within* it. They then began to openly refer to stayers as "they"—explicitly categorising stayers as mobile Europe's very own "internal other", the 'passive' EU citizen.

> *Romanian Female, EU Group 1, UK*: I think, not English. I think, with an English person you'd have a beer and a talk about football. But you meet an Italian or German person the next week for a coffee rather than you'd meet an English person....
>
> *German Female*: I live with only British people and I have, like, only European friends.... I really feel like the Europeans stick together...
>
> *German-Swiss Female*: I have much more European friends than I have English friends, actually. I don't know why that is. Might just be because we have, at least in our course, at least half of the people are European or from...
>
> *Italian Female*: Yeah, there is a kind of mutual understanding.
>
> *German-Swiss Female*: Yeah![2]

In addition to this lack of 'mutual understanding' between EU mobiles and stayers, the large majority of stayers in the EU were expected to find the mere *idea* of EU citizenship baffling. Such reasoning clearly depicted the large majority of stayers and so, by extension, the large majority of the EU's population (Table 1.1) as member or nation state-oriented citizens. The escalation of EU mobility—rights, flows and implications for *national* citizenship—was seen as far removed from the everyday agenda of these nation state-oriented citizens. Even more, the segment of stayers who lack the foreign language skills and economic resources necessary for EU mobility were expected to become *primarily* state oriented. They were expected to "close up between themselves" in response to further European integration and to exhibit increasingly Eurosceptic attitudes. To a large extent, such predictions seemed to echo the 'winners' and 'losers' of European integration (De Vreese et al. 2019).

Interestingly, even when these stayers expressed a sense of excitement about the opportunity to meet with EU mobiles, doing so seemed to have underlined the continued significance of national frames for their lives

(Medrano 2003) and the attractiveness of further mobility endeavours—or possibly international migration—for EU mobiles (Šerek and Jugert 2018).

> I think when you travel, you find that there is a lot of similarities … So that you feel you could bring about change because you can do it together. You get like a family kind of sensation …you don't really feel that if you stay in one country. I feel like, if you don't travel [and] you don't experience new cultures, you will never really feel that connection and you will always assume the worst of others. You've got to like travel, to get just that feeling.… (French Female [3], EU Group 4, UK)

These conversations seemed to support official EU discourse of the importance of mobility (European Commission 2011).

Only one EU group (EU Group 2, UK) expressed some unease with the resulting distinctions between active/passive EU citizens along mobility—and so, the *reality* that stayers could never be "*as* European" as the EU mobiles who "move around" and "actually sort of live in the other places". This group probed the assumption that EU mobiles were indeed the "*better* Europeans" and expressed some discomfort with the tendency to *rank* EU citizens. After all, "if you are perfectly happy with staying in your small town, the more power to you! And you feel European, that's great!" (Finnish Female [2], EU Group 2, UK).

Yet, EU mobiles—including those in the last group—did not stop at drawing distinctions between themselves and stayers. Once EU mobiles admitted that they mainly socialised with other EU mobiles, they were also more candid in disclosing that they were hardly ever likely to socialise with *just any* EU mobiles. The opportunity for more intense cross-border 'transactions' between EU mobiles hence hardly ever translated into a truly European mobile community. Instead, two separate mobile communities seemed to have been formed—an EU-15 and a CEE mobile community. It is interesting to note that the underlying rationale for separating EU-15 and CEE mobiles from one another appeared to be on the basis of cultural differences based on a historical divide between Western and Eastern Europe—a divide these young citizens were too young to experience first hand.

> [W]e keep speaking of the Italians and French and Germans and maybe Spanish, but we've left out all the other Europeans or European Union

members that there are... And I have loads of friends who are from Bulgaria, for example, which are European Union members but are not necessarily as often referred to as being European. But they're just as well my friends as others, as the French are, or the Italians, Spanish or wherever they may be from.... But then there *are* distinct cultural differences. There is still this common denominator that *they* all make the effort to come here [smilingly]... this long way from home and, I think, wherever they may be from, I just doubt that their similarities count rather than their differences. I think that's the important part. (Austrian Female, EU Group 4, UK)

Such claims then made CEE mobiles particularly aware of the significance of geo-cultural differences in Europe. Often coined in terms of national stereotypes, these differences noticeably influenced CEE mobiles' *personal* experiences of EU mobility—and so of their EU citizenship.

> *Bulgarian Female, EU Group 4, Sweden*: I feel that I am discriminated even if I go as a European citizen [anywhere]... because, [coming from] the new EU countries, people all expect that we are beggars and everything bad and negative... [W]e are not even given the chance to show who we are! ...
>
> *Polish Female (1)*: But don't you think it's maybe now a little bit better than if you stayed outside of EU? ...
>
> *Bulgarian Female*: Well, it depends on the country of the EU. Cause in Sweden for example I think I'm better [off] than in the UK, from [the] perspective that I have bigger problems there, for example. But here are some health insurance [issues] and vice versa... So, there is no perfect [European] country.
>
> *Romanian Female (1)*: I come from Romania. I experienced this transition form when we entered the European Union... It's true that by presenting our nationality, people already get a picture ... according to the stereotypes or the image the country has in Europe.

Even if EU-15 mobiles appeared to listen to the concerns of CEE mobiles with sympathy, their subsequent comments were more likely to reinforce the significance of these issues. Describing Eastern states as "a little bit weird" part of Europe that "doesn't feel *so* home"— unlike the 'Western' parts. Such sentiments were not meant to demarcate CEE participants from EU-15 members—apparently. They thus used phrases such as a 'little bit' to ease their weight. Despite the potential 'offence' such claims carried however—something EU-15 mobiles explicitly recognised—these differences were seen as important enough to be articulated.

French Male, EU Group 2, Sweden: I think Sweden and France are close, not *so* different. I think it will be a bigger change if I move to Bulgaria or something. No offence! [Directed at Bulgarian female, who smilingly shakes her head in response].

Portuguese Male: I think in Europe there is also, like, different areas or...

French Male: Yes, there is not one Europe...!

Portuguese Male: I mean, yeah. I agree with you. I go very often to France and Spain, to England. And even Sweden. I feel very-very, almost at home. But when I go to Eastern Europe, again, no offence [to both Hungarian and Bulgarian participants], but I still feel a little bit weird. It's Europe but I don't know. It doesn't *feel* so home. Maybe, [turns to the Hungarian participant] you have something to add?

British-Hungarian Male: I live in England, but I lived in Hungary for the first 8 years of my life. I still go there, and it is different. Comparing the two countries, it's very large variation.

The differences these mobile participants touched upon are quite nuanced compared to the existing depictions of European community building processes in the literature (Isin and Saward 2013; Van Mol 2014; Recchi 2015).

The debate among British stayers especially seemed to have added an extra facet to the emerging portrait of contemporary processes of differentiation. Rather than 'simply' distinguishing themselves from 'continental Europeans'—a basic assumption that was present throughout the nearly two-hour discussion—multiple internal European and EU 'others' were depicted and were presented as divided along geographical, linguistic and cultural differences.[3]

British Male (3), Stayer Group, UK: [I]t comes down to geography as well.... [I]f you live in the west side of Switzerland or something, to get around Europe, you can drive there [in] a couple of hours! And you can take advantage of [the] Schengen [arrangements]. And the language barriers, to a point, aren't [important], if you are a natural, say, French-speaker, if you like. The language barrier to an Italian or a Spanish, at least from what I understand, is, you could get by...! Whereas, we don't have that proximity they have! *They* can feel European because they are all sort of there. Together.

British Female (5): Saying that, we are not *that* far away!

British Male (3): Oh, I know!

British Female (5): I mean, in terms of transportation... like, it takes ... two hours on [the] Eurostar. It's not like it takes seven hours to get

there. Yet, we still have, seem to have, more in common with [the] Americans than with [the] Italians in terms of how we see others...
British Male (2): ...[T]hat's the peculiarities of the Anglo-sphere.

While from an internal perspective participants clearly found it challenging to define what an EU community *should* signify or where its boundaries *should* end, they claimed that such a community was already linked to certain values, namely democracy, freedom and safety, as well as Christianity and a 'European mind-set'. These references introduced the external contours of an emerging EU community—and related processes of exclusion.

For example, the newly arrived French student probed the perceptions of his fellows about the possibility of Turkey joining the EU someday. His questions led to a number of statements about the need for more stable EU borders and heated debates about what is *not*—rather than what *is*—European. While initially seeking to describe a more inclusive European and near-cosmopolitan outlook, by the end, most groups saw Turkey as part of the EU's "other". They referred to Turkish people as "they" compared to "us"—the "*true* Europeans". In this context, Turkish participation in some EU-led initiatives, such as European Capital of Culture, and, even, Cyprus's EU membership emerged as hindering, rather than enhancing internal, *collective* processes of EU identity building (Ross et al. 2012).

> *French Male, EU Group 2, Sweden:* What do you think about Turkey wanting to become a[n EU] member?... Don't you think that the main problem about Turkey is that they are Muslim and we are not?
> *Portuguese Male:* I hope it's not!
> *Hungarian-British Male:* Yeah, but I think for a lot of people this is the main reason.
> *German Female:* Yes.
> *Portuguese Male:* Probably.
> *French Male:* They are Muslim and like [us, we are] European. We are Catholic.
> *Italian* and *Portuguese Male together:* Christians, basically.
> *Bulgarian Female:* In terms of the European identity, it's based on the Judeo-Christian or Roman Catholic [religions]. Something along these lines.
> *Italian* and *Portuguese Male* nod in agreement.

French Male: I think it will be weird for me to say like, 'Yes, Turkey is Europe[an]'. I mean, Istanbul is a very nice city and people there live like us. ... They *can* drink alcohol. They have clubs. Like European [lifestyle found in] Paris or London. But the rest of Turkey is totally different.

Bulgarian Female: But what is confusing is that, actually, Istanbul was a European capital of culture....What I am thinking is, what is European? Because they [Turkish people] do participate in certain European initiatives but yet they are not *truly* European.

Italian Male: If there are no limitations on who joins Europe, then even Israel wants to join Europe someday, which is quite far. So, [there] has to be some process that countries have to follow... It will take some time for them to join even if it's relevant and, possibly, good for them and [for] Europe to let them join. Because you can make them join, ... but where will we stop? We say that St. Petersburg is part of Europe. But now St. Petersburg is part of Russia. Can you give European status to the whole [of] Russia? And it goes all the way to the United States and China. Or should we just give European citizenship to people that are from this [Western] part of Russia? So, there is always this question. Do you *really* want to open this?! Because there is no limit. Everyone wants to be in Europe! ... And it starts taking over. I don't know. It's complicated...

Bulgarian Female: But then you have Cyprus, which is not really that close to Europe. It's closer to Turkey, closer to Asia. How come they are members?

Italian Male: Half of Cyprus!

Bulgarian Female: Well, yeah, politics and such, but still! Part of Cyprus *is* in the EU. So, is it geographical?

German Female: But isn't that funny that when we feel threatened that Europe is going to be too big, then we already say "No, these countries are not European"? Doesn't that say that we already feel European and we can already say well, we have certain habits and certain characteristics that these countries don't have? I think that's very interesting because we started from the point where we said I am here I come from there [referring to a member state], you come from there. But now we already say "No, you know, the rural area of Turkey isn't European enough." I mean, there must be something that we feel as truly European for us to be able to say, "No, they are not!" ... I think that's always a thing with a threat. As soon as [you] feel threatened you create already a community. You say, "Okay, we are this block." And I agree with you [refers to *Italian Male*], we can't expand Europe too much.

While many groups dealt with similar topics, only one participant recognised the preference of her fellows to tackle what is *not* instead of what *is* European—calling them out on this trend explicitly. In response, the others in her group swiftly established how much easier it was to imagine and construct a specific EU community in opposition to "the external other".

At the same time, however, processes of exclusion were complicated by some of the "common references" young citizens were likely to share with some, formally non-EU, European citizens. This, in turn, obscured their resolve to realise an EU community. For example, the fact that Switzerland is not an EU member did not seem to matter for EU-15 participants, because the Swiss lifestyle and sociocultural priorities were seen as inherently "European". After that, participants did not think being part of the EU necessarily translated into community affiliations. In the case of British stayers, numerous references were made to the 'special relationship' they shared with the United States, and its implication for the relatability of Brits and Americans in contrast to the relatability of Brits with *any* EU or European citizen. This issue in fact made a good number of British stayers more attracted to travel and live outside of the EU but within the Anglosphere.

At the other end of the scale, nearly every male EU mobile in Sweden exhibited a 'cosmopolitan outlook'—an often fragile notion which accentuates the importance of openness towards "others", be it people or cultures (Skey 2011a)—and articulated a global sense of belonging. They did not consider the EU as necessarily part of their identification, though their senses of national belonging remained significant in some respects (mainly in relation to exercising citizenship rights and privileges as shown in the next chapter). By comparison, only one female participant seemed convinced about the appropriateness of thinking about the EU with a cosmopolitan ideal or global context in mind.

> *French Male, EU Group 4, Sweden*: It's not that our small Erasmus community is more international than globalised than European. Because you have the exact same thing in American universities, with people from all over the world. Here, of course, we are European. But if you go to student housing, you have people from all over the world and not only Europe... I think, yes, it's Europe, because we are in Europe. But it could be the same in the US or Australia. According to the laws, [Erasmus] is a European privilege. But according to social reality, this is an international student education privilege.

Polish Female (2): ... I think you are right. It's more of a global experience. Of course, it's much harder for people from outside European Union to study here in Sweden or in European Union in general. But I think, it's just..., you travel, you talk to people from other places, you get to know different cultures and it educates you in a way.

However, before and after this comparison, she reverted back to a more 'Eurosceptic' and the rather pro-national community perspective she had exhibited elsewhere. The evidence thus seems to support gendered European identities and nationalisms (Nelson and Guth 2000; Skey 2011b: 102–103).

4.2   Manifold Inequalities in an Ever 'Gated' EU Community

Considering whether and how the resulting tensions were likely to be upheld by the structural inequalities of a mobile European community (Hansen and Hager 2010; O'Brien 2016), participants underscored that some EU citizens, simply, carry less "value" than others. It was anticipated that the financial crisis—and other similar transnational crises in Europe—accentuated these distinctions. The imperfect immigration, integration and labour market policies across member states and also at the EU level were identified as limiting the ability of *some* EU citizens to fully exercise their EU rights, while also ensured that TCNs were kept at arms' length (Hansen and Hager 2010). Although EU learning mobility and the young and educated EU citizens in the focus groups are bound to be the least affected by such policies, the dynamics in the focus groups changed considerably when these issues were touched upon.

When CEE mobiles stressed that their EU citizenship was, at best, fractional, EU-15 mobiles suggested it was not surprising since their country only recently joined the EU. This issue was particularly apparent in EU Group 2 in Sweden, where the dynamic shifted slightly between the Portuguese and Bulgarian mobiles. Once the Bulgarian mobile suggests that she is treated differently, the Portuguese mobile underscores that she is from a recent member state and so should *try to* understand that people do not know about her EU status just yet. When the other participants joined in this debate, they too supported the claim that it should not be expected for EU-15 *stayers*—including officials—to be too familiar with the mobility right of CEE citizens. With no such claims about Swiss or

Norwegian mobilities raised, these exchanges seemed to have granted a privileged status and higher value to Western European mobile citizens.

> *Bulgarian Female, EU Group 2, Sweden*: Here [in Sweden] I have to explain [Bulgaria is] within the EU. Like when I dealt with bureaucracy …
>
> *Portugal Male*: It's a recent member so…
>
> *Bulgarian Female*: 2.5 years! [Referring to the length of time she had spent in Sweden. Bulgaria had been an EU member for at least 5 years at the time of the focus groups].
>
> *Portugal Male*: One of the last ones, or they are the last ones? Croatia is just coming through. So you are the last ones. So that's why. You understand why? No? Well, you are compar[ed] with countries that entered like 20 years ago.
>
> *Hungarian-British Male*: Like, the original members.
>
> *Portugal Male*: I am not saying that I agree with it, but I can understand.
>
> *Bulgarian Female*: No, I also understand and am being very patient with it, but still. It's a bit annoying…
>
> *German Female*: But then again, if you would truly feel there exists a European citizenship then you would be much more interested in if there was another country joining. Right?! I mean, take Germany. We have 16 federal states. If we had a 17th federal state joining, everyone would know about it.
>
> *Italian Male*: … [A] number of countries joined 5 years ago, but if you would ask me to name them now for a million SEK [Swedish Crowns] I would not be able to [do that)….
>
> *German Female*: But I think that's a drawback … I mean, we are not truly there yet with European citizenship that we really feel we are one and we are very interested in one another.

Even more, CEE mobiles from Romania and Bulgaria indicated that their EU citizenship was further limited compared to mobiles from EU8 states, including Hungary and Poland. Although EU-15 participants appeared to agree with these sentiments at first, they did not quite understand how these issues impacted CEE mobiles' ability to exercise their EU rights. Perhaps more importantly, they did not appear particularly interested in finding out more either. The following exchange in EU Group 1 in the UK demonstrates these tendencies well. When a Romanian participant spoke of the limitations she faced in her attempts to secure employment in the UK, there was very little follow up offered by her EU-15 fellows.

Romanian Female, EU Group 1, UK: As a Romanian, I am restricted for my working hours. I don't need a visa, but I needed a residence and working permit, which was more or less the [same] process [as applying for] a visa. It means you have to show that you've got fantastic funds, or you have a very generous sponsor who wants to pay for all your expenses, and other paper works, of course. And, as a student, my working permit ... was quite easy to get in comparison to if I was just a [Romanian] person wanting to come here and work because they have [to pass] even more formalities. I can only work 20 hours a week and I can't go over that because it's registered... The good news is that by 2014 they promised to take that off and I will be able to work just as Polish people and other people do. However, they are trying to write like a petition and cancel it for another five years.

German-Swiss Female: Who wants to put that into place?

Romanian Female: I think it's English people-initiated. So, yeah! In my experiences, it's quite hard. And, it's going to be quite hard because I'm graduating and I need a working permit ... and it's going to be very-very hard to get...

German-Swiss Female: Maybe you won't stay here.

Romanian Female: Yeah, I could go somewhere else.

Once she voiced her concern, the Romanian participant did not really get a chance to speak more about how to resolve the difficulties she had to face while residing in the UK. The proposal from others in the group that "maybe she won't stay" in the UK for that long—a simple, seemingly understated remark, had an underlying message: she *should* stop bringing this issue up and it is time for the discussion to move on. Subsequently, the rest of the group—all from EU-15 mobiles—returned to discussing the advantages of *their* EU rights, and did not dwell on the difficulties of CEE mobiles were likely to face any longer. These exchanges showed even more explicitly that the EU-15 mobiles saw themselves as a special group of "true Europeans", the 'ideal', informed and 'self-aware' EU citizens.

In addition to formally limiting their rights, CEE mobiles also spoke about the detrimental effects national stereotypes had on their experiences abroad, including the chances of being treated equally. This issue emerged as an important sticking point for EU Group 4 in Sweden, which was the only group where CEE mobiles (5) outnumbered EU-15 mobiles (3). Being able to dominate the debate clearly allowed for more in-depth depiction of how rights and the treatment of CEE versus EU-15 mobiles affected citizenship experiences—painting a considerably different picture of the ongoing, supposedly *EU* specific, community building processes. [If] young people like us, keep on travelling and going to different places and meet different people, then perhaps those stereotypes will phase out (Polish Female (2), EU Group 4, Sweden).

Nonetheless, these CEE mobiles also observed—or at least *hoped for*—some progress over time. Their optimism corresponds with that of other focus groups in Sweden about the broader future the EU and EU citizenship were likely to hold. The only exception to this trend was in relation to the continued, unfair treatment of Roma—the EU's largest ethnic minority. The confines of an unharmonised EU citizenship framework negatively affecting the treatment of minorities were expected to persist in the long-term.

> *Swedish Female (6), Stayer Group, Sweden*: [L]ook at how Roma people are treated [in France, being sent home by chartered flights at that time] and that's [a] very clear example [of inequality between EU citizens] ...
>
> *Swedish Female (2)*: Exactly! ... France is [supposed to be] a democracy.... [Y]ou know, it's contradictory, I think. You create this Union to keep the stability and democracy and interdependence [between people]. And then you have some people who are not part [of it]. That is a [form of] exclusion ...
>
> *Swedish Female (5)*: So again, very contradictory, ... when it suits states, [EU citizenship is] great! [A]nd when... [there is] a problem, you just kind of want to get rid of it.... [A]nd it's kind of absurd to have such a big, huge system in all of Europe, because [states] don't really follow *their own* rules.

A similar sense of disappointment appeared to take hold of the British stayer group too, once novel processes of differentiation were placed in the realm of the EU's very own inequalities. British Male (2) touched upon the notion that, coupled with EU mobility, national stereotypes were bound to weaken the position of *stayers* in a mobile Europe. Perhaps unintentionally—in the light of his expressed sense of embarrassment at the end of his lengthy monologue—he underscored how some of the aforementioned EU-15/CEE divides were accentuated in explicitly nationalist frameworks.

> *British Male (2), Stayer Group, UK*: I went to Malta.... I got on the plane the same way [as] a couple of months before... [when] I went to Edinburgh and I didn't really think about it. I thought it was quite novel!

I thought it was quite nice, if you contemplate going on a little break in another country. [Some laughs.] How cosmopolitan it made me feel! But then, ... if you ask a lot of British people ... they would say that [EU mobility] kind of works against us. You're constantly bombarded with [this] rhetoric, which claims that far too many people are coming into this country and that... [there is a] flow of Eastern European migrants who are coming in and snapping up jobs! And there are people like Nigel Farage who, although they aren't implicitly saying things that are racist, ... [they are] kind of quoting ... the fears that a lot of people have about this! [I am] coming from East Anglia where fruit-picking, for instance, is quite a big business during the summer. [Some smiles]. And you end up with a lot of seasonal workers! And I remember, speaking to ... a Polish chap I met in the pub and he had a Masters degree and yet he was coming over to do fruit picking because ... he wanted to work! He really did! ... I thought it was quite admirable. I thought that was quite impressive. I thought he has the initiative to come over here because ... he's following money. Whereas, I don't think if anyone offered me a job, fruit picking in Poland... I would be particularly happy about it! ... But one joke that I heard was that we have a lot in common with the Polish people. We are both from quite heavy drinking cultures [Some laughs], we both have a national love of meat-based dishes and...
British Male (1): Terrible!
British Male (2): ... another shared similarity is that none of us wants to be in Poland! [A lot of heavy, nervous laughs and exchanges]. And as funny as it is, I actually thought, 'Yeah, that's not really something you can say.' But there is, sadly, a little bit of truth in it. [Others still laugh]. I'm the only one in the room whose face has gone red!

The silence of the other British stayers throughout this fairly lengthy monologue and their nervous but non-confrontational reaction to it is also worth noting. While offering no support, they also failed to challenge some of the points offered by British Stayer (2)—despite their apparent recognition that they were, at the very least, borderline offensive.

Furthermore, this monologue hints at a new national/EU citizen category—'the aspiring Eurostar'. Portrayed as a well-informed and fairly well-off segment of stayers, who were more 'inclusive' and receptive towards EU developments. Aspiring Eurostars had considered exercising their EU mobility rights—but nonetheless *decided* not to do so due to personal or professional reasons, and, quite often, because staying home was assumed to be "easier" than undertaking EU mobility. They were clearly distinct from their "lower class" and "older" national fellows, who were likely to be less receptive towards EU developments—and were expected to react more adversely to them. Nearly all stayers in the focus groups—bar British Female (1)—seemed to position themselves as members of this 'aspiring Eurostar' category, expressing broad senses of ambivalence rather than outright scepticism towards the EU (Van Ingelgom 2014).

While participants addressed non-structural inequalities in relation to processes of differentiation among EU and national citizens differently, they all seemed to agree that structural inequalities guaranteed the *formal* exclusion of TCNs. Even the majority of British stayers recognised the similarity in the status of EU *and* UK citizens—note the distinction— because if EU citizens "come over, they will have the same rights as UK citizens, more or less"—but not "international migrants or refugees", who:

> have a certain number of months to find work and if they don't, they are either deported or get food stamps. And the conditions are *so* bad! ... to the point where it's easier for them to go back than stay here! And it's done on purpose.... [T]hey are not treated equally! Whereas for us, we'd be given time to find, we don't have six months' time limit to find work or anything like that [in another EU state]. (British Female [6], Stayer Group, UK)[4]

The Swedish stayer group also recognised the difficulty international migrants faced when in their attempts to move, live and study in Sweden. They touched on the "pretty high" tuition fees international students had to pay in Swedish universities, while Swedish and EU students could study for free. Yet, it was the distinctive 'value system' of TCNs, which Swedish stayers saw as particularly problematic, to the point where it was claimed to have affected everyday Swedish politics negatively. Meaning 'no offence', of course, their claims put the only Swedish stayer with a 'non-European' background on the back foot strongly enough for her to feel the need to clarify her right to hold 'European' and Swedish status.

> I have a Lebanese heritage, from you know, not being a European, but ... for me, anyway, I would say I was born here and I am raised here and I would say that I think I acknowledge that European citizenship more, because I understand the difference perhaps and the contrast, and also the Swedish citizenship as well. I notice it perhaps more than my Swedish classmates. And also, I think when it's a contrast and when you have a

different comparison you understand, perhaps the purpose of it. Well, I do see myself as European because, I'm part of that now and also see the differences and the rights different from what I would have as a Lebanese citizen, yeah! (Swedish Female [2], Stayer Group, Sweden)

Even when the distinctions between EU and non-EU citizens were represented as blurred in the minds of some participants, especially by the 'cosmopolitan-leaning' EU-15 mobiles mentioned earlier, they admitted that they hardly ever socialised with international migrants or indeed international students. Instead of individual preferences, the "separatist culture" of Swedish and British universities was seen as the main culprit (Van Mol 2014)—and one that was observed to have negatively affected international students' experiences in the EU.

French Male, EU Group 3, Sweden: I don't have Indian or African friends here. And it's not because I don't try, but precisely I communicate easier with people from Europe or, maybe, even, Western Europe. There are not so many people from Eastern Europe. Estonia is not in Eastern Europe, yes? But not so many from Romania or Bulgaria. Like, most of my friends are from Germany, France, Spain, Italy and Sweden... And these people I know they are not "Stockholmers". They are also kind of exchange [students] here in Stockholm. [All smile.] ...They *need* to make friends too.

German Female: Actually, there are a lot of Chinese students at KTH [Royal Institute of Technology] at least. But I do not so much mix with them. Because where I live, they have put all the *Asian* [slight generalisation with emphasis] guys together. On one floor, it's only Chinese people and on the next floor it's only European people. So that doesn't really make it easier for us to mix. And I think it's because they *are*, kind of, different. It's easier for *them* and it's easier for *us* actually to stick to our group... let's put it that way.

Therefore, there is some possibility that the decision of Swedish and British universities to separate home, EU and international students from one another—a trend noted in other countries contexts also (Van Mol 2014)—enhances formal and informal processes of exclusion and, by extension, senses of commonality in a mobile Europe.

4.3   Mobiles/Stayers
as Active/Passive Citizens in the EU

The focus group evidence used in this chapter so far illustrates the fascination of participants with EU mobility and its role in redefining EU/European and national community building processes. Their exchanges suggest that the growing relevance of EU mobility has begun to propel forward novel processes of differentiation and exclusion at the national and EU levels—though, perhaps, with some unintended consequences. The implications of these distinctions appear to have become even more pronounced when the issue of participation was tackled—by EU mobiles that is.

Contrary to other studies which found EU mobility had very little impact on approaches to participation, EU mobiles in the groups debated which categories of EU citizens should be allowed to take part in European politics (Chapter 3.2; Muxel 2009; Recchi 2015). Indeed, when probed about this issue, most EU mobiles almost instantly turned to debating *who*, that is *which* category of EU citizens, *should be* allowed to participate in European politics. It was suggested that the 'European mobile community' that is made up of—yet again—well-informed EU mobiles, the 'aware' 'intelligent' and 'knowledgeable'/active EU citizens, was *the best* placed to influence EU political decisions because they could really appreciate the likely consequences of their decisions across the EU. Despite the cross-EU inclusivity they apparently projected as a requirement for 'informed' EU participation, they clearly distinguished themselves from stayers. The latter group was depicted as the "ignorant", 'uninformed'/passive EU citizens, too preoccupied with local issues—which, compared to EU political realities, were described as "nothing" and miniscule.

The resulting distinctions between politically active versus inactive EU mobiles/stayers sustained a long and emotionally loaded debate in EU Group 4, UK. The heightened level of antagonism between mobiles and stayers that was touched upon at this stage not once was directed towards TCNs (by either the EU *or* stayer groups)—though it did appear to have been directed at one another as the discussion progressed. EU mobility was only expected to enhance personal dispositions for EU political participation *in combination with* other factors—especially supporting family structures. Without these, many EU mobiles were expected to be absent from European politics. EU mobile absentees and 'ignorant' stayers were then recommended to be excluded from European *(?)* participation opportunities—a proposition that proved rather contentious.

> *Italian-Mexican Female, EU Group 4, UK*: I swear to God most of the people back at home see me as an alien. Because I'm studying abroad and I've decided to stay here and never go back to Italy. They are like, "Oh my God, I don't know how you can do that?!" And I'm like, "Well, I don't know how you can stay in a small town for your whole life, you know?" [Some laughs.] ... "Do you think that people in the rest of the world are aware of the town where you're living right now? Like, you're nothing!" ... [My difference] is based on ... how I've been raised... My family always told me, "Don't stay in the same place. Go and travel." ...Even though it's in Europe, like, from the differences that you can find between the cultures, you can actually become 'more cultured'. And you can actually learn something from these differences. It's not like you are ignorant.
>
> *French Female (3)*: [I]f you stay in the same country [in your whole life], you are ignorant.... And I feel, like, you still need to travel a lot to... be just intelligent, overall. Like, not even just intelligent school-wise, but just *be aware*. Aware! Aware of, like, ... everyone else...
>
> *German Female (1)*: [But] we have to be thankful to our parents [for that]... We can't just generalise it and just say, well, we travel more so we vote [or] we want to vote [more]. I don't think it's that. Because there are people who travel a lot and [don't vote]...
>
> *Italian Female*: That's true.
>
> *German Female (1)*: And then, at the end, they just don't understand [the EU] because ... they weren't raised in a way that enables them to perceive things in the same way [as us].
>
> *Italian Female*: [Quietly]. So again, not everybody should be able to vote who *are* European!...
>
> *French Female (3)*: No, everyone *should* [be able to] vote....
>
> *Austrian Female*: [Ironically.] Please, let's not! Let's become a dictatorship and nobody should vote.
>
> *Italian Female*: That's not true. But if you don't have the knowledge, you can't vote...
>
> *Austrian Female*: Stop saying silly things like that ...
>
> *German Female (1)*: Let's make an intelligence test before people vote! [Jokingly, joined in by French Female (3)].
>
> *Austrian Female*: Okay, so let me give you an example. People who take action on the far right or the far left, do you think that they are all uneducated and absolutely stupid?

Italian Female: That's not what I'm saying. I'm saying that if you if you *want* to vote, ... at least you *should* know what you're voting for.... [Becomes visible irritated.] ...
Austrian Female: So you want us to have a test before voting?
Italian Female: Yes!
Austrian Female: Nobody would want to vote because nobody would want to sit a test.
Italian Female: Well, if you don't want to vote, if you don't want to study, ... then you ... shouldn't do it and just stop complaining about everything that happens around you. That's what people do *all the time!*

There is a chance that EU mobility and political participation are not only likely to reproduce processes of differentiation between mobiles and stayers but also introduce further distinctions among politically interested and active EU mobiles also.

Where does this leave stayers' approaches to political participation?

The evidence firmly suggests that, for most stayers in the focus groups, political participation remained embedded in national and local political structures. It was removed from the politics of a mobile Europe. 'Aspiring Eurostars' projected enhanced dispositions towards engaging in local politics. Even the potential promotion of EU parliamentary politics was rebuffed as less appealing compared to the opportunity to participate more 'effectively' and addressing 'more tangible' issues.

British Male (3), Stayer Group, UK: [W]e are unusual. Most people in this room are politics students or are very interested in politics. We're weird! People don't like politics! People aren't interested! [Others nod in agreement]. If that supermarket gets taken away or the post office gets taken away, *that* matters to them. If some politics goes on somewhere, people just don't care! And that also affects both, even *the interested ones*. So, protesting for a post office for example, actually tangible things...
British Male (2): You *know* where to go and you know what to do.
British Male (3): Exactly!
British Female (1): Going to the point, about like, [EU] parliamentary promotion... uhm, I don't think that's the problem. I mean I wouldn't vote. Like, I just don't really see the point, *really*.
British Male (2): Really?! [Surprised].
British Female (1): Yeah! Uhm, I don't know, just like the *trust* issue. I mean like ... [it]s just [about] anti-politics, you know?! ... they put

the same people up for elections, you don't know really know much about them before the election…

British Male (3): You've got absolutely nothing to go on [at] the European level…. The EU would do so well if they had someone like Farage speaking for them.

Rather than EU politics, 'aspiring Eurostars' were more likely to participate in alternative forms of engagement. Yet, this issue was then seen as highly susceptible to individual socio-economic characteristics, such as age, education and social class. The debates among the stayers in the focus groups thus echoed some of the more traditional, political participation perspective on active/passive *national* citizenship, and young people's increased preference for alternative forms of engagement (Theocharis and van Deth 2018). Nonetheless, some of these expected distinctions between 'aspiring Eurostars' and primary-national/peripheral EU citizens were much less present in the reflections of the Swedish stayer group. There are likely to be considerable differences in how processes of differentiation along the political participation issue manifest, depending on national frameworks and citizens' mobility status.

Finally, there was no consideration of whether and how TCNs were— or indeed *should be*—allowed to participate in national and EU politics. The silent treatment this issue received is, possibly, the most obvious marker of exclusion that had emerged from the focus group evidence. Whether or not non-citizens could or indeed should be able to claim for national and EU rights simply did not occur to these participants.

4.4 SUMMARY

The focus group evidence in this chapter has provided a complex portrait of what EU and national community building processes, including processes of differentiation and exclusion, are likely to look like in the context of heightened intra-EU mobility. Although the young and educated citizens who participated in the focus groups are likely to be the least affected by national migration policies and stereotypes, their experiences of EU learning mobility appeared to accentuate the importance of such issues, leading participants to classify different categories of

EU citizens, depending on their mobility status (EU mobiles/stayers), country of origin (especially along the East/West and North/South divides, and length of membership in the EU) and socio-economic backgrounds (students/workers, ethnic backgrounds, language skills, economic resources and educational qualifications). The most-oft cited resulting categories of citizens are summarised in Table 4.1 below.

Table 4.1 Categories of active/passive national and EU citizens today

Active citizens=EU Mobiles EU-oriented citizens	Passive citizens=Stayers Member state-oriented citizens
(1) Eurostars	(3) Aspiring Eurostars
(2) Second-class Eurostars	(4) Peripheral EU/Primary national citizens

Four main categories of EU citizens crystallised through the debates on contemporary EU and national community building processes: (1) the so-called Eurostars, in this case EU-15 mobiles (Favell 2008); (2) the second-class 'Eurostars', in this case 'new movers' from CEE states (Recchi 2015); (3) the aspiring Eurostars, *some* EU-15 stayers; (4) and the peripheral EU citizens, including both lower class EU-15 and the vast majority of CEE stayers. Of course, the suggested distinctiveness of some of these categories was much less clear cut at times. Nonetheless, there is considerable evidence presented in this chapter which supports the main theoretical propositions of this book: we should reconsider the dichotomy of active/passive EU *and* national citizens along the mobiles/stayers distinctions.

Once we accept the role of EU mobility in activating EU citizenship—which is what the institutional set up of EU citizenship and EU studies have asked us to do so—we can begin to more comprehensively assess the accompanying changes to contemporary national and EU citizenship in Europe. The next two chapters in this book will turn to these issues.

NOTES

1. Another issue to note is that many of the processes described in this chapter are likely to match some of the broader, global trends around international migration and, especially student migration (Skey 2011; Igarashi and Saito 2014). Accordingly, it is not the objective of this chapter to overstate the distinctiveness of a European-specific trans-and supranational community building process (a similar point is raised at the end of Recchi's [2015: 147–149] recent study).

2. The only EU mobile who did not claim membership in this vibrant EU "mobile family" (French Male EU Group 2, Sweden) had spent a limited time abroad compared to the other EU students—a mere week before the interview. There is therefore a possibility that the length of time EU mobiles spend abroad has an important influence on how they evaluate (their membership) within the EU's mobile community.

3. What is also interesting about this exchange between British stayers is that they observed their English language proficiency as a disadvantage for their membership in the EU's budding community. Yet, it was recognized as *the* European language by all other groups and have also been done so by the extant literature on this issue (Macedo et al. 2015). British stayers' reasoning clearly resonates with the *national-ist* 'framing Europe' thesis in this instance (Medrano 2003).

4. This was not the case for Romanian and Bulgarian nationals at the time of the focus groups.

REFERENCES

Bellamy, R. (2019). An ever closer union among the peoples of Europe: Union citizenship, democracy, rights and the enfranchisement of second country nationals. In Bauböck, R. (Ed.), *Debating European Citizenship* (pp. 47–50). Cham: Springer Open.

Bosniak, L. (2008). *The Citizen and the Alien: Dilemmas of Contemporary Membership*. Princeton, NJ: Princeton University Press.

Brändle, V. K., Galpin, C., & Trenz, H. J. (2018). Marching for Europe? Enacting European citizenship as justice during Brexit. *Citizenship Studies, 22*(8), 810–828. https://doi.org/10.1080/13621025.2018.1531825.

Bruter, M. (2005). *Citizens of Europe? The Emergence of a Mass European Identity*. New York: Palgrave Macmillan.

De Vreese, C. H., Azrout, R., & Boomgaarden, H. G. (2019). One size fits all? Testing the dimensional structure of EU attitudes in 21 Countries. *International Journal of Public Opinion Research, 31*(2), 195–219. https://doi.org/10.1093/ijpor/edy003.

Duchesne, S., Frazer, E., Haegel, F., & Van Ingelgom, V. (Eds.) (2013). *Citizens' Reactions to European Integration Compared: Overlooking Europe*. New York: Palgrave.

European Commission. (1993). *First Report on Citizenship of the Union, COM(93)702 final*. Brussels, 21 December 1993.

European Commission. (2011). *Proposal on the European Year of Citizens (2013), COM(2011) 489 final, 2011/0217 (COD)*. Brussels, 11 August 2011.

European Commission. (2018, Spring). *Standard Eurobarometer 89, Public opinion in the European Union*. http://ec.europa.eu/commfrontoffice/pub licopinion/index.cfm/Survey/getSurveyDetail/instruments/STANDARD/ surveyKy/2180.

Fangen, K., Fossan, K., & Mohn, F. A. (Eds.) (2016). *Inclusion and Exclusion of Young Adult Migrants in Europe: Barriers and Bridges*. New York: Routledge.

Favell, A. (2008). *Eurostars and Eurocities: Free Movement and Mobility in an Integrating Europe*. Oxford: Blackwell.

Ford, R., & Mellon, J. (2019). The skills premium and the ethnic premium: A cross-national experiment on European attitudes to immigrants. *Journal of Ethnic and Migration Studies*. https://doi.org/10.1080/1369183X.2019. 1550145.

Franklin, M. N. (2004). *Voter Turnout and the Dynamics of Electoral Competition in Established Democracies since 1945*. Cambridge: Cambridge University Press.

Guild, E., Peers, S., & Tomkin, J. (2019). *The EU Citizenship Directive: A Commentary*. Oxford: Oxford University Press.

Hansen, P., & Hager, S. B. (2010). *The Politics of European Citizenship: Deepening Contradictions in Social Rights and Migration Policy*. New York: Berghahn Books.

Igarashi, H., & Saito, H. (2014). Cosmopolitanism as cultural capital: Exploring the intersection of globalization, education and stratification. *Cultural Sociology, 8*(3), 222–239.

Isin, E. F., & Nielsen, G. M. (Eds.) (2008). *Acts of Citizenship*. London and New York: Zed Books Limited.

Isin, E. F., & Saward, M. (Eds.) (2013). *Enacting European Citizenship*. Cambridge: Cambridge University Press.

Kuhn, T. (2015). *Experiencing European Integration: Transnational Lives and European Identity*. Oxford: Oxford University Press.

Macedo, D., Dendrinos, B., & Gounari, P. (2015). *The Hegemony of English*. London and New York: Routledge.

McMahon, S. (2015). *Immigration and Citizenship in an Enlarged European Union: The Political Dynamics of Intra-EU Mobility*. New York: Palgrave Macmillan.

Medrano, J. D. (2003). *Framing Europe: Attitudes to European Integration in Germany, Spain, and the United Kingdom*. Princeton and Oxford: Princeton University Press.

Muxel, A. (2009). EU movers and politics: Towards a fully-fledged European citizenship? In E. Recchi & A. Favell (Eds.). *Pioneers of European Integration: Citizenship and Mobility in the EU*. Cheltenham: Edward Elgar, 156–178.

Nelson, B. & Guth, J. (2000). Exploring the Gender Gap: Women, Men and Public Attitudes toward European Integration. *European Union Politics, 1*, 267–291.

O'Brien, C. (2016). Civis capitalist sum: Class as the new guiding principle of EU free movement rights. *Common Market Law Review, 53*(4), 937–977.

Pries, L., & Bekassow, N. (2017). Is there a European refugee citizenship in the making? The still-weak institutional basis of a common European asylum system. In Mackert, J. & Turner, B. S. (Eds.), *The Transformation of Citizenship: Boundaries of Inclusion and Exclusion* (pp. 116–134). New York: Routledge.

Pukallus, S. (2016). *Representations of European Citizenship Since 1951*. New York: Palgrave Macmillan.

Recchi, E. (2015). *Mobile Europe: The Theory and Practice of Free Movement in the EU*. New York: Palgrave Macmillan.

Recchi, E., & Favell, A. (Eds.) (2009). *Pioneers of European Integration: Citizenship and Mobility in the EU*. Cheltenham: Edward Elgar Publishing.

Risse, T. (2010). *A Community of Europeans? Transnational Identities and Public Spheres*. Ithaca: Cornell University Press.

Ross, A., Issa T., Philippou, S., & Aðalbjarnardóttir, S. (2012). Moving borders, crossing boundaries: Young people's identities in a time of change: Constructing identities in European islands—Cyprus and Iceland. In *Creating Communities: Local, National and Global, Selected papers from the Fourteenth Conference of the Children's Identity and Citizenship in Europe Academic Network*, CiCe.

Ross, A. (2015). *Understanding the Constructions of Identities by Young New Europeans: Kaleidoscopic Selves*. London: Routledge.

Ross, A. (2019). *Finding Political Identities: Young People in a Changing Europe*. Cham: Palgrave Macmillan.

Sanders, D., Belluci, P., Tóka, G., & Torcal, N. (Eds.) (2012). *The Europeanization of National Polities? Citizenship and Support in a Post-Enlargement Union*. Oxford: Oxford University Press.

Schwartz, D. C. (2017). *Political Alienation and Political Behaviour*. New York: Routledge.

Šerek, J., & Jugert, P. (2018). Young European citizens: An individual by context perspective on adolescent European citizenship. *European Journal of Developmental Psychology, 15*(3), 302–323.

Skey, M. (2011). *National Belonging and Everyday Life: The Significance of Nationhood in an Uncertain World.* London: Palgrave Macmillan.

Skey, M. (2011a). 'Thank god, I'm back!': (Re)defining the nation as a homely place in relation to journeys abroad. *Journal of Cultural Geography, 28*(2), 233–252.

Skey, M. (2011b). *National Belonging and Everyday Life: The Significance of Nationhood in an Uncertain World.* New York, NY: Palgrave Macmillan.

Theocharis, Y., & van Deth, J. W. (2018). The continuous expansion of citizen participation: A new taxonomy. *European Political Science Review, 10*(1), 139–163.

Turner, B. S. (1997). Citizenship studies: A general theory. *Citizenship Studies, 1*(1), 5–18.

Van Houtum, H., & Pijpers, R. (2007). The European Union as a gated community: The two-faced border and immigration regime of the EU. *Antipode, 39*(2), 291–309.

Van Ingelgom, V. (2014). *Integrating Indifference: A Comparative, Qualitative and Quantitative Approach to the Legitimacy of European Integration.* Colchester: ECPR Press.

Van Mol, C. (2014). *Intra-European Student Mobility in International Higher Education Circuits: Europe on the Move.* Basingstoke: Palgrave Macmillan.

CHAPTER 5

National Citizenship in a Mobile Europe: They *Are* Changing!

This chapter is the first of two which zooms into a *specific* model of contemporary citizenship as present in mobile Europe. In particular, it interrogates the assumed challenges that the exercising of European Union (EU) citizenship, particularly free movement, place on national models, using original evidence from focus groups with young EU mobiles and stayers.

Before turning to the evidence however, it is important to remember that despite the multiplicity of national models and traditions of citizenship in Europe, a notable discrepancy did not appear to define wider, cross-EU discourses on them until quite recently—that is, until 2004. Beginning a race-to-the-bottom for social entitlements across the EU (as expected by Kvist 2004) and especially along the East/West default lines (Scholten and van Ostaijen 2018), a series of coordinated initiatives by EU-15 states seeking to curb the EU rights of Central and Eastern Europe (CEE) mobiles have, in reality, created inequalities between CEE mobiles and other European citizens (Schmidt et al. 2018). They also drew attention to the potential harm recent EU developments can carry for EU-15 models of citizenship. Early 2000s antagonism in mainstream EU-15 discourses towards CEE free movers were country specific. For example, mainstream discourses in the United Kingdom (UK) were preoccupied with the arrival of the 'Polish plumber' and, eventually, the

© The Author(s) 2020
N. Siklodi, *The Politics of Mobile Citizenship in Europe*,
Politics of Citizenship and Migration,
https://doi.org/10.1007/978-3-030-49051-5_5

Romanian builder (Myslinska 2016). The French, by comparison, were worried about the increasing number of Roma CEE arrivals (Shaw 2012).

Only in the aftermath of the EU's economic crisis did these concerns make it to the agenda of EU actors, ultimately calling for a more coordinated policy response (Mikl-Leitner et al. 2013). Accordingly, Spain secured a special, temporary exemption from the EU's Citizenship Directive against the unusually high inflow of Romanian mobiles (European Commission 2011) and the Danes reinforced their symbolic opt-out from the EU's 'ever-closer union' (Adler-Nissen 2011). Hence, right across the continent it became common to limit the scope, and associated rights, of some people's European citizenship. This issue even infiltrated the workings of a supposedly activist EU court. Rulings such as *Dano vs Jobcenter* put the onus on individual mobile citizens for proving their right for EU and, especially, host state social entitlements (see also Voeten 2018).

Substantial research efforts have gone into outlining the broader implications of these developments for contemporary national citizenship in Europe. Possibly due to their overriding assumption that citizenship must entail some collective political participation by individuals (Bellamy 2008; Bellamy and Castilogne 2019), most of the citizenship studies literature has addressed current practices and models in separation from the idea of mobile Europe. Empirical analyses are usually conducted in relation to one or other national models or with a specific European region in mind, with the notable exception of Sanders and colleagues (Sanders et al. 2012) who removed EU mobility from their analysis of the dimensions of national and EU citizenship.

A slightly more complete, empirically underpinned, portrait of the different aspects of national models has emerged from the EU studies literature. By looking at what these developments mean for the EU's political aspirations, these studies have, perhaps unwittingly, uncovered an ever-more ambiguous *EU* population with bolstered senses of *national* affiliations (Bruter 2005; White 2011; Duchesne et al. 2013; van Ingelgom 2014; Ross 2015, 2019). They also confirm that national framings of politics remain the most significant issue for citizens' decisions to participate in EU politics (Fiorino et al. 2019) and that national considerations still rank highly in the everyday lives of the EU's very own 'ideal citizens', the EU-15 Eurostars (Favell 2008; Recchi and Favell 2009; Recchi 2015). Some of these findings have found further support in the context of youth intra-EU mobility specifically (Cairns 2010; Van Mol 2014; Mazzoni et al. 2018).

Considered together, the two strands of the literature from citizenship and EU studies offer important insights into the *multiple* and *parallel* policies, practices and notions of national citizenships which exist within mobile Europe. But, as has been the case with community building processes (Chapter 4), their varied approach to analysis have inevitably led to some fragmentation in our understanding of these issues. Yet, their findings complement each other enormously. For instance, the findings of EU studies on one or another dimension of citizenship (as defined in Chapter 2.3) seem to confirm the original expectation of citizenship studies scholars—namely the primacy of national models. However, a more inclusive assessment of what this primacy translates into *across* the realm of the dimensions of national citizenship and in the context of EU mobility is still missing. This issue deserves an in-depth, empirical consideration not only due to its timeliness and policy implications, but its potential for aiding comparisons across different models of citizenship in Europe, including national and EU models (the latter is, accordingly, examined in the next chapter of this book). After all, such an inclusive approach to addressing the issue of citizenship is, precisely, what citizenship studies scholars have asked us to do (Magnette 2005).

Adopting this framework can, therefore, help us find out what contemporary national citizenship signifies more fully. This chapter uses original focus group evidence and investigates the national citizenship perceptions of young and highly educated EU mobiles and stayers in Sweden and the UK (more information on rationale for research method adopted in Appendix 1). As such, it studies what national models really mean for the burgeoning group of European integration 'winners' (Kriesi 2014). It begins to answer whether there are traces of 'the end of national citizenships', as advocates of a cosmopolitan model would have us believe (Falk 1993)? Or if we are more likely to detect heightened senses of belonging to *national* communities, as primordialists predicted (Smith 1992)? The evidence used in this chapter strongly suggests that rather than challenging senses of national identity, intra-EU mobility is likely to boost *inclusive* national models of citizenship in the eyes of young citizens, a group which previously rejected national identities as banal or irrelevant.

The chapter is structured as follows.

The first part explores and compares EU mobiles and stayers' perceptions of national citizenship, illustrating just how EU mobility appears to reinforce the significance of inclusive national citizenship frameworks.

The second, third and fourth parts discuss EU mobiles' and stayers' perceptions of the dimensions of national citizenship—namely identity, rights and political participation. They show how both mobiles and stayers emphasised that EU mobility enhances positive perceptions of top-down models of national (country of origin) *social* citizenship provisions (Marshall 1950; for EU citizenship see O'Leary 1995). However, when the consequences of the bi-level structure of EU citizenship were taken into account, important differences between the interpretations of EU mobiles and stayers about the pertinent *realm* of contemporary politics emerged. For EU mobiles, it highlighted the contribution of liberal market structures in feeding societal inequalities across the EU (Mitchell 2014). For stayers, it accentuated the requirement of a bottom-up and locally driven citizenship and citizen activism.

5.1   National Citizenship: The Go-to Status for the EU's Stayers *and* Mobiles

There were little if any differences in the initial reactions of EU mobiles and stayers when asked what citizenship meant to them, personally— or indeed across the two countries. Even though all of them had been informed about the topic of discussions prior to the focus groups, they seemed a little puzzled to be asked "such a broad question"—which was often met with silence and comments about how it was an issue they could make sense of "since [they've] studied political science" or related social science disciplines. Their answers were then *claimed* to be "theoretical", "ideal scenarios"—removed from any personal reflection or experiences.

To some extent at least, such reactions are not that surprising. Citizenship is not a topic likely to come up when you share a '*fika*' [Swedish coffee and cake break] or an English afternoon tea (or something stronger) with friends. But the very fact that it is also not a subject many privileged—in a global perspective—and 'ideal' national/EU citizens—in academic and elite circles (Converse 1972: 324; European Commission 2014; Putnam 2000: 68)—appear to pay much attention to might be more alarming. If the prospective values of citizenship—inclusiveness, equality and security, to name but a few, all of which are largely decoupled from the nation state (Joppke 2010)—are muted in everyday public discourses, its place could easily be hijacked by populist and right-wing ideals.

Indeed, with the values of citizenship likely to occupy an even lower priority for the 'average'—for a lack of a better phrase—citizen, compared to the participants in the focus groups to which this chapter refers to. This issue may provide a further explanation about the appeal of right-wing ideals (in addition to the more mainstream and largely institutional explanations of populism, see for example Kriesi 2014). As some participants put it, "ideally, I would like there to be a cosmopolitan citizenship, [because] national citizenships *are* arbitrary," (British Male (1), Stayer Group, UK), and "it would be nice if, wherever you went, you could just become *a* citizen" (British Female (5), Stayer Group, UK).

However, the lack of such a mechanism has meant that, in reality, however even *some* young people have adopted nativist, xenophobic and even authoritarian rhetoric in order to emphasise the urgency of local, regional, and at times global, challenges. The latter has even been traced in some of Greta Thunberg's speeches on climate emergency (Pollock et al. 2015; Rooduijn 2018; Buranyi 2019). These issues swiftly grant contemporary notions of *youth* citizenship a somewhat contradictory character. Its progressive tone is noticeable, but perhaps does not quite deliver on the idealist expectations set out by citizenship scholars (of which, supposedly, Sweden is an excellent example, as per Midtbøen et al. 2018). Indeed, to get the focus group discussions really going, it was necessary to rephrase the first question and ask, more, precisely, what *being* British, Swedish, etc. *national* citizens meant to participants in their everyday lives. This suggests that, contemporary citizenships are likely to have a very specific—and in this sense negative connotation—an assumption that its personal and practical domains are *always* linked to the *nation* state.

Nonetheless, as the discussions in the focus groups began to flow, the idea of citizenship as social rights (Marshall 1950) provided by nation states was formulated quickly. Citizenship was then defined as an "agreement", "exchange" or "contract" between the state and the individuals within them—a dynamic and direct bond with a top-down, rather than active bottom-up connotation.

> To me, it's a guarantee of rights you *get*. It's a contract between you and the state. It's guaranteed. For example, education and other public goods. Uhm, and that when you go abroad you have a place to go to, like an embassy, if you are in a problematic situation. So, you have external and internal dimensions, including defence and police force, and things like that. It's entrusting the state like that. (Finnish Female (1), EU Group 2, UK)

Subsequently, participants highlighted the interdependence of citizenship with democracy and democratic values, because in an authoritarian state "the agreement is not really present. It's, more like subjection than citizenship." Once the legal and democratic connotations of citizenship were accepted, most participants quickly underscored the relevance of *collective* identity.

> *Moderator, EU Group 1, UK*: So, my first question is what does citizenship mean to you? [Everyone is quiet for a minute or so. Moderator continues, jokingly.] I guess this is the worst question I'll ask, by the way, so it will only get better from here. [All start to laugh.]
>
> *German-Swiss Female*: I guess it means to me having certain rights that I can use. Like, having the right to go to a place or taking up services that a state *should* offer. But, also, I don't know, the word for that when you have to go to do something, you like you know, you *have to* pay taxes or stuff like that...
>
> *Italian Female*: Duties?
>
> *German-Swiss Female*: Yeah!
>
> *Italian Female*: I think it also represents a sense of belonging to a place. It's not just about duties and obligations, ...
>
> *Dutch Male*: Kind of agree. It's such a broad question I suppose. Rights and duties and sense of belonging all cover it, I suppose it's not much differently defined at home [in the Netherlands] and here [in the UK].
>
> *German Male*: I am sure there are [differences between EU countries]. I just never thought about this in terms of citizenship, rather nationality or nationalism. That's why I do not have a straightforward answer to the question "What is citizenship?" Cause, that term, is not that, uhm ...
>
> *Romanian Female*: I guess it's what you want to find out. How [do] you *actually* define citizenship? And what you identify with that? I guess that's why the question is so broad. But I agree. I think it's a sense of belonging to a culture or society and giving something like taxes [and] duties in exchange of something, like rights and enjoying some freedom from that particular culture.
>
> *Italian Female*: And I think it's pretty different between countries. It's the political culture or the place. So, for example, in Italy we do not have a sense of belonging at all. And you can tell [laughs] ...
>
> *Romanian Female*: [Surprised.] Really?!...

Actually, the majority of participants seemed to agree about the significance of *social* rights and civic duties (often tied together) *as well as* elements of identity. No mention of the EU, free movement or, for that matter, migration and *related* security concerns occurred. Given the appeal of these issues in contemporary identity politics (see, e.g., Kuhn 2019), the groups really seemed to have been largely made up of by members of the ideal/future 'good' citizens in both national and EU terms, expressing a preference for cosmopolitan or world rather than national citizenships.

Nonetheless, the apparent (wider) appeal of identity is not all that surprising in the light of the focus group evidence either. Even with the obvious disagreement about the importance and weight of the different dimensions of citizenship, considerations of inclusion/exclusion based on national identity were *always* present. In fact, some groups ultimately defined citizenship in national identity terms *only*, namely EU Group 4, UK and EU Group 3, Sweden. This happened despite some injected and probing questions about the other two dimensions of citizenship by the moderator.

There were quite a number of participants who did not seem particularly keen to link citizenship and nationality together. Yet, even they found it difficult to separate these issues—as per the examples cited earlier. Indeed, the identity, understood often as categorisation, aspect of contemporary *national* citizenships fuelled some of the most heated early exchanges (Van Mol 2014: 94–95). Their incendiary nature became even clearer when mentioned by participants from a visible ethnic migrant background.

> It's never been as important before to, you know, associate yourself to where you come from. Ever since I've come here, the first question is always, "Oh, where are *you* from?" Uhm, obviously Austria, which is my nationality, which is where my culture, my home, everything is based. But in Britain I find because they have such a diverse background, it is so much more important to associate yourself with where you come from [ethnically]... They don't have this shared sense of citizenship. I don't think it exists in England. Everyone is very-very, yeah *very* close still to where they come from, if they've immigrated. (Austrian Female, EU Group 4, UK)

One of the most surprising features of the initial discussions was the difference in the attitude of the Swedish stayer group towards citizenship. In their attempts to unpack their own Swedish citizenship, rather than what they would have liked to see as citizenship, Swedes largely described a near clinical top-down process—the *social* "rights", "entitlements" and "benefits" the Swedish welfare state provides to its citizens. Swedish citizenship was seen as considerably different from other national models in Europe. In other countries, considerations of national citizen identifications or even the identity dimension of national citizenship was presumed to be *the* most relevant issue. In the case of Sweden however, the relevance of identity was dismissed early on, seemingly depicting some form of a post-national(ist) model of Swedish citizenship (Tambini 2001; Brochman and Hagelund 2012: 26)—much in line with broader discourses on Swedish neutralism and exceptionalism (Schierup and Ålund 2011). As the debate deepened however, the emotive value of *Swedishness* as well as the issue of exclusion—along with rights and benefits—turned into one of *the* most defining features of Swedish stayers' senses of *personal* citizenship.

> *Swedish Female (1), Stayer Group, Sweden*: For me, it's mostly that we can benefit from the welfare programme, social programmes and that I am paying taxes. ... I have a safety net from the state. It's not so much about culture or tradition or anything... It's more like I belong to Sweden. That it wants to take care of me when everything goes bad.
>
> *Swedish Female (2)*: Rights and duties [and] to be entitled for benefits, but also to have some duties towards the state. I think that's something that I recognise at older stages or when I study political science. But for me citizenship is, definitely, rights. Because I felt these rights more and more, actually.
>
> *Swedish Female (3)*: As you [points to Swedish Female (5)] said, I have not lived in another country either or haven't been applying for some other citizenship. So, maybe, you are not so aware that you are a citizen at all. If you haven't experienced the applying process or anything, it's just a natural state.
>
> *Swedish Female (1)*: It's not like you are proud to be Swedish because you haven't gone through the process to become [a] Swedish citizen.
>
> *Swedish Female (4)*: For me at least citizenship is, I agree with you, that it's rights and duties. But I find it interesting, you said that "I belong to Sweden", and the element of belonging actually took some part in your sense of citizenship. I experienced it when I stayed abroad for a few months, ... that feeling grew stronger. And it's like a rollercoaster ride on how you perceive yourself as a Swede, or if you're drawn towards the other nation, nationality. ...
>
> *Swedish Female (3)*: I think it's about contrasts. When I was working in France for a month, there were some Russians and a guy from Jordan. And, in contrast to them, I really felt like me and the French people

had more in common. Even though here, in Sweden, I would say these French are so different from me. ...

Swedish Female (4): What you brought up [citizenship] as comparison and the inclusiveness, I think that's key, actually. ...[It] depends on where you are and what you choose to include in your sense of citizenship. ...

Swedish Female (5): I don't feel like Swedish people in comparison to other nations, they don't have, uhm, we're not very Swedish. We don't, you know, talk a lot about our own Swedish culture and just identity overall.

Swedish Female (1): A couple of years ago I travelled around the world and I noticed, especially when I was in the US, that people found that my cultural view and my traditions and my approach to food was *very* different. They thought it was quite exotic and it was more exotic for me to be a Swede than a European. And they were really interested, because we have very different views on what to eat and how to eat and stuff like that. So, I really feel like, ... when I go abroad my notion of identity as a Swede becomes much stronger because it doesn't matter here. And it's like everybody else's. ...

Swedish Female (6): I'm also wondering, as you were talking a bit about, if Swedes are not that promoting of their national identity as other nationalities maybe are. If I were living in France, for example, or in another country with a strong sense of national identity, maybe my national identity would grow stronger in comparison with the European notion.

While projected as a somewhat ideal, post-national model, the emphasis on inclusion/exclusion between Swedes and "others", is indicative of the not-so-inclusive Swedish society many EU mobiles also mentioned. These issues have certainly been emphasised by the incendiary headlines and antagonistic political discourses in Sweden (along with the large majority of EU countries, of course) following the refugee crisis (Abdelhady 2019).

While preference for a cosmopolitan outlook of citizenship—along Nussbaum's (1994) understanding of a world citizen, embracing a moral universalism and no particular attachment to a 'rooted' community—also came up in the early part of the UK discussions, as the debates progressed a considerably different assumption took hold of *some* groups.

Indeed, the more they spoke about the issue of citizenship, more and more stayers and EU mobiles (in Groups 3 and 4 especially) claimed it will *always* be "very difficult" to realise a form of regional citizenship that could come *at the cost of* national affiliations. EU citizenship was expected to be relevant in certain contexts and to some extent By comparison, their national citizenship was always present (even if somewhat banally before their mobility).

In fact, EU mobility often reinforced national affiliations—either because, while staying abroad, EU mobiles made references to their country of origin repeatedly or because the people they interacted with did so. While they found that their national (citizenship) affiliations were quite banal at home, it had become more tangible in the context of intra-EU mobility. In most cases nationality served as a 'simple' and inclusive identification mechanism, rather than a signifier of strong senses of *ethnic* national citizenship among these young citizens—albeit with 'recent' arrivals it often seemed that way. Nonetheless, the very fact that nationality *had to* be formulated repeatedly, for example, appeared to grant *national* citizenship a significance that was not noticed previously.

> *German Female (1), EU Group 4, UK*: I think [citizenship is] language and culture mainly. Because, like each country is different, each country has certain rules or perceptions of whatever else is going on, especially in the European Union. So, wherever you come from, you have that implemented perception of your country that you sort of represent, unless you totally disagree with it.
>
> *German Female (2)*: I really agree with [you]... I think that it's about the language you share and the traditions you share with the people you live with. And then, it's like within the national borders. But then I think it can also grow. Like, for example, in the European Union. I think you can feel European. Yeah, I feel European. ...I went to a European school. My dad works in a European institution. All my friends are international, well European. And I grew up in this really European environment. So, I feel really European. Although, I feel really German and I have this strong national feeling, but I feel European as well.
>
> *French Female (3)*: I think it kind of changes. I feel like within Europe, I feel very, like French or associate more with my citizenship. But when I leave Europe, I feel like I represent Europe in general.

In this way then, intra-EU mobility is likely to further senses of national citizenship at *all times*. However banal such references were assumed to be, or may appear to us, the readers, they also fed and, in a few cases, furthered national stereotypes—sustaining to some extent national/European "others" (also touched upon in Chapter 4.2 on differentiation processes towards CEE mobiles, for example).

It is also important to notice that even when citizenship was not qualified as 'national' explicitly—as in the above quote—it was simply understood as such by all members of the group. The same tendency took hold of the other debates too. And while the issue of anticipated contradictions between EU/national senses of citizenships were often challenged, the simple assumption that citizenship was, by default, synonymous with participants' own nationality did not come under much scrutiny. As the debates progressed, *national* citizenship was granted a delicate and emotive value—and one that EU citizenship simply *could not* match, only, at best, reinforce.

> [W]ith national citizenship, there you have also the emotional issue or the familiarity or the connection with your home. But with the European Union, it's still [under] construction. So, rights are there, the legal rights, the social rights... the political rights also. But, still, there is a lack of emotional connection with the big structure. I think it's another layer of citizenship that somehow reinforces the nation state citizenship. (Portuguese Male, EU Group 1, Sweden)

The deceptively heightened role of national citizenships or just simply nationality in the context of intra-EU learning mobility and EU integration surely supports the fixation populist and right-leaning politicians seem to have with these issues.

In the focus groups too, made up of the ideal EU/national citizens who often did not think of their EU citizenship prior to their EU mobility, the emphasis on the EU's heightened role in their everyday emerged as a particularly fertile ground for explicit and *even* emotive senses of *national* citizenships to emerge. The very citizens who often claimed to hold different personalities from the majority of the EU's population, since they were "not scared" but "interested", "aware" and "willing to move" and "work hard abroad" (just as underlined by Kuhn 2012 on the likelihood of pro-EU young citizens taking Erasmus than Eurosceptics). Subsequently, and in order to enhance their professional successes, these EU mobiles found that "the concept of 'where is home'" and, relatedly, citizenship were "evolving".

Their resulting senses of national citizenships emerged as far from exclusive, allowing for senses of EU citizenships to also emerge in most cases. Yet, the fact that the values of *national* citizenships which were not noticed originally received a boost is likely to be 'good news' for those possibly worried by the potential erosion of nationality in the EU context (Aspinwall 2002) or even for those preoccupied with the apparent cosmopolitan outlook of youth notions of citizenship. In fact, the apparent cosmopolitan outlook of youth has, for quite some time, been found to be flexible at best and temporal at worst (Mitchell 2007: 714).

The many twists and turns participants in the focus groups took in the course of the discussions seem to underscore this temporal and rather eclectic aspect of their cosmopolitan outlook.

By comparison, national outlooks were there as a familiar reminder of where participants had come from. Such results and behaviour appear to clearly contradict some of the pro-EU and transactional assumptions about the impact transnational interactions have to shift national affiliations towards a cross- and transnational community (such as Deutsch et al. 1968; Haas 1958; European Commission 2017). This issue is unpacked further in the next section on national identity along the key elements defined earlier in the book–senses of belonging, shared identity, the "us" and the "other" (Chapter 2.3.1).

5.2   Citizenship and More and More National Identity in the Context of EU Free Movement

From the very early stages of the focus groups, the significance of enhanced senses of belonging to the nation (state) and their personal and practical importance to participants was apparent. Despite some slight disagreements, a large majority of EU mobiles suspected that it was in fact "hard to separate" senses of citizenship identity "from the context it comes from". This explained students' basic approach to contemporary citizenships in Europe from within the *nation* state. While not a notion they seemed overly comfortable with, participants appear to stress their *own* senses of belonging was often context-specific and flexible, changing in "scales" from the national to the regional and local, going as far as to an EU or even a global level of citizenship.

> *Polish Female (1), EU Group 4, Sweden*: I think that's how it works, that there are different levels of citizenship... It's like you are citizen of your city and then of your region, maybe of your country and then [the] European Union. And then there [are] some, like, citizens of the world. But..., I don't know about that. ...And then, it's linked to how you feel, the identity. Cause, I guess, there are some people that feel mostly the citizens of their own country. But there are some that feel more like citizens of Europe or the city. ...

French Male: I think it's a kind of belonging. You belong to a community and this community could be small[er] or wider. You have different scales of identity, of community. ...

Bulgarian Female: So maybe we then have to differentiate between the citizenship by nation, by where you are coming from, your country of origin, and citizenship within the boundaries of the EU.

The apparent flexibility in participants' senses of belonging seems to correspond with some of the key assertions in the literature on emerging youth citizenship identity. Simply put, young citizens' approaches to their own senses of belonging is prone to be less vigorous than it has been the case for older generations, who often "had to fight for" recognition (pointing to the presence of internal national "others" along age, as underscored by, for example, Ross 2015, 2019).

Additionally, EU mobiles often asserted that their sense of belonging to the EU was not exclusive or necessarily apparent *at the cost of* their national affiliations. Quite the opposite. Both senses of belonging to the national and EU levels were claimed to have received a boost.

[J]ust because you feel affiliated to the European Union, [it] doesn't mean that your national identity is lost. Nobody is saying that people who feel as EU citizens feel less of [national] citizens. I sort of feel *very* German despite also feeling like an EU citizen. And I wouldn't expect to have the *same* sort of affiliation the other people have, but it's just an added bonus. That's the way, I think, people should see [EU citizenship] as opposed to... [thinking] the EU is taking away power from us [the nation or the country]. I see that as a bonus or [as] an advantage to us ... (German-British Female, EU Group 3, UK)

Nonetheless, when personal senses of belonging to the nation state were perceived to be directly challenged—such as during EU mobility—quite a good number of young EU mobiles felt it much more enhanced than on average (and especially compared to their previously broader senses of citizenship). This was the case even among participants holding dual and potentially conflicting nationalities and identities.

Well, I don't feel European at all. I'm gonna have to go against everyone here. [Smiles nervously.] Especially since I came here, actually, I feel like there's a lot of division among us. When you first come here, everyone asks, "Where are you from?", so you say your home country. I don't feel like there is anyone that links us [Europeans] together. Because the cultural differences are so broad that I still feel like, very, uhm, *connected*, to my country of origin, if that makes sense. (Italian-Mexican Female, EU Group 4, UK)

The same idea was presented by stayers—anticipating to feel 'more' Swedish and British in the context of free movement and perhaps slightly more European outside the continent. While perhaps not all that surprising in the case of the UK, but more so in the case of Swedes who, had previously claimed (and did again throughout most of the debates) that they did not have a specific "Swedish *cultural* identity like other Europeans do". Yet, they too expected to "feel more European ... outside of Europe", because within it their "Swedish background would prevail [over] other feelings" (Swedish Female, Stayer Group, Sweden).

By comparison not only shared senses of national identity but also of EU identity appeared to have been boosted by EU mobility. While the majority of EU mobiles agreed that this experience made them feel they "have something to share" with other EU citizens, it did not always translate into a common sense of *being* "Europeans" from a cultural standing point. The latter was, instead, deemed as much more obvious and stable at the national level (as anticipated by scholars, e.g. Bauböck 1997).

At this point, the question of bonding among EU mobiles is also important to consider, especially in regard to its impact on the categorisation aspect—on inserted or taught perceptions of "the (national) other"—which decides who is not supposed to belong to national communities (Smith 1992: 59f.). This is where EU mobiles became more critical about their own enhanced sense of national identity and, more broadly, about the continued significance of nationalistic and static affiliations in European affairs today.

The "bond" they were seemingly building with their (non)EU mobile fellows allowed them to see the many 'commonalities' which often cut across superficial national boundaries. Such recognition appeared to have fed into novel processes of differentiation at the national level, whereby internal, national "others" emerged along the stayer/mobile distinctions (specifically).

Such distinctions were quite obvious of course when we consider the position of EU mobiles and stayers in the two host countries—and their very little interaction (discussed in much detail in Chapter 4.1). In the

UK, for instance, the emphasis on multiculturalism appeared to have further stressed the presence of multiple *ethnic* mobile/stayer communities. Such practices in turn ensured that, ultimately, none of the EU mobiles developed a sense of belonging to either host countries—regardless of the length of time they had spent there.

By comparison, the significance of internal, national "others" was often stressed by the emotionally driven and perhaps even all-encompassing claims of EU mobiles. In this context, they reflected upon a growing mutually perceived distance from some of their national fellows, the home country stayers, which could easily include members of the general public and also friends and family.

> *German Female (1), EU Group 4, UK*: I *hate* national identity. Whenever someone asks me where I'm from, I kind of have a mental breakdown in front of me, cause....
>
> *Austrian Female 1*: Yeah, I have the same!
>
> *German Female (1)*: ... I would say *if* this European citizenship happens, I would be the first one to go there. Because the amount of times I had to explain that I speak Italian, but I have no Italian blood. That I'm French, but I've never lived there. It's just, such a mess! I feel like there are *so many* people who are in the same situation as me ... Like, for the longest time, I always said I'm Italian, because that's the values I associate with. That's where I was born. ... But, in my experiences, a lot of Italian people will push me away because they say "No, you're actually not Italian, because you're *something else*." ... I feel like people will push you away, cause you are not like *100 per cent* [similar]. ... I feel like a lot of people do hang on to their identity and ... sometimes it makes me feel awful, when I don't know where I'm from. It actually drives me crazy. It's nice to have the European [level], cause I know I can be European, but I can't be French or Italian, or English...
>
> *Austrian Female*: Yeah, I agree! I agree a lot. Cause I am not in the same, but in a similar situation, growing up in a mixed heritage household, obviously in mixed-ethnic heritage as well. Most people are like, "Yeah, but you're not Austrian!" Yes, I am! Like, all the way. The way I grew up. The food I ate. The language I spoke. *Everything* about me is Austrian. There is not a single part, there is not a single thing that I can relate to being Nigerian. Not at all. There is not a single ounce. And people don't understand it. "Yeah, but, you know, *look at you*! You can't be Austrian." And I'm like, "But that's unfair, ... is ethnicity now, basically what makes you be part of a nationality? That's not the way it *should* be." [Obviously upset.] I suppose, ...I can still be fully European, because that's where I was born and that's the values I grew up

with. I couldn't associate myself with any African values or any African nationality in a way. So, in that sense, I'd always be more European than anything else.

German Female (2): I agree with both [of you]. Before coming to the UK, I never really thought about what it means to be German. Obviously, because nobody asks you the question when you are at home, 'Are you German or are you from somewhere else?' And I felt really European, especially because I grew up in that European environment. And I came here, and everyone asks me, "Where are you from?" ... Obviously, you can't say, "Well, I'm European." You say, "I'm German." ... That's how I've developed this national identity. But I think, it's something you associate *with*. I *feel* German. I *am* German. I grew up there. German is my mother tongue. But there is more than that to me than just being German. ... And then again, there's so much negative, like there are *so many* negative views on the German culture and I've heard so many negative things about the German people when I came here...

German Female (1): Ahham! I have that a lot.

French Female (3): Really? [Surprised.]

German Female (2): I tell them I'm German and people will tell me, "Oh, you're a Nazi." [Visibly very worked up.] I'd be the first one to be, like dying in a gas chamber! Because I'm not blonde! I don't have blue eyes! My dad is Egyptian, my Mom ... [Others begin shuffling uncomfortably in their chair.]

Italian-Mexican Female: *Oh dear*!

German Female (2): I'm sorry what was... Nah. It's just like, I'd be the first to be *outsourced*. So, I just get this feeling that people, *other* people make you create this [ethnic] national identity. And that's exactly how, historically, like the German nationality, national identity was brought about. Through this xenophobic definition. ...

German Female (1): Don't worry, *I* will save you!

While positive for the potential of what EU citizenship might offer once realised—clearly not yet as per the earlier quote—there seems to be little in the form of an 'institutional' safety net that could assist in coming to terms with the apparently widening distinctions between internal, national "others"—mobiles/stayers—in both host *and* sending countries. Since even these ideal EU citizens—likely to make up the most desired to-be members in host and home countries—felt so strongly about the changes in their senses of *national* citizenship, it is very likely that other EU mobiles do so as well.

The evidence is strongly indicative of some prospective fundamental changes to member state citizenships against the backdrop of heightened EU free movement. While empirical studies have often been pre-occupied with the effects or lack thereof of EU mobility for senses of EU citizenship, the changes it brings about to senses of national citizenship (and identity), including senses of belonging, reflections on the community and the emergence of novel internal/national "others" are, at the very least, equally fascinating (perhaps a somewhat similar conclusion is reached by Favell [2008] in relation to the EU-15 adult Eurostars).

Given the continued competence—perceived by EU mobiles and stayers as well as institutionally guaranteed at by the bi-level structure of EU citizenship (European Commission 2017)—of national citizenships in the EU, this issue warrants further inspection.

5.3   There Is No Place like Home—Even for (Citizenship) Rights

There were plenty of examples in the early part of this chapter demonstrating how participants linked citizenship and rights together (especially at the start of Sect. 5.1). Clearly, rights seemed to have been at the heart of most approaches to citizenship. The list of entitlements and even questions about equality and membership within nation states were mainly interpreted in terms of who had access to basic social and welfare provisions—provisions not benefits—or indeed to political rights, ensuring political representation in the host state for EU mobiles, for instance. This is probably not surprising given the oft-cited top-down connotation these participants afforded to their understanding of (national) citizenship.

Even when some of the most lauded, by participants, beneficial, EU social provisions were discussed, quite a few were in fact never really used by them. Instead, by zooming in on the foreign, unfamiliar and at times expensive features of the host countries' welfare systems, EU mobiles often expressed a preference to travel home and receive treatment there.

This was true for most EU mobiles, regardless of the length of time they had spent in Sweden *or* the UK—or in another EU country in which they, at times, held dual citizenships.

German Female, EU Group 1, Sweden: For example, the health care thing. I mean even though you have this European health care card, I've experienced in Sweden, a lot of people, including me, that rather go home

and see their doctors than go to the doctors here. Because the system
is fairly difficult... and it's quite expensive. And then you never know
how much you get reimbursed. So, I do [go home] as well when I get
ill. ... So even though there is this sort of [EU] benefit, I've seen a lot
of people [do the same] ...

Hungarian-British Male: I don't know the Swedish system so well, so I
can't really comment, but I do the same. I go back to Hungary as well.

Returning home for healthcare provisions—among others—is prone
to strengthen senses of national citizenship by sustaining, however
mundanely, a formal membership in the community. The apparent quarantining of EU mobiles' access to some basic social provisions in EU-15
host states is likely to deepen such feelings (Kramer et al. 2018), despite
some attempts by the EU courts to ease member state restrictions
(Blauberger and Schmidt 2014).

With EU mobiles increasingly asked to 'prove' their eligibility to access
welfare provisions, it is likely that quite a good portion—at the lower
end of the socio-economic spectrum especially—remain absent and will
continue to use services at home instead. Since contemporary notions of
citizenship in Europe appear to be largely associated with social rights,
these practices are bound to weaken democratic issues more broadly
(Hooghe and Oser 2018), as well as EU mobiles' ability to integrate
in the host state or even possibly to develop senses of EU citizenship.
Offsetting these trends would require quite a bit of pro-EU activism, for
instance in the form of a large-scale EU healthcare policy, an intrusive,
controversial and expensive idea (Greer et al. 2014).

So, it seems even some aspects of (home) citizenships' rights are likely
to be boosted rather than dented in the context of EU mobility. Participants were well informed, interested and quite a few studied politics. Yet
they did not feel "it was *their* place" to challenge the socio-economic and
political structures of the host state by participating in politics. This was
the case with the large majority of EU mobiles regardless of the length
of time they had spent in Sweden or the UK. Indeed, most discussions
on rights abroad were framed in the EU's mobility and rights perspective. So, they were almost forgiving of host state responsibility for the
challenges they had encountered, often deeming them as a result of 'cultural' differences. By comparison, they became ever more critical about
the consequences of the EU's inherently marketized structures, which

were seen to have resulted in shrinking national social rights and opportunities to access education and employment opportunities for both EU
mobiles *and* non-EU migrants.

It is fascinating how, in all other contexts, the host society was
approached from a fairly antagonistic position. Here however, any attempt
to make the challenges EU mobiles seem to have experienced as squarely a
British or Swedish issue was quickly re-buffed by the others. While most
EU groups in Britain referred back to the issue of national stereotypes
(discussed in detail in Chapter 4.2), those in Sweden focussed on broader,
cultural and structural differences that they had come across.

Italian Male, EU Group 1: I am *very* embarrassed in answering this question because I think that the problems, we highlighted in this discussion
were partly inherent to political rights, but they're problems that fall on
us from the [EU's] market structure. So, where do you have to poach
in order to change the market structure? That's a really almost, not to
say ideological, but metaphysical question. It's very difficult to answer.

German Female: I don't really think that it's only the market that is responsible for that. It is a matter of an aspect of culture [French Male nods
in agreement], and I think it's not only [a] Swedish phenomenon. It
might be a bit stronger here and it's even harder to get in to [and]
actually being part of Swedish society in the manner that you get a job,
you get a flat, whatever... And if you don't have a support system from
somewhere, it is hard. You just have to leave the country again, because
you can't afford living here. That's the basic problem, I think. But I
don't think it's *only* the market. It's a cultural development. [Others
nod in agreement.] ...

French Male: Okay, officially, we are open. We grant people rights and
opportunities and stuff like that. But, after that, you face reality, ...
it's *economic* reality, ... as you said it's the market. And okay, if we
are not in a global period of wars, there will be national preferences
in *every* aspects of life. The job, education, okay. I think they are really
advanced in education... Because still for Europe, yeah, it's perfect! You
don't pay anything, and you can do what you want, as long as you want
to. Although, you have to find housing... that's also hard.

German Female: The interesting part is that at the same time where there
is opening up for EU students to come here and like get granted this
really great educational system, it's closing up towards other countries!
After opening up to all EU students, last year they introduced a fee. So
now it's almost impossible for non-EU students to come here, sustain
this cost of living, that's really, really high, and pay for those enormous

tuition fees. It's like there is always some trade-off, in Sweden. When you consider equal rights, like, "Oh yeah, we are so open. We always have unisex toilets!"...

Portuguese Male: Which is good!! [All begin to laugh.] ....

French Male: But at the end I think they are closing up because it's not a will. I think they are kind of *forced to* do [so], because they were the only country where you did not have any student fee [regardless of] wherever you come from. The only country in Europe, in the world I don't know, but the last country we could say [in Europe] ...

When it came to the negative effects of EU integration and globalisation on perceived or actual cultural and societal inequalities (Kuhn et al. 2014; Bourguignon 2015)—EU mobiles exhibited a sense of reflexive understanding and even went as far as to defend host countries.

They were not quite as 'lenient' towards state- and nationality-generated processes of exclusion and differentiation, such as continued and negative European national stereotypes.

Ironically, stayers were more ready to defend EU-induced equality provisions. They simply appeared more ready to consider the role of states in sustaining or even breeding inequalities and inequality of opportunities, not just when we compare one EU country with another, but also when we look at internal state policies and their impact on different regions and districts.

The discussion about formal inequality of EU citizens was in fact the only occasion where the ideal of the EU or even EU citizenship were not rejected outright by UK stayers. The exchange between them is also extremely important in that it illustrates that this group too was made up of extremely well informed and interested young citizens—who nonetheless had a generic tendency to follow national, i.e. British Eurosceptic frames in their approach to EU integration and EU citizenship elsewhere.

British Male (3), Stayer Group, UK: [T]he EU has a name for trying to make us equal. But each individual member state has its own nuances and things. So, some countries are, like, Italy's stereotype is a bit sexist, perhaps, ... you know what I mean? And the EU is trying to homogenize that. But then, again, it's not an unrealized thing. It's a process. The EU is a process and it's purely influencing on common concepts. ... This is a kind of thing it's trying to create. And the way they're doing it, it's gonna take decades!

British Female (5): But it's the kind of thing that has to be done on the smaller scale as well. You can't just have the EU implementing the policy. Like, this has gotta go beyond that. Like, you know, countries have to actually make way to, [and] go towards equality, rather than just having the EU doing it on its own. As it wouldn't be able to influence it properly.

British Male (1): [W]e are talking about formal equality, right? But then I think we should also consider equality of opportunity and equality of outcome. And definitely, like in the European Union [people] don't have homogenous opportunity. I mean we have way more opportunities than, let's say a citizen from Poland because of the nature of what's at stake. Although that's increasingly coming under attack. [Laughs ironically.] And, I am sure, in certain respects, from what I understand, ... the French have more opportunities than we do. Like I say, in certain respects. So, it really-really depends on what we mean under equality. And if we ever gonna have a homogenous equality of opportunity, I'd imagine that would require very stiff fiscal unity, which is very controversial in itself!

British Male (3): But that's the thing! And, it's not the unity [but that] it's not being that harshly implemented... the EU puts up a directive, whereas some Europeans, where civil service is very efficient or the government's very efficient, they will stingily follow. Certainly, the Equality Act. Like, what we have here, they will stingily follow it. The other countries, well, they'll take a bit of it, here and there. "Oh, we *love* that bit! Can't have *that*!" And they'll take a third of it! ... So even [EU] efforts of homogenizing everything, the idea is right, but until you have that proper unity, and people identify with Europe, I think, it's not gona happen. ...

British Female (6): Yeah, ... it's interpreted differently by all the member states. Whereas, we, in Britain, we have a habit of, ... overanalysing the treaty and the constitution and redefining it and making it more complicated than it really is. Whereas the Italians, for example, will just take it at face value and just implement the bits, the small bits that they want! So, they just, cherry-pick, almost! So again, [the implementation of EU rules is] completely different between all the member states. The aim is the same, but in terms of how it's implemented, it's different.

British Male (1): I just think how problematic that is! Because I mean, ... we can't even say that equality of opportunity is homogenous *within* our own borders! Could we? I mean not, not in terms of, not just regions but neighbourhoods. [Sarcastically] So-o-o... [Laughs], maybe, maybe that doesn't, undermine, uh, the idea of, you know, European citizenship. I'm not saying it's not a problem, but, yeah...!

These examples may suggest that sufficient time and a safe space provided, in-depth debates about significant societal issues—as seen by citizens themselves—may in fact contradict some of our expectations. In the case of continued inequality and inequality of opportunities within the EU, EU mobiles attempted to mitigate the responsibility of the member states, while stayers—including Eurosceptics (!)—were wary of blaming the EU only.

On the surface then, the evidence challenges the national framing of EU politics (Medrano 2003) and the 'blame it on Europe' theses (Hobolt and Tilley 2014; De Vries 2018). But, in light of their other responses, these exchanges are more likely to be the first clear-cut examples where distinctions were drawn by participants about *essentially* EU and national political issues. With EU mobiles striving for equality *within* the EU market and stayers at the local level, these findings might just be indicative of how basic points of socio-economic and political reference are prone to shift due to intra-EU mobility experiences (or lack thereof) (Mitchell 2014).

While seemingly good news for advocates of mobility for senses of EU citizenship, there is also of course an explicit demand and sense of urgency presented by these ideal EU/national citizens—and on inequality; a topic that even member states continue to struggle addressing.

5.4   Political Participation: *If* Anywhere, *Probably* at Home

How did the participants expect to hold the politicians accountable for delivering on their manifesto promises? There were quite extensive debates in the focus groups about how citizens generally and their own young, highly educated and mobile 'elite' group could and *should* make their voices heard in politics—in response to quite a bit of prompts by the moderator.

Initially, every group—regardless of mobility status—seemed to confirm the recent propositions on how young citizens' preferences in political participation has shifted to alternative forms of engagement. A lot of examples of issue-specific and personal examples were cited, from membership in and leadership of student unions to online petitions and green consumerism.

The basic assumption that their participation was issue-specific shaped how EU mobiles selected at which level, local, national or EU they wished to or had participated at. In particular, most EU mobiles adopted a multi-level approach to participation—similarly to their approaches to identity—and suggested citizens are most likely to select one or the other level available to them on the basis of what they conceive as the most effective route to making their voices heard.

> I think the subsidiarity principle should be applied to [participation in] Europe. Where you get these European issues that the European level should be dealing with, and there are national issues that should be dealt with at the national level.... The European level should be dealing with foreign policies, defence. But then if you take them to be the most important, then definitely [the EU-level is important for you]! But if you think it's more about education and things like that, then maybe it's the national level that's more important. (German Male, EU Group 1, UK)

Accordingly, those EU mobiles who previously exhibited traces of a cosmopolitan outlook seemed to prefer participating in alternative forms of engagement, especially so when the issue had an international scope.

> I went to the 1st of May march with Swedish friends. [All laugh.] Precisely, the workers' day is international and by walking there with the Swedes, I was actually kind of walking with also French people, or everybody in the world! That made sense for me. (French Male, EU Group 3, Sweden)

These examples suggest that the approaches of most EU mobiles to participation were inclusive, dynamic and issue-specific, with a wide range of traditional and alternative forms of engagement. As such, they appear to echo the expected shift in how young citizens approach participation (see, e.g., Sloam and Henn 2019).

But as the discussions progressed, EU mobiles' claims became increasingly contradictory. While these EU mobiles' participation in alternative forms of engagement could have been guided by issue-specific considerations, the issue of impact—just as in the above quotes—kept reappearing.

> *Romanian Female (2), EU Group 4, Sweden*: I volunteered in an NGO wh[ich] had projects funded through [the] EU. But in a way, they only worked with people from the [national] ministry that filtered the money from the EU. So, everything was also inside the country, except the money was coming from [the] outside.
>
> *Polish Female (2)*: I participated in couple of training courses, like the European Youth in Action programme. [M]y organisation [has] also

established ... [the] 'National Youth Organisation Council' and all of the European countries have this. Its responsible for whenever, for example, the Commission wants to introduce new laws [and] ... consult the youth. ... And I know, it's [a] very little thing, but I think it helps. There is also something called a 'Structured Dialogue.' It's basically the idea that in every country [we] consult the youth ... on topics like unemployment ... or participation in democracy and so on... [The resulting recommendations] go to the European Commission. And, of course, it has no real legal force, but I think it's good that youth has some kind of voice.

Bulgarian Female: Do you really think that the Commission reads this? [Sarcastically.]

Polish Female (2): Oh, they *have to*! Because some people are attending this conference and there are some people from the European Commission that are involved... Uhm, I don't know what they do later with it.

Polish Female (1): At least it exists!

Polish Female (2): As I said, it might be a little drop in the sea...

Indeed, even when some EU mobiles expressed a sense of enthusiasm about participating in alternative forms of engagement on issues that they felt closest to—including at the EU level—there were always a couple of EU mobiles who appeared less than convinced about the difference such practices could *really* make. Similar attitudes emerged in the other groups as well, suggesting that the majority of EU mobiles (in both countries) selected both the level of their participation and the forms of their engagement according to the *perceived impact* they were likely to have.

In the few instances where the right to participate in the host country was mentioned, quite big differences between EU mobiles' perceptions emerged, depending on the length of time they had spent in Sweden and the UK. Those EU mobiles who stayed in Sweden or the UK on a semi-permanent basis or for a longer period of time, over 3 years in most cases, had a tendency to participate in the host country as well as in their country of origin. They were also much more likely to support the granting of national electoral rights to EU residents—an option the EU has also been thinking about for a few years (see, e.g., European Commission 2010).

Yet, there was never quite a consensus on this issue within the groups. In the case of Sweden in particular, EU mobiles often said they did not know enough about Swedish politics to make an informed choice. Moreover, a long-term EU mobile mentioned that Swedish parties never "really reach[ed] out to migrants" and instead "focused on Swedes". As a result, only one of the 25 EU mobiles had participated in Swedish politics prior to the focus groups.

[E]ven though we live outside of our home countries and some longer than others, we still vote in our national elections... But we don't actually live in that country! ... [W]e don't participate in the policies that are taking place where we live that could actually benefit us. (German Female, EU Group 2, Sweden—Full time student, lived in Sweden for 3.5 years)

More recent and temporary EU mobiles—i.e. those on Erasmus for example—only ever *considered* participating in politics their country of origin. They identified a number of reasons for their abstention from Swedish and UK politics, including a lack of knowledge about their electoral rights and a sense of unease about participating in a society of which they were not full members. These mobiles then assumed it was not "their place" to participate in the politics of the host country.

In response, EU mobiles with semi-permanent residency were critical of the reasoning behind these abstentions. The ensuing debates then revealed that, quite often, these young and educated citizens were not familiar with the residency requirements that were attached to EU mobiles' right to participate in the local elections of the host country.

Italian Male, EU Group 1, UK: The thing with participating in another country is that, firstly, I wouldn't like the person who comes [here] for one month to have a voice. Not because he can't, but because it's not really *right*. Live there for one year, two years and then you decide. Obviously, if you live there for a long time, you work there, you live there, you have family there – it's right that you can actually vote. But, like, last year, there were some council elections and I didn't even *think of* going. Because it wouldn't feel right! Why would I do that, you know? I came here in September, why would I vote in October?...
German-Swiss Female: But maybe if that had happened at the end of your three years here, you would have had something to add. Just because other students will be living here in Egham, in the university...
Italian Male: Yeah of course! If you live for a long time in one place... But I didn't know anything about it!
German-Swiss Female: ...Yeah, I know. I'm saying if it had happened after [some time]...

Dutch Male: I would also feel the same way as well. Even, for instance, in the Netherlands I studied in Maastricht which is not my hometown. I didn't feel like I could vote for them [or] I could make a decision for them. Even if I lived there for three years! It would still feel just *wrong*.

There seems to be a sense of 'community' belonging that is required for EU mobiles (or indeed intra-national movers) to propel them to participate in the socio-political debates of their host society. As long as EU mobiles do not feel part of this community, they are likely to maintain participation in their country of origin or even town.

This is problematic for EU citizenship participation of course. EU mobiles use of their voting rights in the host country's local elections, appears to be dependent on their *perceived* membership in the host society. None of the EU mobiles in the groups appeared to have fully achieved this. However, if they would have done so, it was expected to be a sign of integration into the host society—at the cost of their EU status. And so, while n focus group participants engaged in mostly ad hoc and issue-based participation, such as in the union of their universities, at no point was their engagement likely to enhance the importance of any *other* citizenship (status) than that of nation states.

Even more, the evidence does not seem to suggest that EU mobiles became particularly engaged in the host city's sociocultural political landscape—contrary to what older generations of EU-15 mobiles were found to have done in the past (Favell 2010). This finding could, however, be the result of selection bias—all EU mobiles were in full-time education at the time of the research and the educational context would have shielded them from experiencing the political adversities of the local host society. Importantly, some EU mobiles recognised this issue (as seen in the examples earlier).

Similar to their understanding of individual-level rights and equality, stayers clearly preferred to participate in local level politics, which was seen to have a clear relevance to their lives. Importantly for these young citizens also, local issues just did not feel *as political* as the national or EU ones.

British Female (1), Stayer Group, UK: But also, … if you want something done at the local level, it doesn't feel political. Whereas, if you get it to [the] European-level or [the] national-level, it does. …

British Male (2): It's got the *weight* to it. But then, the kind of effectiveness with which you can deal with, just really dissipates the bigger and
bigger the issue becomes. [Others express their agreement.]

Hence most stayers appeared to echo the well-documented shift
among young citizens in the EU, who prefer participating in alternative
rather than traditional forms of engagement *and* at the local level—the
one they perceived as having *the most* relevance to their lives *and* with
the least 'political' outlook (see, e.g., Sloam and Henn 2019).

While alternative forms of engagement appeared to be slightly more
common among EU mobiles in Sweden than in the UK, the opposite was
true in the case of stayers. Swedish stayers only discussed different levels
of participation in traditional forms of engagement, while British stayers
debated the convenience and—for once—broader awareness raising role
of alternative forms of engagement. Once again, the discussion among
British stayers was framed around the proposition that their participation
was *always* issue specific.

British Male (1), Stayer Group, UK: [S]ometimes, [participation] is just
about [raising] visual awareness and..., obviously, [protests] didn't stop
the Iraq War. It wasn't successful. But ... the student protests here,
like, the tuition fees, which I hope we all went to?! [Passionately – to
which others begin to laugh.] Uh, millions, well not millions, you know,
thousands... – *how many was it?*
British Female (3): Quite a lot!
British Male (4): It wasn't millions.
British Female (2): *Not* millions!
British Male (1): No, not millions! [*British Female (2) and Male (3) begin
to laugh again*]. ... Obviously, not like 10 million people, but, uhm,
you know, there was, a visualisable amount of people against that. And
that in itself meant that the government couldn't use the discourse,
"Well, everyone's in agreement, this is the right thing to do." Just little
things like that, it is visibly aware that there are people against it and,
and that in itself can have, uhm, consequences that aren't necessarily
visibly tangible, but have their effect.
British Male (5): I was gonna say, I don't think participation should *ever*
be judged on whether it was effective or not.
British Male (1): Yes! [Thinks a little and changes his mind.] Well, ...
British Male (5): And that means, anyone who voted in that kind of way
..., which [is] about the idea, "We shouldn't vote, because it kind of,
wouldn't be successful.:" ... So even though, you know..., you are right,

the protests didn't stop the Iraq war. It was still a really significant, really important protest in itself! You know?

British Female (5): I think, it's difficult, cause especially with the students protests, if anyone wanted a student protest after they realized it [increased fees] went through, uhm, it's like, all morale was gone. And people don't carry on trying to protest again that often… Yeah, they just lose confidence once they pass through a bill, … Anyway yeah, … so it's difficult and…, people say protesting work, but, unfortunately, people need to have critical mass … Actually trying, like carry on having at the government rather than just like breakaway as soon as it doesn't [work out.] But that's just [what happens, i.e. carrying on], if it's a problem that's close to the protesters.

British Male (1): And we, we still talk about these protests. They still contextualise our discussion. So it's already, already, uh, having an effect. And with Iraq, it did. It did. I mean, I stick to your point [pointing to British Male (5)] as you don't have to measure success. But it also, because it was very successful, it did undermine Tony Blair quite a lot. It was like, "Oh, he's not listening to people!" You know? "He's full of it!" and blah-blah-blah.

British Male (2): It still haunts him. …

British Female (6): Rightly said!

It is interesting to note the similarity between the perceptions of EU mobiles and stayers when it came to explaining their reasons for participating in politics. For EU mobiles, participation was seen as "a little drop in the sea", but still worth the effort. Similarly, some UK stayers clearly believed that participating in politics should *not* be about making an "impact" but instead, e.g. creating "visual" awareness on a broader scale.

The sense that people were only ever likely to carry on participating if an issue was close to their hearts—and possibly even after a policy decision was formalised—once again, stressed stayers' assumption about citizens' chiefly personalised and issue-specific approach to political participation. Given that the EU level hardly *ever* seemed relevant in their everyday lives, they were likely to refrain from participating in EU politics.

By comparison however, *national* issues were likely to be on their agenda—even if often on an individualistic basis. While this does not replicate 'persistent nationalism' and strong national identities which then entirely hamper the presence of *any* supranational concern (Recchi 2015: 106), there is a sense that only when EU issues breach the 'national' or local sphere will they be the target of citizens everyday political participation. The sudden surge of pro- and anti-Brexit activism suggests that even when the supranational is under extreme threat (Cram 2012), it must first pierce national political processes for it to be a sufficient backdrop of activating citizen's EU participation (Siklodi 2019).

5.5 SUMMARY

This chapter explored and compared young and educated EU mobiles and stayers' senses of national citizenship against the backdrop of heightened intra-EU learning mobility. Despite what some of the pro-EU integration mobile literature and policymakers suggest, EU mobility did *not* appear to lessen EU mobiles' senses of national citizenship.

Quite the opposite.

The importance of national citizenship for mobiles was equal to or at times appeared even more important than it was for stayers. While the national framework was the basic reference point in all matters to do with citizenship, the relevance of *inclusive* national citizenship—across its three dimensions—became more noticeable *whilst* young citizens were using their EU learning mobility rights. The only time EU affairs appear to have trumped national politics were in relation to addressing inequalities affecting citizens. These issues were seen to cut across national borders and originate from the EU's very own market structures. While EU mobiles clearly saw the EU level as responsible for and best placed to addressing these issues, stayers demanded change at the local level.

While not entirely consistent, the findings in this chapter challenge the anticipated distinctions between the senses of national citizenship between EU mobiles and stayers—as part of a budding EU community. Instead, they accentuate the primary character of national citizenship. However, EU mobiles' approaches to national citizenship were largely inclusive—possibly more so towards traditional national "others" from elsewhere in the EU, than towards some of their own national stayer fellows, including, at times, personal friends and family members. The question then becomes how these changes in senses of national affiliations are likely to affect notions of EU citizenship in the context of mobility. The next chapter will explore this issue further.

References

Abdelhady, D. (2019). Framing the Syrian refugee: Divergent discourses in three national contexts. In M. R. Menjivar & E. Ness (Eds.), *The Oxford Handbook of Migration Crisis*. New York, NY: Oxford University Press. https://doi.org/10.1093/oxfordhb/9780190856908.013.16.

Adler-Nissen, R. (2011). Opting out of an ever closer union: The integration doxa and the management of sovereignty. *West European Politics, 34*(5), 1092–1113.

Aspinwall, M. (2002). Preferring Europe: Ideology and national preferences on European integration. *European Union Politics, 3*(1), 81–111.

Bauböck, R. (1997). *Citizenship and national identities in the European Union* (Jean Monnet Working Papers. 4/1997). Harvard Law School.

Bellamy, R. (2008). Evaluating union citizenship: belonging, rights and participation within the EU. *Citizenship Studies, 12*(6), 597–611.

Bellamy, R., & Castiglione, D. (2019). *From Maastricht to Brexit: Democracy, Constitutionalism and Citizenship in the EU*. Lanham, MD: Rowman & Littlefield International.

Blauberger, M., & Schmidt, S. K. (2014). Welfare migration? Free movement of EU citizens and access to social benefits. *Research & Politics*. https://doi.org/10.1177/2053168014563879.

Bourguignon, F. (2015). *The Globalization of Inequality*. Princeton: Princeton University Press.

Brochman, G., & Hagelund, A. (2012). *Immigration Policy and the Scandinavian Welfare State 1945–2010*. Basingstoke: Palgrave Macmillan.

Bruter, M. (2005). *Citizens of Europe? The Emergence of a Mass European Identity*. Basingstoke: Palgrave Macmillan.

Buranyi, S. (2019). Greta Thunberg's enemies are right to be scared. Her new political allies should be too. *The Guardian*. https://www.theguardian.com/commentisfree/2019/sep/30/greta-thunberg-enemies-inaction-climate-crisis.

Cairns, D. (Ed.). (2010). *Youth on the Move: European Youth and Geographical Mobility*. Wiesbaden: VS Verlag.

Converse, P. E. (1972). Change in the American electorate. In A. Campbell & P. E. Converse (Eds.), *The Human Meaning of Social Change* (pp. 263–337). New York: Russell Sage.

De Vries, C. E. (2018). *Euroscepticism and the Future of European Integration*. Oxford: Oxford University Press.

Deutsch, K. W., Burrel, S. A., Kann, R. A., Lee, M., Jr., Lichterman, M., Lindgren, R. E., et al. (1968). *Political Community and the North Atlantic Area*. Princeton: Princeton University Press.

Duchesne, S., Frazer, E., Haegel, F., & Van Ingelgom, V. (Eds.). (2013). *Citizens' Reactions to European Integration Compared: Overlooking Europe.* Basingstoke: Palgrave.

European Commission. (2010). *Report on the Election of Members of the European Parliament and on the Participation of European Union Citizens in Elections for the European Parliament, COM (2010) 605 final.* Brussels, 27.10.2010.

European Commission. (2011). *The Commission accepts that Spain can temporarily restrict the free movement of Romanian workers, MEMO/11/554.*

European Commission. (2014). *Erasmus+.* http://ec.europa.eu/programmes/erasmus-plus/index_en.htm.

European Commission. (2017). *White paper on the future of Europe: Reflections and scenarios for the EU27 by 2025.* COM/2017/2025 final.

Falk, R. (1993). The making of global citizenship. In J. Brecher, J. B. Childs, & J. Cutler (Eds.), *Global Visions: Beyond the New World Order* (pp. 39–52). Boston: South End Press.

Favell, A. (2008). *Eurostars and Eurocities: Free Movement and Mobility in an Integrating Europe.* Oxford: Blackwell.

Favell, A. (2010). European identity and european citizenship in three eurocities?: A sociological approach to the European Union. *Politique Européenne, 30*(1), 187–224.

Fiorino, N., Pontarollo, N., & Ricciuti, R. (2019). Supranational, national and local dimensions of voter turnout in European Parliament elections. *JCMS: Journal of Common Market Studies, 57,* 877– 893.

Greer, S. L., Fahy, N., Elliott, H., Wismar, M., Jarman, H., & Palm, W. (2014). Everything you always wanted to know about European Union health policies but were afraid to ask. *World Health Organization.* WHO Regional Office for Europe.

Haas, E. B. (1958). *The Uniting of Europe: Political, Social and Economic Forces 1950–1957.* Stanford: Stanford University Press.

Hobolt, S. B., & Tilley, J. (2014). *Blaming Europe? Responsibility Without Accountability in the European Union.* Oxford: Oxford University Press.

Hooghe, M., & Oser, J. (2018). Social and political citizenship in European public opinion: An empirical analysis of TH Marshall's concept of social rights. *Government and Opposition, 53*(4), 595–620.

Joppke, C. (2010). The inevitable lightening of citizenship. *European Journal of Sociology/Archives Européennes de Sociologie, 51*(1), 9–32.

Kramer, D., Thierry, J. S., & van Hooren, F. (2018). Responding to free movement: quarantining mobile union citizens in European welfare states. *Journal of European Public Policy, 25*(10), 1501–1521.

Kriesi, H. (2014). The populist challenge. *West European Politics, 37*(2), 361–378.

Kuhn, T. (2012). Why educational exchange programmes miss their mark: Cross-border mobility, education and European identity. *JCMS: Journal of Common Market Studies, 50*(6), 994–1010.

Kuhn, T. (2019). Grand theories of European integration revisited: Does identity politics shape the course of European integration? *Journal of European Public Policy, 26*(8), 1213–1230. https://doi.org/10.1080/13501763.2019. 1622588.

Kuhn, T., Van Elsas, E., Hakhverdian, A., & van der Brug, W. (2014). An ever wider gap in an ever closer union: Rising inequalities and euroscepticism in 12 West European democracies, 1975–2009. *Socio-Economic Review, 14*(1), 27–45.

Kvist, J. (2004). Does EU enlargement start a race to the bottom? Strategic interaction among EU member states in social policy. *Journal of European Social Policy, 14*(3), 301–318.

Magnette, P. (2005). *Citizenship: The History of an Idea*. Colchester: ECPR Press.

Marshall, T. H. (1950). *Citizenship and Social Class and Other Essays*. New York: Cambridge University Press.

Mazzoni, D., Albanesi, C., Ferreira, P. D., Opermann, S., Pavlopoulos, V., & Cicognani, E. (2018). Cross-border mobility, European identity and participation among European adolescents and young adults. *European Journal of Developmental Psychology, 15*(3), 324–339. https://doi.org/10.1080/174 05629.2017.1378089.

Medrano, J. D. (2003). *Framing Europe: Attitudes to European Integration in Germany, Spain, and the United Kingdom*. Princeton: Princeton University Press.

Midtbøen, A. H., Birkvad, S. R., & Erdal, M. B. (2018). *Citizenship in the Nordic Countries*. Copenhagen: Tema Nord, Nordic Council of Ministers.

Mikl-Leitner, J., Friedrich, H. P., Teeven, F., & May, T. (2013). *Letter to Allan Shatter*. http://docs.dpaq.de/3604-130415_letter_to_presidency_f inal_1_2.pdf.

Mitchell, K. (2007). Geographies of identity: The intimate cosmopolitan. *Progress in Human Geography, 31*(5), 706–720.

Mitchell, K. (2014). Rethinking the 'Erasmus effect' on European identity. *JCMS: Journal of Common Market Studies*. https://doi.org/10.1111/jcms. 12152.

Myslinska, D. R. (2016). Post-Brexit hate crimes against Poles are an expression of long-standing prejudices and contestation over white identity in the UK. *LSE Brexit Blog*. https://research.gold.ac.uk/26564/1/index.html.

Nussbaum, M. C. (1994). Patriotism and cosmopolitanism. *Boston Review, XIX*(5), 3–16.

O'Leary, S. (1995). The social dimension of community citizenship. In A. Rosas & E. Antola (Eds.), *A Citizens' Europe in Search of a New Order* (pp. 156–181). London: Sage.

Pollock, G., Brock, T., & Ellison, M. (2015). Populism, ideology and contradiction: mapping young people's political views. *The Sociological Review, 63,* 141–166.

Putnam, D. R. (2000). *Bowling Alone: The Collapse and Revival of American Community.* New York: Simon & Schuster.

Recchi, E. (2015). *Mobile Europe: The Theory and Practice of Free Movement in the EU.* Basingstoke: Palgrave Macmillan.

Recchi, E., & Favell, A. (Eds.). (2009). *Pioneers of European Integration.* Cheltenham and Northampton: Edward Elgar Publishing.

Rooduijn, M. (2018). What unites the voter bases of populist parties? Comparing the electorates of 15 populist parties. *European Political Science Review, 10*(3), 351–368.

Ross, A. (2015). *Understanding the Constructions of Identities by Young New Europeans: Kaleidoscopic Selves.* London: Routledge.

Ross, A. (2019). *Finding Political Identities: Young People in a Changing Europe.* London: Palgrave Macmillan.

Sanders, D., Belluci, P., Tóka, G., & Torcal, N. (Eds.). (2012). *The Europeanization of National Politics? Citizenship and Support in a Post-Enlargement Union.* Oxford: Oxford University Press.

Schierup, C. U., & Ålund, A. (2011). The end of Swedish exceptionalism? Citizenship, neoliberalism and the politics of exclusion. *Race & Class, 53*(1), 45–64.

Schmidt, S. K., Blauberger, M., & Martinsen, D. S. (2018). Free movement and equal treatment in an unequal union. *Journal of European Public Policy, 25*(10), 1391–1402.

Scholten, P., & van Ostaijen, M. (Eds.). (2018). *Between Mobility and Migration: The Multi-Level Governance of Intra-European Movement.* IMISCOE Research Series, Springer Open. https://link.springer.com/book/10.1007/978-3-319-77991-1.

Shaw, J. (2012). *EU citizenship and the edges of Europe* (Citizen Working Paper Series). University of Edinburgh, School of Law.

Siklodi, N. (2019). The Brexit crisis: Potential implications for the EU and its citizens. In Europa Publications (Ed.). *European Union Encyclopedia and Directory 2020* (20th Ed.). Abingdon, UK: Routledge.

Sloam, J., & Henn, M. (2019). *Youthquake 2017: The Rise of Young Cosmopolitans in Britain.* London: Palgrave Macmillan.

Smith, A. D. (1992). National identity and the idea of European Identity. *International Affairs, 68*(1), 55–76.

Tambini, D. (2001). Post-national citizenship. *Ethnic and Racial Studies, 24*(2), 195–217.

Van Ingelgom, V. (2014). *Integrating Indifference: A Comparative, Qualitative and Quantitative Approach to the Legitimacy of European Integration.* Colchester: ECPR Press.

Van Mol, C. (2014). *Intra-European Student Mobility in International Higher Education Circuits: Europe on the Move.* Basingstoke: Palgrave Macmillan.

Voeten, E. (2018). Populism and backlashes against international courts. *Perspectives on Politics.* https://doi.org/10.1017/S1537592719000975.

White, J. (2011). *Political Allegiance after European Integration.* Basingstoke: Palgrave Macmillan.

CHAPTER 6

EU Citizenship and Mobility: A Less Than Perfect Partnership

The institutional framework and official discourses on European Union (EU) citizenship appear to neatly reflect the multidimensional requirements set out by citizenship studies scholars (Chapter 2.3). Accordingly, EU citizenship is presented as the source of citizens' collective European, more precisely EU, identity, associated series of EU rights (and duties) and EU participation. Together, these dimensions, when realised by citizens, expected to nourish the EU's political thirsts (as apparent in the European Commission's three yearly EU citizenship reports starting in 1993). Yet, it is the legacy of the market citizenship—emphasising intra-EU economic mobility among EU nationals—which has resonated with the majority of academics. This chapter draws on original focus group evidence in order to interrogate whether and how EU citizenship emerges in the best-case scenario—during young and highly educated citizens' intra-EU learning mobility.

Much of the literature on EU citizenship has followed the same pattern of duality that is present in official EU discourses. Legal scholars have tended to accentuate the ever-expanding supra- and post-national scope of citizens' EU rights, whereby a supranational model is in the making as per the liberal traditions of citizenship (Kostakopoulou 2001; Jenson 2007; Kochenov 2014; van den Brink and Kochenov 2019). The hopeful tone of these accounts is matched by the far-reaching criticism of scholars who investigate EU citizenship's institutional and empirical

© The Author(s) 2020
N. Siklodi, *The Politics of Mobile Citizenship in Europe*,
Politics of Citizenship and Migration,
https://doi.org/10.1007/978-3-030-49051-5_6

frameworks. Far from a progressive and dynamic model, these interpretations accentuate how a market-orientated model of citizenship is failing in its attempts to stimulate citizens' senses of *collective* EU identity and enhance their input into EU politics (Bellamy et al. 2004, 2006; Bellamy and Castiglione 2019). Criticism has been especially harsh when the *exact* scope of EU citizenship's challenge to the "the exclusive sovereignty of national citizenship" in Europe (Delanty 1997: 296) came under closer scrutiny. Accordingly, comparisons have been made between citizens' senses of EU and national citizenship, testing whether the EU can develop a 'European-nationality' similar to that of member state nationalities (White 2011; Sanders et al. 2012; Duchesne et al. 2013; Guiraudon et al. 2015).

To some extent, the aforementioned approaches have all expected EU citizenship to closely replicate national models. Yet, the emphasis on citizens' intra-EU mobility—as *the* activation element of EU citizenship—signals an important shift. EU studies scholars, as indicated in the previous chapters of this book, have tended to be more responsive to this issue in their assessment of the role of EU citizenship in Europe's integration efforts. However, they have reached rather inconclusive and contradictory conclusions about how mobility experiences affect EU mobiles' and stayers' senses of EU citizenship (Chapter 3; Favell 2008, 2010; Recchi 2015). The same contradictions seem to characterise findings about intra-EU learning mobility and EU citizenship (Bruter 2005; Sigalas 2009, 2010a, b; Van Mol 2011, 2013, 2014; Wilson 2011; Mitchell 2012, 2014; Ross 2015, 2019; Siklodi 2015).

This chapter brings EU citizenship's "future-looking" (European Parliament 2017: 18) character under closer scrutiny and probes the extent to which it is likely to signal a "*political* link between the citizens of Member States and the European Union" (European Commission 1993: 2, emphasis in original) *during* intra-EU mobility. More to the point, it examines the *political* rationale of intra-EU learning mobility and its ability to "enhance [students'] development as active citizens" in an ever-more mobile Europe (European Commission 2010: 2), using original focus group evidence from Sweden and the United Kingdom (UK). The official EU discourse seems to imply that stayers—80% of all formal EU citizens (European Parliament 2017)—have been provided with barely any opportunity to develop a sense of EU citizenship. The European Parliament (2009: 16, 14 emphasis added; see also 2017: 18–20) has been particularly perceptive of these potential shortfalls and set a new requirement "to improve communication with the *average* Union citizen". Against this backdrop, the current chapter seeks to illustrate the likely distinctions and similarities between the perceptions of EU mobiles *and* stayers about EU citizenship, and across the interlinked dimensions of citizenship as set out by EU scholars—identity, rights and participation (Chapter 2.3).

Overall, the chapter demonstrates that, as the upper level of a bi-level citizenship structure in a mobile Europe, EU citizenship is likely to signal a "novel" but temporary notion for EU mobiles and a second-order extension of national statuses for stayers (Delanty 1997). Nonetheless, it also shows that both groups are likely to readily accept that EU citizenship is only ever apparent *during* intra-EU mobility—emphasising the requirement to adjust academic and policy expectations and examine EU/national citizenship realities as present in a mobile Europe today.

The chapter is structured as follows.

The first part explores and compares EU mobiles' and stayers' perceptions of EU citizenship. The second, third and fourth parts investigate EU mobiles' and stayers' perceptions of the dimensions of EU citizenship—namely EU identity, EU rights and EU participation. Overall, the chapter illustrates that even in the best-case scenario, EU citizenship is still likely to be deemed as "something for the future"—when and where intra-EU mobility becomes more accessible and normal part of the experience of the everyday citizen.

6.1 EU Citizenship—Not for Us, *Just Yet*

Unlike their initial approaches to and understanding of national citizenship (Chapter 5.1), there were considerable differences between EU mobiles' and stayers' approaches to EU citizenship. Most importantly, none of the stayers appeared to hold durable senses of EU citizenship—especially one that could resist some of the key challenges raised in the course of the focus groups—while the majority of EU mobiles at least appeared to do so.

This might please *some* EU actors.

EU mobiles appeared as generally more optimistic about what EU citizenship signifies—something "novel", an "extra feature of citizenship" that is "more of a guarantee" and "security" especially during intra-EU travels (Bruter 2005). There was an assumption, often repeated, that citizens tend to have at least an abstract and shallow sense of EU citizenship, stemming from the everyday personal benefits EU citizenship offered to them at the individual level, such as using the European passport outside the EU and travelling without visas within it, as well as paying with the Euro in most EU countries (European Commission 2017; Bruter 2005; Favell 2008). These benefits were believed to afford a generic sense of "freedom" to the public—and to EU mobiles participating in the focus groups.

> *Swedish Female, EU Group 3, UK*: [EU citizenship] opens up more possibilities for you. It's more freedom, I would say! Like, you have this kind of citizenship, or it's a sense of belonging. You belong in the European Union. Like, *everywhere* is home! You're allowed everywhere. You can do the same things almost as you can do at home in whatever country you choose.
>
> *Dutch Female*: It really just means that I have less passport checks. It's, like, really easy to travel and that's literally all it means to me. It's probably because I'm not a taxpayer... Like for me, it's just easier to travel. It's easier to pay with Euros everywhere.

Nearly every EU mobile were ready to expand on a *personal* story of their EU citizenship, though never thought of introducing themselves in 'European' terms. "[I]f you speak about European citizenship, I never felt so European than this year as an Erasmus student. And I see that I can share much with the other people from Europe" (French Male, EU Group 3, Sweden).

In comparison, stayers did not seem to have a personal investment in EU citizenship and seemed to make sense of it by comparing it with their national citizenships. Their descriptions were about the "extending [of] national citizenship" and a "belonging to a wider community", granting a second-order character to EU citizenship (Delanty 1997). Initially at least, Swedish stayers seemed excited about the prospects of assessing EU citizenship and almost all of them believed that it was an important aspect of everyday life in Sweden. However, two of them openly admitted that they had never heard of the notion of EU citizenship prior to their university studies or the focus groups. One of them seemed puzzled for the seemingly little 'promotion' of her *own* EU citizenship status by policymakers, never quite pondering on the possibility of developing her familiarity with or from an individual incentive (i.e. from a bottom-up perspective).

Swedish Female (2), Stayer Group, Sweden: We have extended our rights outside the national borders and it means that it should be easy to live in another European country the same way that you live in your own country. You can work, study or travel without any problems. And, therefore, we are now European citizens. That identity has now been prolonged, stretched and I think that's the ambition of the EU is to create the notion of European citizen.

Swedish, Female (4): I heard about [EU citizenship] for the first time in our political theory course and we were talking about citizenship. I've never come [into] contact with the concept of 'the European citizen' before. And I found it surprising because I consider myself being, well, at least not ignorant. [Some nervous laughs, probably given the topic of the research and my presence as the moderator]. I try to follow current events and also news about the European Union. So, I was also surprised that I haven't been, uhm well, *no one* had tried to convince me that I am a European citizen.

British stayers assessed EU citizenship in quite the opposite manner. They distanced themselves from the rest of the EU from the very beginning of the focus groups, justifying their position with references to the UK's *outlier* position.

Another, more widely cited, exclusive quality was granted to EU citizenship as the groups turned to EU mobility (related processes of differentiation were investigated in detail Chapter 4). They suggested that the well-off, educated and (longer-term) EU mobiles are the *only* category of EU citizens—from the 500 million total—possibly holding an *explicit* sense of EU citizenship. By comparison, occasional EU mobility (in fact any type of temporal movement, such as cross-border shopping) was often depicted as the portrait of the EU's very own "parochial tourist" (Thompson and Tambyah 1999: 216)—crossing borders with a specific aim in mind and without an interest in engaging with the members of the host community. Such practices made it highly unlikely for stayers to develop a sense of EU citizenship or a broader cosmopolitan outlook (Münch 2017).

When I look at my friends that have never left Germany, they don't feel European. They *really* don't. It's nice for them to go [outside of Germany]; once in a while for a summer holiday, all inclusive, staying at the hotel, doing a bus-trip and going to the beach... [T]hey go on holidays, but not to feel part of [the host] community. (German Female, EU Group 2, Sweden)

With the benefit of *some* hindsight, EU mobiles *and* stayers also drilled into another issue apparent from the quotes above—the temporal character of EU citizenship. Claims of being EU citizens were always followed by references to *some* "occasions" and the "not structural" sense of EU and European identity it led to. Besides, once on the move, the implications of country contexts also mattered considerably. For participants, the "West German-Dutch-Belgian joint" was identified as *the* place "where you can experience that a form of European *Union* has already been reached" thanks to its "multi-speaking" and "really moving communities". However, such places were seen as far from common in the EU—they were in fact claimed to have been "isolated spots". Such assertions have then begun to crack open the fault lines of contemporary EU citizenship.

The longer-term *and* constructive limitations EU mobility granted to EU citizenship were then further probed by two (returned) stayers' assertions, one in each country. They very strongly insinuated that *their* previous experiences of EU mobility did not lead to a lasting bond with the EU. They had only ever identified as EU citizens *during* their experiences of EU mobility—at which point they had also often related to *other* EU citizens. However, since returning home, they have identified as national citizens first and foremost.

When I was working in France for a month, I met some... Russians and a guy from Jordan... In contrast to them, I really felt like me and the French people had more in common. ...Even though here, in Sweden, ... these French [people], they are so different from me! But there, I really felt this European notion. (Swedish Female (3), Stayer Group, Sweden)

I think that living in a different European country makes you *slightly* more European. I don't think I would have ever considered [being a European] if I haven't lived in Spain for a year. And now... I have done that, been living there and I can speak Spanish, I probably relate [to this European feeling] more than before. (British Female (6), Stayer Group, UK)

Hence, it seems as if though EU citizenship is—at most—likely to be a temporary phase in citizens' lives, just as is the case with their EU mobility. Since the majority of participants assumed that citizens "*always* see national government[s] first" (Chapter 5.1), it is plausible that once EU mobiles return home or, in the case of longer-term residency abroad, integrate in the host country, many lose *their* previous EU sentiments. With a self-prescribed enhanced ability to notice differences between themselves—as national citizens—and as EU mobiles, there is even a possible 'danger' for returning EU mobiles to adopt stronger and possibly more 'exclusive' senses of national citizenships. Similar findings were also noted by colleagues looking at youth EU mobility elsewhere (especially Van Mol 2014; Mazzoni et al. 2018).

On a slightly more positive note, when participants turned to addressing the 'future' of EU citizenship, the large majority—bar the UK stayer group—believed it already begun to assist the EU's state building aspirations and expected its significance to be enhanced further in the future. "I think this European Union citizenship is going to be more visible in the future because... we are travelling so much now" (Polish Female (1), EU Group 4, Sweden). Accordingly, the majority of participants observed the economic crisis as an important event, showcasing the positive outcomes a 'newly' integrated Union already offered to its citizens.

> [W]e've got a nascent institution and a nascent form of "supranational", in quotation, for the record, democratic institutions. And just because it's so new and now because of the euro crisis... it's going through a lot of dispute. It's going through a lot of political argument to disassociate and create infighting in the European Union. Probably the state when it emerged, it didn't seem to tie people together the way it has now. Political institutions change and, I think, that the public sentiment towards the European Union will change and the idea that we can still be who we are ... we'll adopt with the European Union, if that makes sense? It's just so young at the moment that it hasn't been as accepted as it perhaps will be by future generations. (Finnish Female (1), EU Group 2, UK)

While largely anticipatory in tone, what this quote nonetheless indicates is that even more enthusiastic EU mobiles in the focus groups quickly resigned to admitting EU citizenship is not *yet* a reality.

6.2   EU Citizenship as Identity: EU Mobility, EU Signals and Some Senses of 'Geo-Proximity'

Identity is, perhaps, the most researched aspect of EU citizenship—so much so that EU studies scholars have used and continue to use these two terms interchangeably. This tendency is not surprising considering the role EU actors foresaw for citizens' EU identity in European integration (e.g. Council of Ministers 1987). Given the multifaceted character of citizens identity, it is nonetheless the least institutionalised and most personal aspect of emerging senses of EU citizenship (Herrmann et al. 2004).

This section examines EU citizenship as identity along its key elements; senses of belonging to the EU, shared EU identity and the EU's "other" (as defined in Chapter 2.3). The tendency by participants to expand/limit their discussions of EU identity so as to 'fit' the given topic is likely to be illustrative of the broader ambiguity in senses of EU identity (Van Ingelgom 2014). Participants did not seem to feel comfortable enough with a single issue which could demarcate (their) EU identity. This issue may also exemplify the ambiguity expected to be present in empirical research on political identity (Brubaker and Cooper 2000: 2).

The majority of groups observed EU mobility as effective in developing EU mobiles' civic senses of belonging to the EU (Bruter 2005; Recchi 2015: 123–144). They suggested that mobility was *necessary* for making the EU "relevant to [their] lives" as EU citizens.

> When you move out and you travel, you can develop this sense of 'Europe' [and] 'Western membership'. I think we are developing this kind of identity in this vague sense. We are an elite compared to our national fellows, compatriots. I mean, it's easier for us to feel European or Western in general than people that don't move away. (Italian Male (1), EU Group 4, Sweden)

However, EU mobiles were also quick to underscore the ambiguity prevalent in citizens' EU identity, suggesting various domains from multi-layered to context-specific factors as key to unpacking this issue. Doing so, however, complicated interpretations of the role of EU mobility in building EU identity. Indeed, nearly all EU mobiles suspected that EU mobility strengthened *both* their senses of belonging to the EU *and* their country of origin, referring to home stayers as their "compatriots" (also discussed in Chapter 5.2. in relation to national senses of belonging).

> I define myself as a 'Berliner'. I feel German. But I also feel European. So, in a way, you could argue that there is a multilevel identity thing going on. [Others nod in agreement.] But, I think, it sounds sort of weird, I guess. I like to think of it spatially. So, my base is my home city but the people who speak my language, who vote for the same parliament, I guess, you could say that's sort of the next level, the country. But then, at the same time, Europe is sort of the wider geographical base where I can move around freely, where I can enjoy the rights of being a citizen without feeling foreign, I suppose. So, yeah, I would say that there is sort of a two-level identity going on. (German Male, EU Group 2, UK)

Participants often touched upon how Sweden and the UK were unique member states—positioned as being "more/less European" by stayers and EU mobiles, respectively. Through their everyday interactions, EU mobiles often made claims to experiencing Euroscepticism in both countries. Such claims echoed the continued importance of national framing of European politics (Medrano 2003). But there was something more present in these discussions. National frames were interpreted in the light of common assumptions which are often prevalent in EU mobiles' host country. Accordingly, it was claimed that "people from the European continent feel more European than British people do" (French-British Female, EU Group 2, UK). And, similarly, "many Swedes feel that they are not part of Europe... and would [prefer] to have a 'Scandinavian Union' and shut everyone else off" (Hungarian-British Male, EU Group 2, Sweden).

The latter perception seemed to have been particularly effective in enhancing EU mobiles' *direct* senses of belonging to the EU.

> Actually, most of my Swedish friends that I have, and there is a quite a couple of them, I do speak English with. I don't speak Swedish with them. I think, the language is not a barrier at all. It's more that cultural thing ... Everything that comes from the outside is viewed as quite sceptical, first of all. So, they keep their distance. ...They are friendly. But they don't get so attached in the first place. And they're not, like, *really* open. (German Female, EU Group 1, Sweden)

This 'exclusivist' character of socialisation practices in Sweden and the UK was assumed to have been particularly effective in promoting EU senses of belonging among mobiles. However, as the debates progressed, it became ever more likely that for EU mobiles in the UK a sense of belonging to continental Europe rather than the EU per se was developing.

> I even feel that [European identity] here in the UK. And that's not so much European, but more "continental-European". Well, the difference is mostly made by the British themselves. [All laugh.] So, if they ask me about, like, "How do they do this or that in Europe?" I thought we were already in Europe! So, I started out from seeing all of Europe and now I do see a distinction. And that makes me more kind of conscious about the fact that I relate more to, say, the French and the Germans than I do to the English, perhaps. (Dutch Male, EU Group 1, UK)

In comparison, stayers did not really perceive EU mobility as effective in enhancing their senses of belonging to the EU. Swedish stayers said they felt "dull" when they were mobile in the EU because their nationality was not as interesting as other EU nationalities. They believed that the lack of an outspoken Swedish citizenship culture (Midtbøen et al. 2018) made Sweden a peculiar member state. After all, "Swedes don't treasure their national identity [as] much [as other EU nationalities do] and ...[our] European feeling [as a result] maybe stronger" (Swedish Female (3), Stayer Group, Sweden). They portrayed a somewhat post-national and idealised Swedish community (similarly to that of the literature on Swedish citizenship, for example, Roth 2004), where shared values, including "equality" and "justice" promoted a sense of belonging to Sweden and, by extension, to the EU. As the discussion progressed, however, Swedish stayers appeared more and more jumbled about what the EU—or indeed EU citizenship on the whole—actually signified to them and about who bears responsibility for these apparent contradictions.

A good portion of Swedish stayers then claimed to have felt a sense of belonging to the EU—whatever the depth—and appreciation of "European values" enhanced through specific civic values, including "peace" and "democracy", and key EU symbols, especially the European Health Insurance Card (EHIC). They generally expected the EU to be the most visible to them through "little things like that" (Bruter 2005; Ross 2015, 2019).

> I think also when I received my European Health Insurance Card and that was some kind of symbol [Others nod in agreement] … I haven't used it. But I kind of *knew,* I think, that we have a common health insurance system. Those kinds of benefits or entitlements are… strengthening the [European] feeling. (Swedish Female (6), Stayer Group, Sweden)

While some Brits seemed to have agreed with this sentiment, far from all did so. In observing certain aspects of EU mobility as relevant to underlining senses of belonging to the EU, the others remained vocal about a (continued) distinction between British and other 'European' citizens.

> *British Male (2), Stayer Group, UK*: In some specific ways I always feel, like, when I travel inside the EU and have my EU [EHIC] card with me, it's like my mind is calm. It's little things like that. And thank goodness I never actually had to use it for anything! Touch wood! But I… actual feel that by having it on me, just this tiny piece of purple, laminated plastic … there is a kind of symbolic aspect to it.
>
> *British Female (1)*: I don't think that, really. I guess, … this is probably *really optimistic of me,* but I believe in the competence of our government to be able to do anything … if, you know, anything happens to us, uhm [Smiles.] *elsewhere*! You know?
>
> *British Female (3)*: Well I think, people find it hard to name things that are specifically beneficial because of the EU…
>
> *British Male (1)*: Yeah, the conceptions of Europe that we have is always to refer to something *other* than ourselves. Whenever you hear it mentioned in the news or you have a kind of substantial discussion about European citizenship, the European Union or aspects of the European identity, you often hear with reference to decisions the Europeans made. Being referred to as "Europe said this". And European [Union is] being presented as *something* "otherly". And there is Europe and there is Britain somehow sucked into it, but doesn't really belong.
>
> *British Male (2)*: [Smiles] That's true, actually. It doesn't really come across as we are a part of [the EU].
>
> *British Female (6)*: …It's "them and us." … It's never "*We* decided this".
>
> *British Male (5)*: Europe is something like a very easy scapegoat for things that have gone wrong, it's like "Oh yeah, it's Europe's fault! It's not our fault. We have to do it because of Europe!"

Perhaps as a result, some UK stayers spoke candidly about not seeing the UK as part of the EU nor the European continent. Often relying on post-imperialist and, in traces, a populist logic, they then drew attention to the UK's geographical proximity relative to the rest of the EU, including the British "moat" which surrounds "our little island" and positions the UK "far away... from Europe". These claims seemed to have echoed some of the now more mainstream pro-Brexit discourses and are very much in line with recent research on 'English' identity specifically (Leddy-Owen 2019). More to the point, distinct territorial identities and 'geographical imaginaries' (Bruter 2004) were crucial to unpacking UK stayers' approaches to their senses of belonging. Even those UK stayers who were originally more enthusiastic about discussing their EU citizenship and expressed some senses of belonging to the EU, later acknowledged the negative impact British public, elite and media discourses of the EU and its political system had on their own perceptions.

Compared to these somewhat jumbled discussions, there seemed to have been a general agreement among the focus groups that EU mobility had a constructive impact on citizens' shared EU identity, supporting the expectations of transactionalist and neofunctionalist approaches (Haas 1958; Deutsch et al. 1968). The majority of EU mobiles suggested that their experiences of EU mobility assisted in developing a shared *cultural* EU identity, since it intensified cross-border interactions with the "other"—from a national perspective—who came from elsewhere in Europe (Ross 2015, 2019).

> [I]t's like when you are here, when you are out with your friends and you feel like it's an international community of Europeans. ... We are Europeans, but noone kind of says it. It's just in the air. You *feel it*, like we are from kind of the same place but different areas of it. (British-Hungarian Male EU Group 2, Sweden)

Even stayers recognised that EU mobiles were more likely to "stick together" and claimed that *certain* EU citizens were more inclined to be mobile than others, especially from France, Germany or Italy.

> I think, if you lived in another country and spoke another European language ... language is a big part of it. I mean, being in Spain and being in the Erasmus programme, ... I was meeting people that were German but then spoke six other European languages. And, I think, they would

associate more with being European citizens because they spend so much time in other European countries and can speak to so many other European people. But for me, it was just English and Spanish. So, I think, living [abroad] and speaking other European languages makes you more of a part of that community. (British Female (6), Stayer Group, UK)

It is interesting that British stayers' perceptions about proficiency in English were observed as an insufficient basis to developing a sense of shared EU identity with other EU citizens. For everyone else, English was recognised as *the* European language, mimicking the academic literature on inter-cultural mingling (Mitchell 2012). Swedish stayers also claimed that a shared EU identity required EU mobility *and* knowledge of European languages. They then criticised the current elitist quality of shared EU identity and were clearly worried about the extent to which it could ever be realised by *all* EU citizens.

As the discussion progressed, both EU mobiles and stayers became agitated by the *requirement* to move within the EU in order to belong to the 'community of Europeans', however (Pukallus 2016). So, the idea that EU mobility led to a genuine, unifying force in identity terms was questioned even further. This adds perhaps another layer to the apparently endless inconsistency present in EU identity research (most notably McLaren 2006; Hooghe and Marks 2009; Fligstein 2008; Medrano 2010; Gaxie et al. 2011; White 2011; Duchesne et al. 2013; Van Ingelgom 2014; Kuhn 2015). Nonetheless, even when admittedly present, EU mobiles' shared senses of EU identity was characterised by contrasts, e.g. distinctions were drawn between CEE and EU-15 mobiles (Chapter 4.1). This issue may illuminate why we have such a wide-ranging diversity of findings about the effects of EU (learning) mobility on EU identity (compare, for example, King and Ruiz 2003; Sigalas 2010a; Van Mol 2011, 2014; Kuhn 2012; Mitchell 2012, 2014).

Nevertheless, given that EU mobility also strongly underscored processes of differentiation (Chapter 4), a number of participants suggested external migration as perhaps a better alternative to underlining the differences between EU and non-EU citizens—and by extension the similarities among EU citizens. They felt it was natural to consider nationality and national stereotypes as the first point of call within the EU. However, nearly all participants expected differences between EU citizens and the EU's "other" to be more noticeable *externally*.

Lithuanian Male, EU Group 3, Sweden: I think you cannot be more or less European. You just *are [European]* … There are many things in common [referring to Europe, not the EU, necessarily]. I think everybody sees themselves as European but also, it's different levels of identities. You have probably your identity with your family and friends and city, then you have your town, your country and then you have the European level and then you have world citizen. But to create a European identity, how will we create a binary identity, an opposition? Like, as you said, you were in Canada and then there you were not Canadian, not American, you *were* European, you know? So, you are different compared to us, [compared] to *something*. So, it's always [a] negative binary.

Hungarian-South African Female: What's [a] negative binary, sorry?

Lithuanian Male: Like you are not *that*, you are something else.

Hungarian-South African Female: Yes, it's "the other".

Lithuanian Male: Yes "the other", exactly! That's why you are European but not [the] native [Swedish]…?

Hungarian-South African Female: I think so too. That's different when you get out of Europe. It changes completely.

Lithuanian Male: Yes, exactly! It's about different levels.

French Male: I would feel very uncomfortable to having to answer a question about whether I feel more European or French, because I *feel* both.

Hungarian-South African Female: I don't know. Maybe if someone did not travel outside of Europe might think of that. But I think if you do experience it, then [it's different]…

French Male: I can imagine! I haven't been to the United States or China. When you are there…, did you feel that there was something different from not only Germany, Hungary but from Europe?

German Female: Yes! One time I was in the United States and someone asked me where I was from. And I was like, "I'm from Germany." And they were like, "Yeah, I know someone from Italy" … [Others start to laugh.] And then I was like, "That's totally different. That's nice, but I'm German". And so, they see Europe, really, as *one* thing and America as *one* thing. And yes, there are different countries in Europe but that does not really matter to them. That was my impression.

While strongly optimistic about their benefits for senses of EU identity—or even *European* identity—it is important to notice participants understood external migration quite differently from EU mobility. The costs and prerequisites of EU mobility were often a heated topic, but only one group evaluated the economic and social prerequisites of external migration. Actually, quite a few groups agreed that they preferred to continue their studies within the EU because it was easier and cheaper to do so. Yet, there were little or no considerations about the costs external migration carried before it could really elevate senses of EU citizenship—which, of course, would have been substantially greater than that of intra-EU mobility.

Broader—and perhaps more accessible—discourses on "the other", the non-European, notion, culture and people were also touched upon, especially considering how EU and international students were treated in Sweden and Britain.

> You always have this special status as an EU student ...in Sweden, you have an extra line, which goes a lot quicker than the other applicants from non-EU countries. And, also studying here, it's always about I'm a member of the European Union. .... And there's something else here, the non-European citizen. This distinction of others that makes you feel more European. (German Female, EU Group 1, Sweden)

Such claims then started to build an EU-specific geo-proximity. For instance, quite a few participants in the UK considered the EU safer and more democratic than the rest of the world.

> [W]hen I went outside the EU this academic year, and it wasn't a completely unsafe place, but it was on my mind that, "Now you are outside of the EU. No one is coming to get you help if all goes wrong here". And there ... [is a] perceived [sense of] security maybe that you are safe here. Your rights are safer within the EU. (British Male (3), Stayer Group, UK)

This claim is particularly interesting coming from a British stayer. Only one EU mobile in Sweden made a similar comment—in a somewhat failed attempt to explicitly underscore that EU citizenship *already* exists.

> Just coming back to European citizenship, I kind of wanted to disagree [with what has been said]. Because you said that there is no way soon, at least, that there will be something like European citizenship. I think we [already] have it. It's just that if we look at citizenship in a very traditional way, like we have police execute the laws and so on [and] then of course it's not gonna happen. We are not gonna have *a* European police

very soon and an [EU] army ... But I mean, there *is* European citizenship. It's just a completely different concept and it's also a new concept.
That's why it's also not that widespread. Maybe it takes a lot of time to
get adjusted to it and to get used to it. But I think there is something
like this and [it] might be a very silly example, but even me, when I travel
around and, I'm sorry to say it, but even in my country or in Eastern
European countries, sometimes, I'm having these thoughts, "Okay, should
I drink water from the tap or not?", or how something works. Then I
think something like, "If this country is in the European Union, probably
there are some umbrella laws that have some standards and it can't be that
bad, I guess." I mean there are a lot of stupid laws, like define what's a
"vegetable" and what's a "fruit" and stuff like this. And it's hilarious. But
on the other hand, there are a lot of standardising laws and I think that
this might benefit [us]. (Polish Female 1, EU Group 4, Sweden)

However, the others in her group did not quite follow her apparent
eagerness about EU citizenship. A couple even questioned the extent
to which "EU standards", for instance drinking water standards, were
genuinely relevant to the functioning of the EU "market" today. The
large majority felt citizens have largely "misunderstood the European
Union", the sole purpose of which is to promote regional economic
integration. Developing a common sense of EU identity and then recognising an EU-defined "us" or, indeed, a non-EU "other" was then
deemed as pointless.

6.3   EU Citizenship as Rights:
Disadvantageous Supranationalism

Since rights were central to participants' understanding of their national
citizenship (Chapter 5.1), perhaps a clearer depiction of the significance
of EU citizenship was to emerge through a focus on EU rights. And, in
fact, initial approaches to EU rights were largely complimentary. Participants quite often underscored that EU citizenship is a "kind of citizenship
that belongs to rights, to travel, to choose your partner considering the
sexuality you feel you belong to". Participants also recognised the "liberal
principles... concerning your personal choices". Both EU mobiles and
stayers appeared to be quite optimistic about the EU's 'homogenising'
effect in this liberal realm and depicted the EU as an area of 'freedom',
'security' and 'guarantees'.

However, they were worried that people "often forget" such benefits come *directly* from the EU and so they probably "take them for granted". Yet, when the same provisions are applied slightly differently between states, as is the case of Schengen/non-Schengen access for instance, mundane practices can turn into a "hassle".[1]

> *Moderator, EU Group 2, Sweden*: Can you think of any advantages of being EU citizens?
> *Bulgarian Female*: Free education.
> *Hungarian-British Male*: Easy travel, no border control[s].
> *German Female*: Although, you do have border control when you come from the UK!
> *Hungarian-British Male*: Yeah, it's true. But, do you know how tight that border control is? You just walk through...
> *Portuguese Male*: The health insurance we have... You just take it in your country and it's available everywhere.
> *Hungarian-British Male*: That's a good one!

Besides their intra-EU rights, four EU mobiles also mentioned their rights to consular protection from the embassy of another member state outside the EU—in the UK across three EU Groups (1, 2 and 3) and in Sweden in EU Group 1. Only two female EU mobiles—in the UK EU Groups 2 and 3—linked their right to vote in the EP to EU rights. However, not once did the same EU mobile mention both of these rights together—or in the same group.

Moreover, the fact that a couple of EU mobiles in the UK were the only ones to mention EP voting rights in positive light counters the expectations laid down at the outset of this book, whereby Sweden was identified as ideal for civic citizenship to emerge and, by extension, one of the most likely contexts within the EU for moving beyond nation state-based citizenships (Chapter 2.1).

Similarly to EU mobiles, both Swedish and British stayers spoke of the "pragmatism" that is associated with their EU rights, listing the benefits of EU mobility rights. But their claims seemed quite paradoxical. EU mobility was seen as the most positive benefit of EU citizenship broadly speaking—but not for them, personally.

> I think that accessibility, to be able to move and travel and study abroad and have the same opportunities in Sweden as in the rest ... of Europe. I think, that's the way I've been in touch... with the [EU] rights... [F]or

example, [I'd] prefer to study in Europe than the US because it's much easier. And it's much cheaper. And you have Erasmus, and you have these other [programmes] that make you feel the incentive to study in Europe. (Swedish Female (2), Stayer Group, Sweden)

To some extent, stayers' embracing of EU learning mobility rights might be seen as supportive of EU institutions' attempts at extending EU *mobility* rights with explicitly 'supranational' goals (Blauberger et al. 2018). Indeed, such strategies for EU rights have been considerably more 'intrusive' than in the case of EU identity, for example (as apparent in the dynamic notion of EU citizenship as rights, Olsen 2012). There might be some evidence to support such approach. Existing literature has shown that developing senses of EU identity or even participating in EU politics can occur even among those who do not hold citizenship from member states (e.g. Juverdeanu 2019).

Once on the move, however, EU mobiles were also quick to underscore the many obstacles they experienced when attempting to benefit from their EU civil, social and economic entitlements—the entitlements *supposed to* accompany their EU mobility rights. Since "implementing market justice" via "the European welfare state" was deemed to have failed, some of the supposedly country-specific challenges, such as the opening of bank accounts, taking out of mobile contracts or accessing health care services, were frequently mentioned by EU mobiles as prevalent issues.

> *Dutch Female, EU Group 3, UK*: [But] as a Dutch citizen, I couldn't get a bank account here. It was impossible! It only worked when I was there [in person] and they [were] like, looked at their international bank accounts. They wouldn't let me have one [until then]! And they wouldn't let me have a phone contract unless I paid extra...
>
> *German-British Female*: I think that's bank specific to be honest.
>
> *Swedish Female*: But there are so many other things like... [when I] first came here, it was a year before I started studying ... and I wanted to work. But for that I needed a national insurance number. So, I went to get a national insurance number and they told me, "But you don't have a job, so you can't get a national insurance number." And then I was like, "Ok, I'll get a job!" And then, I tried to get a job and they [prospective employers] were like, "No, you need a national insurance number to get a job". So sometimes it feels like the country is working against you a little bit ...

German-British Female: I think that's England specific. I don't think it has anything to do with being an EU citizen... Yeah, I think that's just a lack of organisation ...

Dutch Female: I think it wouldn't make a difference for me... Like, [EU citizenship] didn't make it easier for me to get a bank account at all or a phone contract ...

Importantly though, responsibility was not usually left at the EU's doorstep. It was squarely placed with member states who seemed much less inclined to cooperate. By comparison, a couple of EU mobiles observed the 2005 Constitutional Treaty as a crucial (and failed) attempt by EU actors to put "market justice" on the political "agenda".

While EU mobility debates were not just lively but in-depth and fairly well-informed, the dialogue about EU participatory and consular protection rights often fell flat with no follow-up questions offered. Even when one participant cited, correctly, that consular protection is written in all EU passports, the other members in his group queried, sarcastically, "*who* reads that?*". While such rights became quickly side-lined, some participants noted that, from a broad legal perspective at least, the international outlook of EU citizenship as status was often "hailed to a higher account" than their nationality placing EU citizens "on the same level with an American citizen". Clearly, a 'westernised' discourse on legal citizenship struck a chord with these young citizens.

Nonetheless, as soon as the discussions appeared to move away from *any* type of movement, participants clearly struggled to identify the broad appeal and advantages of EU citizenship as status. If anything, their silence reinforced the inherently individualist character of EU citizenship and the intrinsic disparity between EU mobility and immobility (just as was the case with processes of differentiation, Chapter 4).

French Male, EU Group 1, Sweden: I think what's quite specific in the EU is that since it's not a state, well, not yet or, maybe, never, we are citizens of a union or community, depending on your preference ...[and] it's an interesting kind of *personal* estate. ...Here for example, since I am not Swedish, I am an exchange student, I meet a lot of people from around the world. And whether they are European or non-European, I feel like *we are a community* of people. I don't mind their nationality or stuff like that. But still, we're basically similar and, I think, that's the kind of feeling European citizenship *can* grant you. After[wards], of course, we have some rights. But, basically, mostly have the right to do 'things', travel or stuff like that. There is not really a European welfare state or a thing that could create like an alliance, a trust of close relation with the European institutions. Because we are still are very close to our national states whenever we have to receive our welfare rights, for example. But since we can move, it starts to be relevant to be European. But that's the problem I think, not for us but for people that don't move. *Why should they feel European?* They do not take advantage of it. Okay, it's like an 'extra-upper institution' that they don't really understand. I think it will create very soon a gap between cosmopolitan citizens, whether they are European or not, and national citizens [who] can't be anything but national citizens. It will be just a social difference.

Portuguese Male: Do you think that might replace class structure in a sense?

French Male: I think class will still be relevant but like in foreign relations, because our lower classes won't be able to travel or meet the other people of the world or of Europe or whatever. They will close [up between] themselves. And that's actually what'd happened because, unfortunately, quite an important part of our lower classes turned their vote from left parties to far-right parties. Sweden might be different, but in Denmark, in France, in Germany, in Switzerland [that is what's happening]. There will be really a distinction of people that *could* feel European or citizen of the world or whatever, and the people that can't because they just don't have the opportunities even to experience international travel. So, [EU citizenship is] not ...a general citizenship. At least, I think, national citizenships will be the same at the end. You can be French, British or whatever. But it does not mean that you are co-national [EU] citizens.

The "class struggle" EU citizenship and mobility have brought about was introduced in every group—and was usually supported by French students. This is very much in line with the basic expectations of the value of citizenship in France—a preoccupation with social belonging and equality among citizens, rather than an association with the state or political institutions (Duchesne 2003).

Fazed by the challenge of bringing citizens together or underscoring the relevance of EU citizenship to stayers, an alternative interpretation of EU citizenship was suddenly offered. EU citizenship was no longer about EU rights, i.e. EU mobility, but EU identity—the relevance of which dimension they had previously been dismissed. So, once a particularly problematic aspect of contemporary EU citizenship was detected, almost all groups attempted to make up for it by pointing to other prospects.

Such practices were probably present because of a researcher-effect—participants *really* wished to assist in my "search for" EU citizenship. Of course, for a more optimistic reader, such tendency may indicate the interrelatedness between the dimensions of EU citizenship—albeit superficially. For a sceptic, it is likely to underline the challenges inherent in public—and many scholarly and policymaker—understandings of what citizenship in the EU *should* signify. Ultimately, citizenship approaches are bound to draw inspiration from national models and look for some parity with its dimensions. That means at least 28 (at the time of writing) different concepts of citizenship in the EU with 29 official statuses in place.

> *German Female, EU Group 1, UK*: [M]aybe with European citizenship it's more about identity than knowing about your rights and obligations. Like, I think, not many people know what are their [specific EU] rights and obligations. Like, what are the national rights and what are the European rights; you don't make really a distinction.
>
> *Romanian Female*: I think most of the European citizens just know that they can travel. They can travel without a visa. I think, that's the main thing that all Europeans know. And other than that, I think, no one knows. I mean, aside from European Studies students.
>
> *German Male*: It's not very practical, I would say. I mean, if we go to the airport and then there you have a row for EU citizens when you have to show your passports. And then there is another row for others. And then you feel a bit European, I would say. But that's, well, the exception.

The political, social and economic differences between member states (Chapter 5.3) have thus made it quite difficult for participants to consider their EU citizenship as a legal *guarantee* of their membership in a budding EU community.

For example, in Sweden, most EU mobiles identified proficiency in the Swedish language and assimilation into an allegedly peculiar socialising culture as especially difficult. On top of these issues, a number of EU mobiles, particularly those who planned to stay for a shorter period of time—up to 10 months under the Erasmus exchange programme—found obtaining a Swedish personal identity number an almost impossible and tedious task. While the first two issues were likely to hinder participants' socialising prospects in the host society, the latter clearly infringed the ability of EU mobiles to live their lives on an equal footing with Swedish stayers.

French Male, EU Group 1, Sweden: I don't speak Swedish.
Everyone together: Yeah, that's a big problem!
Portuguese Male: That's a big problem in terms of circulating in the European Union. Okay, you want to work here and there. But, if you don't know the [national] language [in the host country]...
German Female: No. But, I think, in Sweden that's not actually the problem at all, if you don't speak Swedish.
Portuguese Male: Why? Can you get a job? [Shakes his head in disagreement.]
German Female: Maybe not when it comes to working, but regarding participating in Swedish life. It's not necessary...
Portuguese Male: But how do you participate in Swedish life without money, without working?
Italian Male: When it comes to work, language is still detrimental. However, compared with the rest of the [EU] countries, there are lots of levels of interaction that can actually take place without [speaking] Swedish. Only the most structural thing at all cannot take place. ...
German Female: Consider life in Sweden without a personal number!
Italian Male: You can't even rent a DVD!
German Female: That's the main issue in Sweden! [All nod in agreement.] If you don't have those ten digits, you don't exist. You can't even get into the system without it! They need to create it. If you come somewhere with an emergency, you can't get treated because you don't fit in the system. Because you don't have ten digits.
Italian Male: You are a pain in the ass for any type of administration.

EU mobiles in the UK adopted a somewhat different approach to the same issues. Their discussion was particularly interesting because a good number had attended a European (projected as very elite) school before coming to a British university. It is precisely these type of pre-university schools that have been portrayed as the most favourable to providing access to an increasingly globalised and hierarchically structured higher education (Igarashi and Saito 2014).

The evidence suggests that EU mobiles were *aware* of this benefit and identified international educational contexts as particularly effective in raising young and educated citizens with a cosmopolitan outlook (as defined by Skey 2011). They spoke of their learning mobility and previous educational qualifications as a form of embodied and institutionalised cultural capital in the cosmopolitan context. For example, they were quite outspoken about their previous educational experiences as being much stronger than that of British stayers. They then identified their EU mobility as helping them becoming even more "aware" of EU similarities and national differences. Yet, for EU mobiles these alleged differences were not recognised by the UK higher education system—much to their annoyance.

> *French Female, (3), EU Group 4, UK:* I think the biggest disadvantage I ever felt … it's kind of the level of education you need to come into the UK [higher education system]. Like they expect so much more from non-UK students in order to study here. … I did the international bachelorette … [and it] is worth 20 A-levels …it's ridiculous! I don't know, my first year, it was actually a joke. There are people who didn't know how to write their essays. And I had written so many essays… they were just catching up with me …!
>
> *Austrian Female:* Yes.
> *German Female (1):* Yes, I totally agree with you.
> *Austrian Female:* I think the same.
> *German Female (1):* Because last year, I felt like I am on summer vacation.
> *French Female (3):* I felt like I went back a few years!
> *German Female (1):* I felt like, I don't know, I felt like I could have taught some of the courses, because, I knew these things … And I think that is also one of the key differences [between stayers and the] people that come from abroad… And we have to know so many different things. When we come here, we are more open-minded. And then the people, the students here are rather limited in what they, not knowledge-wise, I won't say they're stupid, I wouldn't say …
> *Italian-Mexican Female:* Yes, they are!

It is possible that registration processes and migrant integration requirements at the national level are deliberately stopping the integration of EU mobiles. All EU groups mentioned that their *actual* access to welfare services was hindered by their lack of knowledge about these processes. Indeed, EU mobiles said that the EHIC—the very symbol participants previously observed as being effective in cementing a sense of EU citizenship—did not always help them.

Although most EU mobiles in the UK seemed to have found it easy to register with the National Health Service (NHS) than those attempting to get health care in Sweden, a few seemed disappointed about the lack of information about how to use the NHS exactly. Subsequently EU mobiles established that member states make it deliberately difficult to take advantage of their EU civic, social and economic entitlements.

German Female (2), EU Group 4, UK: [T]he   medical   system,   for example,... I have [a] health condition and when I go to the doctor here, it's just awful! ... [I] don't get the right medication ... and the things is..., I tried to explain to them [my condition] and they don't want to give me antibiotics. It's just that they are so strict, narrow minded on their things. And they didn't even give me like the address, or the opportunity of me seeing another doctor... [I] have to go to the healthcare centre of the university and [I am] not allowed to go somewhere else. But if I want to see someone else, I *can* see someone else... this system is so weird! They don't make it possible for you as a foreigner to understand it or to integrate. ...

Italian Female: But that's not Europe...

German Female (2): It's the system [that] exploits you.

Italian Female: But, it's the country!

Austrian Female: In terms of medical treatment, for example, you are always allowed to get a second opinion.

German Female (2): ... I know I'm allowed, but where the hell am I supposed to go if I don't know any [other options]?

The latter issue may not be intentional, at least where EU students are concerned. Its negative impact on young EU mobiles' senses of EU citizenship and broader study abroad experiences maybe one to be easily addressed by EU actors. Alternatively, given the positive effects antagonistic country contexts can have for emerging senses of EU citizenship, these too could prove as another source of keeping EU mobiles on their toes or indeed on the move—which then adds some *required* longevity to their otherwise temporary mobility.

6.4   EU Citizenship as Participation: Secondary at Best, Irrelevant at Worst

Traditionally, citizens' participation in politics grants their bond with the political community a dynamic character, and, as a result, has dominated most of the literature within the field of citizenship studies on the dichotomy of active/passive citizenship (Magnette 2005; Welge 2015). However, the introduction of EU citizenship appeared to have shifted the dichotomy of active/passive citizens to the stayers/mobiles distinctions in the EU (Chapter 4.4). What role is left then for EU participation? This section suggests that EU participation is *the* weakest dimension of EU citizenship for both EU mobiles and stayers and one that is likely to call into question the relevance of the other two dimensions of EU citizenship altogether—not least in the light of national considerations (Chapter 5).

Almost every participant—regardless of his or her mobility status— suggested that their participation was increasingly personalised, issue-specific and dynamic. Yet, while such characteristics directed participants' approaches to *national* politics (Chapter 5.4), it quickly became apparent that related approaches to EU politics were anything *but* dynamic, with only one group actually discussing EU participation as EU citizenship without prompts (EU Group 3, UK). Furthermore, two groups did not discuss participation in any great detail even though they were directly probed about it (EU Group 3 in Sweden and EU Group 4 in the UK).

Hence, EU participation was largely understood as voting in the EP elections and, while claimed to have been important to them, only *seven* of the total 52 EU mobiles who participated in the focus groups had voted in the EP elections (two across all EU groups in Sweden and five across all EU groups in the UK). Abstention was mostly seen as a result of the EU institutions being "too abstract" and "complicated to really understand", as well as a perceived lack of "any real influence" citizens had at this level of policymaking.

Bulgarian Female, EU Group 2, Sweden: ... I don't think anyone gets European politics, like voting for your MEP in the European Parliament. *I* don't get it! I don't understand what these people do there. Like, what decisions they make [or] how they make them. I was a bit annoyed a couple of years ago when they voted the European President [Herman Van] Rompuy. *Who* voted [for] him?! ...

Portuguese Male: Yeah, *you* didn't vote for him... I would agree with you, that with European politics you don't really know what's happening. But then suddenly you see all these things happening, the certifications and ... these common laws. *I* like it. So, I'm not going to criticise. I think they are doing a good job. Maybe, they are doing such a good job that it's not so political or *cheap* political!

Italian Male: [The EU] only comes up, ... to show people if they have done [something] really good or [if there is] something that they are about to do. So, these two moments that I see things from the European [Union]. It's hard to say that we *feel* democratic, because Europe is *so* big. They have to divide the voting system in such a complex way that when they elect someone inside their committee, it seems to be very undemocratic. But, in a way, it's the most democratic way they can find to make the whole European Union, unified Europe, to actually vote... They couldn't ask the whole population of Europe, 20-30 countries, so who else is going to decide this? So, I think, it *seems* to be undemocratic, but I think it's *the most [democratic]* that they can do at the moment.

Perhaps these claims are not that surprising in the light of the generally low EU turnout levels, often explained with references to the second-order character of EP elections, the EU's enlargement to CEE states with historically lower levels of citizens' political participation, as well as changing (youth) public attitudes towards European integration, EU institutions and national politics (Schmitt 2005; Muñoz et al. 2011; Dahl et al. 2018).

Indeed, quite a good number of EU mobiles suggested it was *acceptable* not to participate at the EU level at all, because it was perhaps "not so political" as national politics. Even if citizens abstained, "everything still worked". They appeared to grant the EU a largely "bureaucratic" and "regulatory function", which does not require ordinary citizens to *really* understand or engage with (echoing to some extent at least the case put forward by Majone 1998). Nonetheless, it is also probable that such responses served a very specific purpose—to justify participants' own abstention from EU politics. If 'ideal EU citizens' do not consider EU participation as a necessary part of their EU citizenship, it is even less likely that others—e.g. the stayers—do so.

Similarly to the above example, and despite their more extensive attention to EU participation compared with the other groups, the discussions that took place in EU Group 3, UK supported the same point: EU mobiles were not likely to adopt a *genuinely* dynamic approach to EU participation, even if its potential benefits were directly presented to them. In this group, one EU mobile—German-British Female—tried really hard to find an alternative route to enhancing citizens' EU participation (and, consequently for her, senses of EU identity). She belonged to a handful of participants, three female EU mobiles, who assumed that realising a political form of EU citizenship—that stems from citizens' participation in EU-level politics—was already possible. She suggested introducing an EU-wide list of candidates for the EP elections—so as to draw attention away from national parties and national politics and to turn these elections into a truly 'European' affair.

In retrospect, her idea was already on the agenda of EU bureaucrats and was suggested as an option to fill the empty seats of British MEPs following their Brexit departure (Chopin et al. 2019). However, there is little to suggest that such a list resonates with the EU's electorate. Even in this 2013 pre-Brexit times, it was deemed as an absurd idea by most focus group participants.

> *German-British Female, EU Group 3, UK*: I would feel much, *much* more European if I voted for example for a Hungarian candidate, let's say, for example, or an Italian candidate...
> *Italian Female*: But ... you wouldn't have the knowledge to do that. That's what I think.
> *German-British Female*: Why wouldn't I? I can read about it, can't I?
> *Dutch Female*: You don't know whether [the candidates] are capable. You don't know. Like, you would have to do research... I don't think many people would [do that].
> *German-British Female*: But that would make it European!...
> *Italian Female*: I think only a really rich politician [could run an EU-wide campaign] ...
> *Swedish Female*: But then I think there is a national bias as well. Because I think it's, like form a perspective from someone from Sweden, to say that an Italian person is a best person, no offence, to be in the EU, first we will be like "No! A Swedish person is the best!" Because that's what you know ...
> *Dutch Female*: Patriotism, yeah! ...
> *German-British Female*: I don't believe that...
> *Swedish Female*: I think a Swedish person would say, "But what does this Italian person know about Sweden?" We're like, on different poles! Like we are cold and ... population wise really tiny country compared to Italy or the UK. Why would we want someone who ... doesn't understand our society?

While quick to dismiss the transnational MEP list, the others failed to offer any alternatives on how to enhance citizens' EU participation—or, more likely, this issue never really made it into their agenda.

These examples underline that, in reality, EU mobiles' approaches to EU participation—and, potentially, to participation more broadly—were anything *but* issue-based. Instead, the perceived impact and the role of rational cost-benefit calculations seemed to have shaped participants' perceptions the most (for an overview see Smets and van Ham 2013). In the case of EU participation, both issues stirred EU mobiles away from, rather than towards EU politics.

Polish Female (2), EU Group 4, Sweden: I don't think we have any real influence in politics on a bigger level, like [the] EU-level or any actual big decisions. I'm a bit pessimistic about it... I think that where there is money involved, lots of money especially, no one will back [away from] the decisions that will allow him [or her] to earn millions... Of course, it's important for people to be heard and for people to have a medium to voice their opinion. But, I really don't think that we have any big influence on the things that happen on this huge [EU-]level...

French Male (1): It's also a technical question. *How* to participate? Where is the European-level when you are in your county? [It is] difficult to find it. You're more used to know your average realities... Of course, to be a volunteer is maybe the [simplest] way to engage... But for the election, ... I'm a bit more pessimistic. Because we voted against the European Constitution and it still passed!

Nonetheless, quite a few EU mobiles, especially those in the UK, set themselves on course for participating in future EP elections—as the quote from the Finnish Female (2) suggests.[2]

A couple of EU mobiles also spoke about the other structural opportunities the EU offered to its citizens in order to encourage their EU participation. However, these were mentioned only fleetingly and without generating much discussion. For example, petitioning the EP or the European Ombudsman was only cited in one group and by the openly pro-EU participant who was also keen to make the EP elections truly 'European' (German-British Female, EU Group 3, UK, quoted earlier).

Only one EU mobile in Sweden spoke of the European Citizens' Initiative (CI), in an attempt to underscore the likely weaknesses of an EU-level direct democracy (Mendez and Mendez 2017). He was especially sarcastic about the genuine purpose and scope of CI. His tone echoed the other EU mobiles who previously seemed to have a 'cosmopolitan outlook'.

I'm *really* looking forward to the day it will be used, the [European citizens'] initiative. Because one million of Europeans, yeah, okay... I think, it's only possible if [the] European Union decided to attack the United States. Then you will have 200 million [or] so of Europeans signing the petition "No we should *not*!" [All laugh.] Otherwise, I don't want to be pessimistic, but look at the turnout for the European election[s]! It's so *low*. [Portuguese and Italian males nod in agreement.] ... [It is] even lower in [the] recent countries that have joined the Union. Whereas, it should be so high [there], because it's *so* important for them! (French Male, EU Group 1, Sweden)

Hence, EU mobiles only really seemed to have agreed on one issue—the distant character of EU politics, which offers very little in return for their efforts. This questions the extent to which their EU citizenship was genuinely seen as a "huge and incalculable advantage". Surely, if it is 'huge', it deserves sustaining or defending. Yet, there was very little if any evidence implying that EU learning mobility made it more likely for students to think along these lines. Instead, the findings echo previous empirical research that has shown that EU mobility does *not* enhance mobiles' disposition to participate in politics—and indeed may affect their actual levels of political participation negatively (Mattila 2003; Muxel 2009; Favell 2010; Strudel and Michalska 2012; Recchi 2015: 105–122).

Similarly, to EU mobiles, rational considerations appeared to guide stayers' approaches to EU participation and, as a result, hardly any had engaged in EU politics. Most found the local level to be the most relevant outlet for their activism, where it was "easier" to influence decisions.

> *Swedish Female (6), Stayer Group, Sweden*: I guess I have a more passive participation because I've never voted, I was underage [at the last elections]. I never voted and not even at school, because I was not part of the [Students Union], so I did not vote here also. But I have been studying politics, reading politic's but I've never been like, you know, participating as a *democratic citizen*. And it's really awful!
>
> *Swedish Female (4)*: Well, I'm like a step up from your passiveness. I've voted at all levels except the European [level]. I never voted for the European elections. [Couple of others in the background meanwhile claim to have voted for the EP.]
>
> *Swedish Female (5)*: I think it's easier to do something at the local level. Just closer [to you] and, I do not know, I'm involved in the school politics as well as [serving as the] chairman of the student sociology council. ...It's *easier* to actually make a difference in the local level.

UK stayers established that citizens' approaches to participation should not, *ever*, be decided on the basis of their likely impact.[3] It should "just" be about raising "visual awareness". Yet, their exercising of EU participatory rights clearly depended on the extent to which doing so was deemed to impact EU politics or not.

British Male (5), Stayer Group, UK: I think that the fact that voting didn't come up [in the previous discussions about EU citizenship], shows the kind of change in notions of contemporary citizenship ... So, you know, the idea of voting in the European elections is something so *distant*. Whereas, you know, ... we want to... be involved with participatory acts that we can see having the benefits [of]...

British Male (2): There are so many great problems, I think, with participation at the European-level and the fact that we fight the elections on national issues. They seem to be an extension, ... a little sub-act to our national elections. If they occur separately from a national election, it's your opportunity to punish a government for things that it's done domestically. Rather than because you admire any kind of views that they have on Europe. Unless [sarcastically], you're a UKIP voter and just want to spoil your ballots...

While maintaining the second-order quality of EU elections (and politics, perhaps), some stayers appeared to be almost more critical about citizens' abstention from EU politics than EU mobiles did. In fact, a Swedish stayer actively encouraged her fellows to participate in future EP elections.

Swedish Female (3), Stayer Group, Sweden: When I think about it, the Commissioners and the people in the Council [of the EU], they are representatives of the [national] government[s] or are appointed by the national governments. So still, the national governments have a say in the European Union. So, by voting in the national level, you also interact in the European Union.

Swedish Female (1): Sometimes I think, well I don't have to know so much to vote in the European Union, because you can... vote [for] the socialists, the conservatives or if you choose the extreme, vote for the Greens! You can choose your political ideology and vote for that, [and] then, hopefully, things will turn out fine. I mean, ... you do not have to know *so much* to go to vote. I do not think we should take it as seriously as some do, because it's hard to get to know information about the European Union, [or about] what will [candidates] do if they come to power. Just go there and vote!

Nonetheless, the apparent readiness to increase citizens' willingness to participate in EU politics appeared to accentuate, yet again, the second-order character of EU elections (Schmitt 2005). In fact, the idea that citizens "should not take" EU participation "as seriously" did not only grant a secondary character to EU participation but also, by association, to EU citizenship. This is a considerable shift from the initial suggestion by the very same stayers who said they felt almost 'more European' than Swedish.

Though participants largely abstained from EU participation, their explanation often alluded to the contextual implications of senses of citizenship and the interlinked nature of its dimensions. Interestingly, even the Swedish stayers, who originally adopted a value-based approach to EU citizenship, mentioned that their abstention from EU participation might explain their lack of EU identity (again, previously part of their national identity). "I might not feel much like a European citizen because it doesn't feel like *anything* I will do will make a difference on [the] European-level" (Swedish Female (1), Stayer Group, Sweden).

EU Group 1 UK appeared to reach similar conclusions—not only about participants' abstention from EU participation but more broadly about how young citizens are likely to approach this issue today. As a result, they could not see how citizens could *ever* develop a meaningful bond with the EU. They stressed that *every* other EU citizen was likely to know, "do" and "feel" very little about the EU.

> *Romanian Female, EU Group 1, UK:* I think there are so many things happening and you can watch the news everyday, on the BBC, and you're not gonna see *anything* [about the EU]. I think if we don't have that information [delivered by the media], you do have to do the research on your own. But that takes a lot of initiative, to awake that kind of willingness to go and vote, and contribute to something...
>
> *German Female:* British people [especially] don't really have [a] big connection to the European Union... They are, like, not connected *at all.* ...This feeling about Europe or the European Union is just not as present [as elsewhere]. ...
>
> *Dutch Male:* I think, everywhere in Europe it's going downhill in the sense of activeness and 'informed-ness' in politics... And in terms of the EU, yeah, definitely! British people are probably way less interested in the EU than other European countries. But even in other European countries... My football friends [in the Netherlands] really don't do anything about the EU and probably don't know anything about [it]...
>
> *Italian Female:* I really would like to know which country really believes in the cooperation of countries ... that's why also, maybe, people don't feel very European, as we didn't build *yet* this kind of sense of cooperation between states.

This issue was expected to be even further challenged by the EU's (then pronounced) financial woes and the rise of populist politicians. Considered through a more inclusive lens of the institutional setting of the dimensions of EU citizenship, these findings are not particularly surprising. For example, the EU's citizenship discourse seems to suggest that its focus on EU participation is temporary and selective at best—and are on the agenda only when EP elections are near (compare, for example, European Commission 2010, 2013). Even then, due to an almost exclusive focus on EU mobiles' participation, the discourse itself may probe the extent to which EU citizenship is here to enhance the EU's democratic legitimacy to begin with.

6.5   SUMMARY

This chapter explored and compared EU mobiles' and stayers' senses of EU citizenship. The main findings seem to raise serious questions about the relevance of EU citizenship today. EU mobility altered observations of EU citizenship considerably, with EU mobiles appearing as more vocal about their *status* as EU citizens. Nonetheless, most participants clearly did not consider their EU citizenship as an appealing alternative to their national status. An obvious question arises here: On what basis could their senses of EU identity emerge and *why* would they then participate in EU politics? The focus group evidence appears to suggest that they simply do not—or at least not *yet*.

Indeed, only a small segment of participants claimed to have held senses of EU identity or recognised their exercising of EU rights *within* the framework of EU citizenship. Even then, EU participation hardly ever faired on the agenda of these young, ideal EU citizens. These findings are in sharp contrast with recent Eurobarometer data, which suggests that more and more citizens are aware of their EU citizenship (see, e.g., European Commission 2018). This inconsistency goes to the heart of current debates about the significance of the EU and the role of EU citizenship in integrating citizens at the EU level. In order to begin answering some of the questions this chapter raised, the final chapter will recount some of the main findings of this book about contemporary citizenship politics in mobile Europe.

NOTES

1. However, EU mobiles in the UK often felt that this "hassle" was in fact constructive towards their sense of EU identity.
2. This was more apparent in the EU groups in the UK, probably because of the timing of the focus groups—they took place almost a year after the Swedish interviews and just a year before the 2014 EP elections. At the time a possible 'Brexit' referendum was already flaunted by the Conservatives and the popularity of the United Kingdom Independence Party (UKIP) was on the rise.
3. Interestingly, the same participant (British Male (5)) spoke about how important it was to "see the benefits" of participation (in the EU context especially) in order to mobilise citizens. Yet, he later concluded that "participation should [n]ever be judged on whether it was effective or not". His shifting opinion illustrates well the often sporadic and contradictory points put forward by these young and educated citizens about citizenship as participation. Evidently, discussing a sense of citizenship is and can prove a difficult topic to tackle.

REFERENCES

Bellamy, R., & Castiglione, D. (2019). *From Maastricht to Brexit: Democracy, Constitutionalism and Citizenship in the EU*. London, New York: Rowman & Littlefield International.

Bellamy, R., Castiglione, D., & Santoro, E. (Eds.). (2004). *Lineages of European Citizenship: Rights, Belonging and Participation in Eleven Nation States*. Basingstoke: Palgrave.

Bellamy, R., Castiglione, D., & Shaw, J. (Eds.). (2006). *Making European Citizens: Civic Inclusion in a Transnational Context: Civic Inclusion in Transnational Context*. London: Palgrave Macmillan.

Blauberger, M., Heindlmaier, A., Kramer, D., Martinsen, D. S., Sampson Thierry, J., et al. (2018). ECJ judges read the morning papers. Explaining the turnaround of European citizenship jurisprudence. *Journal of European Public Policy, 25*(10), 1422–1441.

Brubaker, R., & Cooper, F. (2000). Beyond identity. *Theory and Society, 29*(1), 1–47.

Bruter, M. (2004). On what citizens mean by feeling 'European': Perceptions of news, symbols and borderless-ness. *Journal of Ethnic and Migration Studies, 30*(1), 21–39.

Bruter, M. (2005). *Citizens of Europe? The Emergence of a Mass European Identity*. Basingstoke: Palgrave Macmillan.

Chopin, T., Fraccaroli, N., Giovannini, A., Hernborg, N., & Jamet, J. F. (2019). The European Parliament after Brexit: what would it look like? *LSE Brexit Blog*. https://blogs.lse.ac.uk/brexit/2019/06/05/the-european-parliament-after-brexit-what-would-it-look-like/.

Council of Ministers. (1987). Council Decision of 15 June 1987 Adopting the ERASMUS, OJL., L166, 15.6, 20–24.

Dahl, V., Amnå, E., Banaji, S., Landberg, M., Šerek, J., Ribeiro, N., et al. (2018). Apathy or alienation? Political passivity among youths across eight European Union countries. *European Journal of Developmental Psychology, 15*(3), 284–301.

Delanty, G. (1997). Models of citizenship: Defining European identity and citizenship. *Citizenship Studies, 1*, 285–303.

Deutsch, K. W., Burrel, S. A., Kann, R. A., Lee, M., Jr., Lichterman, M., Lindgren, R. E., et al. (1968). *Political Community and the North Atlantic Area*. Princeton: Princeton University Press.

Duchesne, S. (2003). French representations of citizenship and immigrants: The political dimension of the civic link. *Immigrants & Minorities, 22*(2–3), 262–279.

Duchesne, S., Frazer, E., Haegel, F., & Van Ingelgom, V. (Eds.). (2013). *Citizens' Reactions to European Integration Compared: Overlooking Europe*. Basingstoke: Palgrave.

European Commission. (1993). *First Report on Citizenship of the Union, COM(93)702 final*. Brussels, 21 December 1993.

European Commission. (2010). *Youth on the Move: A Guide to the Rights of Mobile Students in the European Union, SEC(2010) 1047*. Brussels, 15 September 2010.

European Commission. (2013). *EU Citizenship Report 2013 EU Citizens: Your Rights, Your Future, COM(2013) 269 final*. Brussels, 8 May 2013.

European Commission. (2017). *EU Citizenship Report 2017: Strengthening Citizens' Rights in a Union of Democratic Change*. Luxembourg: Publications Office of the European Union.

European Commission. (2018, Spring). *Standard Eurobarometer 89: Public Opinion in the European Union*.

European Parliament. (2009). *Resolution of 2 April 2009 on problems and prospects concerning European Citizenship (2008/2234(INI))*.

European Parliament. (2017). *Report on EU Citizenship Report 2017: Strengthening Citizens' Rights in a Union of Democratic Change (2017/2069(INI))*.

Favell, A. (2008). *Eurostars and Eurocities: Free Movement and Mobility in an Integrating Europe*. Oxford: Blackwell.

Favell, A. (2010). European identity and European citizenship in three "Eurocities": A sociological approach to the European Union. *Politique Européenne, 30*, 187–224.

Fligstein, N. (2008). *Euroclash: The EU, European Identity and the Future of Europe*. Oxford: Oxford University Press.

Gaxie, D., Hubé, N., & Rowell, J. (Eds.). (2011). *Perceptions of Europe: A Comparative Sociology of European Attitudes*. Essex: ECPR Press.

Guiraudon, V., Ruzza, C., & Trenz, H. J. (Eds.). (2015). *Europe's Prolonged Crisis: The Making or the Unmaking of a Political Union*. Basingstoke: Palgrave Macmillan.

Haas, E. B. (1958). *The Uniting of Europe: Political, Social and Economic Forces 1950–1957*. Stanford: Stanford University Press.

Herrmann, R. K., Risse, T., & Brewer, B. M. (Eds.). (2004). *Transnational Identities: Becoming European in the EU*. Lanham: Rowman and Littlefield Publishers.

Hooghe, L., & Marks, G. (2009). A postfunctionalist theory of European integration: From permissive consensus to constraining dissensus. *British Journal of Political Science, 39*(1), 1–23.

Igarashi, H., & Saito, H. (2014). Cosmopolitanism as cultural capital: Exploring the intersection of globalization, education and stratification. *Cultural Sociology, 8*, 222–239.

Jenson, J. (2007). The European Union's citizenship regime. Creating norms and building practices. *Comparative European Politics, 5*(1), 53–69.

Juverdeanu, C. (2019). The different gears of EU citizenship. *Journal of Ethnic and Migration Studies*. https://doi.org/10.1080/1369183X.2019.1632697.

King, R., & Ruiz, G. E. (2003). International student migration and the European 'year abroad': Effects on European identity and subsequent migration behaviour. *International Journal of Population Geography, 9*(3), 229–252.

Kochenov, D. (2014). EU citizenship without duties. *European Law Journal, 20*(4), 482–498.

Kostakopoulou, T. (2001). *Citizenship, Identity and Immigration in the European Union: Between Past and Future*. Manchester: Manchester University Press.

Kuhn, T. (2012). Why educational exchange programmes miss their mark: Cross-border mobility, education and European identity. *Journal of Common Market Studies, 50*(6), 994–1010.

Kuhn, T. (2015). *Experiencing European Integration: Transnational Lives and European Identity*. Oxford: Oxford University Press.

Leddy-Owen, C. (2019). *Nationalism, Inequality and England's Political Predicament*. Abingdon: Routledge.

Magnette, P. (2005). *Citizenship: The History of an Idea*. Colchester: ECPR Press.

Majone, G. (1998). Europe's 'democratic deficit': The question of standards. *European Law Journal, 4*(1), 5–28.

Mattila, M. (2003). Why bother? Determinants of turnout in the European elections. *Electoral Studies, 22*(3), 449–468.

Mazzoni, D., Albanesi, C., Ferreira, P. D., Opermann, S., Pavlopoulos, V., & Cicognani, E. (2018). Cross-border mobility, European identity and participation among European adolescents and young adults. *European Journal of Developmental Psychology, 15*(3), 324–339. https://doi.org/10.1080/174 05629.2017.1378089.

McLaren, L. M. (2006). *Identity, Interests and Attitudes to European Integration.* Basingstoke: Palgrave Macmillan.

Medrano, J. D. (2003). *Framing Europe: Attitudes to European Integration in Germany, Spain, and the United Kingdom.* Princeton: Princeton University Press.

Medrano, J. D. (2010). Unpacking European identity. *Politique Européenne, 1,* 45–66.

Mendez, F., & Mendez, M. (2017). The promise and perils of direct democracy for the European Union. *Cambridge Yearbook of European Legal Studies, 19,* 48–85.

Midtbøen, A. H., Birkvad, S. R., & Erdal, M. B. (2018). *Citizenship in the Nordic Countries: Past, Present, Future.* Denmark: Rosendals.

Mitchell, K. (2012). Student mobility and European identity: Erasmus study as a civic experience? *Journal of Contemporary European Research, 8*(4), 490–518.

Mitchell, K. (2014). Rethinking the 'Erasmus Effect' on European identity. *JCMS: Journal of Common Market Studies.* https://doi.org/10.1111/jcms. 12152.

Münch, R. (2017). European citizenship between cosmopolitan outlook and national solidarities. In J. Mackert & B. S. Turner (Eds.), *The Transformation of Citizenship: Boundaries of Inclusion and Exclusion* (pp. 169–191). London: Routledge.

Muñoz, J., Torcal, M., & Bonet, E. (2011). Institutional trust and multilevel government in the European Union: Congruence or compensation? *European Union Politics, 12*(4), 551–574.

Muxel, A. (2009). EU movers and politics: Towards a fully-fledged European citizenship? In E. Recchi & A. Favell (Eds.), *Pioneers of European Integration* (pp. 156–178). Cheltenham: Edward Elgar.

Olsen, E. D. H. (2012). *Transnational Citizenship in the European Union: Past, Present and Future.* London: Continuum Books.

Pukallus, S. (2016). *Representations of European Citizenship Since 1951.* Basingstoke: Palgrave Macmillan.

Recchi, E. (2015). *Mobile Europe: The Theory and Practice of Free Movement in the EU.* Basingstoke: Palgrave Macmillan.

Ross, A. (2015). *Understanding the Constructions of Identities by Young New Europeans: Kaleidoscopic Selves.* New York: Routledge.

Ross, A. (2019). *Finding Political Identities: Young People in a Changing Europe.* London: Palgrave Macmillan.

Roth, H. I. (2004). The Multicultural Sweden. In K. Almqvist & K. Glans (Eds.), *The Swedish Success Story?* Stockholm: Johnson Foundation.

Sanders, D., Magalhães, P., & Tóka, G. (Eds.). (2012). *Citizens and the European Polity: Mass Attitudes Towards the European and National Polities.* Oxford: Oxford University Press.

Schmitt, H. (2005). The European Parliament elections of June 2004: Still second-order? *West European Politics, 28*(3), 650–679.

Sigalas, E. (2009). Does ERASMUS student mobility promote a European identity?. *Webpapers on Constitutionalism & Governance Beyond the State,* 2009/2.

Sigalas, E. (2010a). Cross-border mobility and European identity: The effectiveness of intergroup contact during the Erasmus year abroad. *European Union Politics, 11*(2), 241–265.

Sigalas, E. (2010b). The role of personal benefits in public support for the EU: Learning from the Erasmus students. *West European Politics, 33*(6), 1341–1361.

Siklodi, N. (2015). Active citizenship through mobility? Students' perceptions of identity, rights and participation in the EU. *Citizenship Studies, 19*(6–7), 820–835.

Skey, M. (2011). *National Belonging and Everyday Life: The Significance of Nationhood in an Uncertain World.* Basingstoke: Palgrave Macmillan.

Smets, K., & van Ham, C. (2013). The embarrassment of riches? A meta-analysis of individual-level research on voter turnout. *Electoral Studies, 32*(2), 344–359.

Strudel, S., & Michalska, K. K. (2012). European citizenship in action: EU movers as voters. In E. Recchi (Ed.), *MOVEACT "All Citizens Now": Intra-EU Mobility and Political Participation of English, Germans, Poles and Romanians in Western and Southern Europe.*

Thompson, C., & Tambyah, S. (1999). Trying to be cosmopolitan. *Journal of Consumer Research, 26*(1), 214–241.

Van Den Brink, M., & Kochenov, D. (2019). Against associate EU citizenship. *JCMS: Journal of Common Market Studies.* https://doi.org/10.1111/jcms.12898.

Van Ingelgom, V. (2014). *Integrating Indifference: A Comparative, Qualitative and Quantitative Approach to the Legitimacy of European Integration.* Colchester: ECPR Press.

Van Mol, C. (2011). The influence of European student mobility on European identity and subsequent migration behaviour. In F. Dervin (Ed.), *Analysing the Consequences of Academic Mobility and Migration* (pp. 29–50). Newcastle: Cambridge Scholars Publishing.

Van Mol, C. (2013). Intra-European student mobility and European identity: A successful marriage? *Population, Space and Place, 19,* 209–222.

Van Mol, C. (2014). *Intra-European Student Mobility in International Higher Education Circuits: Europe on the Move.* Basingstoke: Palgrave Macmillan.

Welge, R. (2015). Union citizenship as demoi-cratic institution: Increasing the EU's subjective legitimacy through supranational citizenship? *Journal of European Public Policy, 22*(1), 56–74.

White, J. (2011). *Political Allegiance After European Integration.* Basingstoke: Palgrave Macmillan.

Wilson, I. (2011). What should we expect of 'Erasmus generations'? *JCMS: Journal of Common Market Studies, 49*(5), 1113–1140.

CHAPTER 7

Conclusion: Where Is Mobile Citizenship in Europe—And Elsewhere—Heading?

The prospect of a 'global community' remains alluring despite the plethora of recent examples—from the refugee crisis to Brexit—indicating its deep-rooted contradictions. It is this paradox which has been the starting point and the recurring theme of the present book. To elucidate citizens' notions of a 'global community' and their senses of 'one world citizenship', the book examined the only exemplar of post-national community and citizenship we have—as apparent in the European Union (EU). Specifically this book looked at how far the EU has come in its attempts to create a truly inclusive political community—above and beyond territorial communities—and how its attempts have changed the role of citizens in Europe.

The EU does, within certain limitations, offer a unique instance of post-national community building and a groundbreaking citizenship practice. In particular, the national communities and citizenship of member states are 'complemented' by a new, transnational community and EU model of citizenship. Despite its 'secondary' character as apparent in EU law (Delanty 1997), EU citizenship does signify EU nationals' 'fundamental' status. The convoluted dynamics between national and EU communities and models of citizenship as a result of their interdependence are further complicated by the reliance of nearly all EU citizenship provisions on citizens' cross-border, intra-EU mobility. Yet, it is precisely,

© The Author(s) 2020   191
N. Siklodi, *The Politics of Mobile Citizenship in Europe*,
Politics of Citizenship and Migration,
https://doi.org/10.1007/978-3-030-49051-5_7

this reliance on citizens' intra-EU mobility which has already been found to strengthen the position of national models (Favell 2008).

In its attempt to "reinterpret the long-term social and political transformation of European states and societies in facing new global challenges" (Guiraudon et al. 2015: 3), this book gave EU developments the 'benefit of the doubt' and viewed national and EU models of *mobile* citizenship as a Pangloss microcosm. Specifically, it explored the perceptions of a small group of 'ideal citizens', young and highly educated EU mobile and stayer (or home) university students who get to experience the budding EU community to the fullest and within higher educational structures in a shielded context. Accepting that the 'united in diversity' mantra is probably present even in this context (Van Mol 2014), the study compared experiences in two EU states—both of which had adopted an open door policy to EU mobiles in the early days of heightened intra-EU mobility, namely Sweden and the United Kingdom (UK).

This final chapter brings together the main findings of the study presented in the various chapters of this book and considers their broader academic and policy implications.

The chapter is structured as follows.

The first part recounts the key conceptual and empirical findings of the book as presented across the conceptual (Chapter 2) and empirical chapters (Chapters 3–6). The subsequent part considers the implications of these findings for contemporary scholarly and policy debates, including the democratic credentials of a 'one world', or at least regional, transnational mobile community.

7.1   MOBILE CITIZENSHIP IN EUROPE: WHAT IS IT?

This book has set out to complement the extant literature on contemporary mobile citizenship in Europe, which has emerged from the citizenship and EU studies prisms (Chapter 2). It demonstrated the benefits of adopting a citizenship studies approach to empirical research in order to aid the comparability of distinct models of citizenship—namely national and EU models of citizenship. It also illustrated that, despite the dissimilarities in historical and political models of citizenship (an excellent overview is provided by Heater 2004), the significance of recent EU developments, especially those within the Union, has often been overlooked by citizenship studies scholars. Apart from the 'acts of citizenship' agenda as introduced by Isin and colleagues (Isin and Nielsen 2008; Isin and Saward 2013) and the dedicated assessment of Sanders and colleagues on national and EU attitudes towards European politics (Sanders et al. 2012), most of the literature has focussed on either the national or the EU model—and mostly ended up observing EU citizenship as not worthy of its citizenship status.

Genuine empirical assessments of the implications of EU citizenship provisions have in nearly all cases been carried out by EU studies scholars. Understandably, their studies placed EU citizenship as one in the long list of efforts supporting European regional integration. As such, there has been a preference for unpacking the identity dimension of national and EU communities—too often removed from the broader citizenship framework. This has been the case despite the introduction of a dedicated EU citizenship by the Union and here with notable exception by Recchi and colleagues (Recchi and Favell 2009; Favell 2010; Recchi 2015). Without underestimating the progressive implications of EU political developments (Guiraudon et al. 2015), these studies offer significant insights of where pro-EU expectations do not translate into reality—even in the case of high-flying 'Eurostars', i.e. EU-15 highly skilled mobiles, Erasmus students or other pro-EU young people (also notable Bruter [2005], Van Mol [2014], and Ross [2015, 2019]).

Even if not enthusiastic in their conclusions, the contribution of these scholars still suggests that a sizeable number of citizens in the EU hold varying senses of national and EU affiliations and that these affiliations shape individual political attitudes. Even more, once intra-EU mobility is thrown into the equation, including the idealised intra-EU learning mobility aspect, senses of EU identity have been found to gain some ground. This book attempted to contribute to the ongoing conversation by citizenship and EU studies scholars in the way of introducing the conceptual framework proposed by citizenship studies to the EU case. In so doing, it argued, a more inclusive approach to the study of contemporary mobile national and EU communities and models of citizenship could be developed, which supports their comparability with one another and with broader, global citizenship developments.

A secondary analysis of EU-wide quantitative data (EB 89.1 2018) was used to illustrate resulting national and EU citizenship attitudes and changes in approaches towards different migrant groups, including internal EU mobiles and external, third country nationals (TCNs) across the EU, and in Sweden and the UK specifically (Chapter 3). In particular, multivariate analysis was used to demonstrate the significant explanatory value of intra-EU mobility, migration attitudes, as well as the different dimensions of (EU) citizenship—bar participation—along with sociological factors, especially education, as key to unpacking senses of European citizenship in the EU-28. Considered in the light of the aforementioned citizenship and EU studies literature, this finding underscored the urgent requirement to assess notions of community building and senses of national and EU citizenship along with the issue of EU mobility in more depth, in the light of educational implications and from a comparative perspective.

Hence, the rest of the book systematically applied the conceptual approaches of citizenship studies to contemporary community building processes and national and EU models of citizenship, using original focus group evidence. Albeit relying on qualitative evidence, these chapters strongly challenge the optimism which progressive expectations have placed on the link between EU mobility, EU community and EU citizenship—all, supposedly at the cost of exclusive, national attachments—among young and highly educated EU mobiles and stayers in Sweden and the UK.

In the course of novel community building processes, including processes of differentiation and exclusion, key changes emerged as a result of intra-EU mobility experiences—and in contrast to the non-EU citizens (Chapter 4). Clearly, a "community of Europeans" among mobiles and stayers or heightened transactions between them hardly ever materialised (Deutsch et al. 1968). Nor did such exchanges occur with TCNs. Quite the contrary.

These ideal EU citizens—who spoke a common language, usually English, and did not have to 'compete' with one another for jobs or their livelihoods—appeared to feel somewhat distant from one another on the basis of their mobility experiences. Even the 'shielded contexts' of higher educational institutions did not mitigate the impact of national stereotypes (Van Mol 2014: 5–8). Rather, EU processes seemed to have enhanced pre-existing regional and national stereotypes—an impression perhaps strengthened by the 'peculiarity' of Sweden and the UK as outlier countries within the EU.

Similarly, stayers' exposure to EU mobiles and TCNs only seemed to sustain long-standing processes of national exclusion and also reinforce their membership within national communities. Ironically, these communities had been not so apparent to stayers *prior* to them taking notice of the 'elitist' communities of EU mobiles. The evidence provided a nuanced angle on senses of ambivalence towards the EU (White 2011; Duchesne et al. 2013; Van Ingelgom 2014). Specifically, it suggested that ambivalence is likely to end with increased exposure to the EU mobile and TCN communities—at least in the case of young 'aspiring Eurostars'.

Viewed through the key dimensions of citizenship, including and importantly, EU participation, the evidence suggested that a series of new categories of citizens are emerging in the EU: (1) the so-called Eurostars, including EU-15 mobiles (Favell 2008); (2) the second-class 'Eurostars', including the 'new movers' from CEE states (Recchi 2015); (3) the aspiring Eurostars, including some EU-15 stayers; and (4) the peripheral EU citizens, including both lower class EU-15 and the vast majority of CEE stayers (Table 4.1). As these categories indicate, more often than not, the intra-EU mobility of young citizens was likely to lead to separate EU mobile and stayer communities along the EU-15 and CEE divisions, and sustained the national orientation of stayers, though with some variation in their (professed) EU mobility aspirations.

Both mobiles and stayers seemed quite aware/conscious of these issues and proposed external migration as a possible alternative to promoting a single EU community—and so boosting EU processes of exclusion. However, none of them acknowledged the costs associated with external migration, even though the socio-economic costs of intra-EU mobility had been cited previously as *their* rationale for studying within the EU in the case of mobiles, and for remaining at home in the case of stayers. Hence, participants ended up replacing one elitist process of EU community promotion—EU mobility—with another, possibly even more elitist process—external migration.

The rest of the book offered specific empirical insight into senses of *mobile* national (Chapter 5) and EU (Chapter 6) citizenship. In particular, the chapters illustrated the many ways in which national citizenship remained or even became the most attractive—and distinguished—status for both EU mobiles and stayers in the context of intra-EU mobility. Actually, the basic idea of citizenship emerged as embedded within national structures for both groups in both countries. Importantly, this assumption stemmed from young citizens' experiences of or heightened exposure to EU mobility.

Despite the apparent attractiveness of hypothetical post-national models of citizenship, in reality, for the large majority of these groups, citizenship was always equated with nationality (Chapter 5). Even more, instances of European integration, including the ideal scenario of intra-EU learning mobility, sustained the primacy of *national* models of citizenship across the dimensions of citizenship, including identity, rights and participation. This was especially noticeable in young citizens' broad interpretation of citizenship as social rights (Marshall 1950). EU mobiles quickly identified a range of obstacles they had to face while residing in Sweden or the UK (when they had attempted to open a bank account for example). Both EU mobiles and stayers then spoke about the diversity in European languages, cultures and welfare state provisions (especially those related to health care and education) (Favell 2008; European Commission 2017), and the uneven influence of national governments at the EU level (Moravcsik 1998) as underscoring the prevalence of national over EU status. The only instance where the EU became a clear reference point was during the debates about securing 'equality' in the realm of the EU's elitist market structures that was assumed to guide its mobility and citizenship provisions.

Hence, the ensuing deliberations on identity politics and, even, preferences for 'alternative forms of engagement'—mainly present in the UK groups—were firmly embedded within national frames (Medrano 2003). Both EU mobiles and stayers were quick to underscore the context-contingent and "kaleidoscopic" character of their citizenship identity (Ross 2015). Although participants expressed a sense of unease with 'national frames', they eventually admitted to it being their principal point of call—especially within the EU. Importantly, while stayers appeared or were expected to carry traces of 'exclusive' nationality, EU mobiles repeatedly felt their national identity to have progressively 'opened up' and made them aware of the similarities and differences among European (not only EU) nationals. Such 'inclusive' nationality then seemed to have required a 'banal' admission of cross-national differences in the EU. Too much emphasis on these differences however, such as apparent in 'multicultural' Britain, was expected to lead to antagonism between EU nationals.

A closer inspection of EU citizenship appeared to have replicated the rights-focussed interpretation of citizenship and mobile/stayer distinctions in senses of citizenship yet again (Chapter 6). There was a tendency among the focus groups to substitute the advantages of their EU citizenship with EU mobility rights (Férnandez 2005; Carins 2010; Van Mol 2014). EU mobiles then saw their mobile EU citizenship as a "novelty" that could be effective in enhancing their identification as EU citizens.

Stayers perceived it as a mere "extension" of their national status. Actually, quite a few stayers seemed surprised to learn that they could already be regarded as 'EU citizens' in legal terms. In a similar vein, though perhaps not as extensively, a good number of EU mobiles and stayers assumed that EU citizenship was something for the future and did not yet exist.

Subsequent debates were then indicative of how EU mobility might, someday, turly serve as a dynamic bond between the EU and its _educated_ (including, interested, active and informed) citizens—which is precisely how scholars in the field of citizenship studies define the concept of 'citizenship' (especially Isin and Turner 2002; Heater 2004; Magnette 2005; Bellamy 2008; Isin and Nyers 2014; Mackert and Turner 2017). However, for now, EU citizenship was seen as 'temporary' at best, ending with the end of intra-EU mobility experience. Furthemore, it was deemed as irrelevant for a large group of stayers and anticipated to remain as such for the foreseeable future.

The "kaleidoscopic" character of participants' identities meant that perceived antagonism rather than welcoming or neutral member state contexts was identified as constructive for emerging senses of shared EU identity (contradicting the findings by Mitchell 2012, 2014; Van Mol 2014). However, antagonism was seen as 'exceptional' within the 'truly European', EU-15 region. Yet EU mobility experiences in such contexts, as described in Sweden and the UK appeared to contribute towards a contradictory sense of civic EU identity—and one that firmly assigned the cultural aspect of EU mobiles' citizenship identity to an 'inclusive' national identity (Bruter 2005; Ross 2015, 2019). Against this backdrop, the large-scale abstention of participants from EU participation was interpreted as a sign of their fragile EU identity and a perceived lack of "knowledge" and interest in EU politics. Alluding to the interlinked dimensions of (EU) citizenship (Chapter 2), EU rights and especially mobility and EU identity were seen as having a positive reciprocal effect on one another.

However, EU participation—clearly the weakest dimension of EU citizenship for both EU mobiles and stayers—called into question the relevance of all of these dimensions and, potentially, even that of EU citizenship. Promoting EU participation in order to strengthen citizens' sense of EU identity and awareness of EU rights (beyond mobility) (Sanders et al. 2012) might be futile as a result. A preference for issue-based approaches to participation was largely over ridden by rational cost–benefit calculations, which then fed young citizens' abstention from

EU participation and also served as another opportunity to manifest the second-order character of EP elections (Schmitt 2005). These tendencies also ehcoed the broader trend of declining participation (Franklin 2004; Sloam and Henn 2019). Some differences did emerge in EU mobiles' approaches to EU participation, depending on the length of time they had spent aboard. Since EU mobility flows are circular and temporary in character (Kahanec and Zimmermann 2010), the differences between short- and long-term EU mobiles' perceptions may shed light on why the majority of EU citizens do not participate in the host country (Strudel and Michalska 2012; Recchi 2015), but prefer to do so in their country of origin (Muxel 2009) or through alternative forms of engagement (Favell 2010).

Overall, the key findings of this book correspond nicely with the argument presented by previous EU studies about the importance of personal advantages, including mobility opportunities, in developing senses of EU citizenship which could then sit 'comfortably' alongside national affiliations (Bruter 2005; Favell 2008; Recchi and Favell 2009; Van Mol 2014; Ross 2015, 2019). The evidence suggests that the traditional citizenship studies lens is equally useful in developing a more politically embedded and comparative explanation of current community building processes and the interdependence between the dimensions as well as the models of national and EU citizenship (Isin and Turner 2007; Bellamy 2008; Bosniak 2008; Isin and Nyers 2014; Mackert and Turner 2017).

Perhaps most importantly, the evidence illustrated, in quite some detail, that the current, lived experiences of national and EU communities and citizenships are likely to be substantially interdependent on, yet distinct from one another. The implications of these findings for academic and policy considerations are the topic of the remainder of this chapter.

7.2   The Politics of Mobile Citizenship in Europe and Beyond—Why Should We Care?

The European Union has been beset by a series of economic and political woes in the past few years, culminating in Brexit—the first example of a member leaving the club. However, there is little reason to doubt the survival of the EU block. Nor is there reason to question the longevity of mobile national and EU community building processes and models of citizenship. This section considers the likely implications of the findings of the study presented by this book, broadening its scope beyond the EU's boundaries. After all, the EU is meant to signify an example of 'global community'—and one that is, clearly, defined by mobility and migration. As such, the actualities in the EU are likely to hold relevant messages for policymakers and scholars anywhere in the world.

First, based on the inspection of novel processes of community building along EU mobility, this book presents a compelling case for replacing the dichotomy of active/passive citizen categories with a distinction between mobile and stayer citizens. Accordingly, the active citizens are the 'EU mobiles', for whom notions of 'good' national *and* EU citizenship are redefined by a sense of inclusivity and awareness, though not political participation. As a result of static EU and member state participation structures, EU active citizens often refrain from too much participation. Yet, it is precisely these citizens for whom EU citizenship is an 'advantage.' They are most likely to enjoy and experience the genuine notion of EU citizenship, however temporarily. While prone to be supportive of EU-level integration attempts, they often seem to find it difficult to shape related policies and, in the reality of the circular- and temporal-migration character of their EU mobility (Kahanec and Zimmerman 2010), may have little interest in doing so (Favell 2010; Recchi 2015). As a result, the pressure on nation state democracies is bound to grow. It is the young, affluent and highly skilled who are most able and most likely to move. This group gets the most help from EU institutions if they do choose to move. However, doing so seems to turn these citizens into "passive" national citizens, from a political engagement perspective who also often become uprooted from national communities.

Nonetheless, we should be mindful that the pro-EU or transnational outlook of these active citizens is likely to have very clear parameters. After all, EU mobiles decide not only about 'where to go' within Europe, but who to go with—or, even, who to meet while staying abroad (Van Mol 2014). The novel processes of differentiation which takes place within their mobile citizenship ranks separates EU-15 and CEE mobile communities. Such separation then contributes to and perhaps even sustains processes of exclusion which were previously apparent within national communities. The increased hostility towards CEE mobiles across EU-15 countries is a clear example. In reality then, national and nationalist processes of exclusion in Europe are likely to find further impetus in the course of intra-EU mobility—even during the ideal intra-EU learning mobility scenario—and so we can expect little sign of national differences diminishing or even 'slowing down' in an ever-mobile Europe.

In this mobile Europe, the passive citizens are, inevitably, the nation state-oriented 'stayers'. Given the 'kaleidoscopic' character of contemporary senses of citizenship (Ross 2019), for stayers, EU or transnational political developments, including citizenship considerations, are likely to have an inherently second-order character and emerge on the basis of national and, for some, even nationalist reflections. Stayers' political engagement is also bound to be 'localised.' This is likely to be equally true for the segment of stayers who have an appetite for engaging in alternative forms of participation—as it has been traced among young, EU-15 stayers (Sloam 2014; Sloam and Henn 2019). Ironically, this issue may, in the long term, benefit the working schedule of EU and national actors. After all, if recent developments taught us anything, it is possibly that *more* participation—or more opportunities for participation—leads to the more political fragmentation. At the same time, as long as 'official' participation channels through which citizens feel they can 'make their voices heard' and the benchmarks against which participation is measured remain static in a mobile Europe, these are bound to challenge the democratic legitimacy of national and EU politics in equal measures.

Despite some of the cautionary tales emerging in relation to both groups from the qualitative evidence in this book—and elsewhere (especially Favell 2008; White 2011; Duchesne et al. 2013; Van Ingelgom 2014; Recchi 2015)—we are often tempted to refer back to the gap between the 'winners and losers of globalisation and European integration' as the liberal and high-flying EU mobiles and nationalist stayers. We use these stories to explain recent political developments from popular responses to the financial crisis or Brexit (Kriesi 2014; De Vreese et al. 2019). In reality, however, many of these developments are set to be the result of "long-term social and political transformation of European states and societies"—all of which requires in-depth 'reinterpretation' (Guiraudon et al. 2015: 3) that reflects upon the more complex processes which actually shape and refine contemporary politics of mobile citizenship in Europe.

Accordingly, if policymakers are *truly* interested in building a "community of Europeans" and for sustaining their national communities, it might be useful to develop methods which aims to start addressing the differences apparent *within* and *between* these new active/passive citizen communities across the EU. This is perhaps a feasible step to take towards the EU's budding community—however flawed this ideal may be—and could also prove beneficial in preparing national communities for the inevitable changes in the role of their citizens in the context of heightened mobility. Even though young and educated citizens form an ideal segment of the EU's citizenry, those who are safeguarded from the adversities of member state policies, they too found their EU mobility experiences particularly important in accentuating differences based on national stereotypes. This finding echoes previous studies on youth mobility (Cairns 2010) and Erasmus exchanges (Van Mol 2014). It shows just how problematic it is to simply expect highly globalised educational contexts to 'brush aside' longer term processes of exclusions—the very processes which had been a central feature of European societies at the local, regional, national and, as the findings here would suggest, supranational levels. They simply cannot be eradicated by one or two targeted policies. This is certainly what studies of an ever more 'globalised' higher education system have also found.

It is probably better to think of universities as "central institutional mechanisms that legitimate cosmopolitanism as a desirable attribute of the person living in a global world, while distributing this universally desirable attribute unequally within a population" (Igarashi and Saito 2014: 2). A redistribution of cosmopolitan—and in the EU's case pro-EU and transnational attributes—surely requires a bottom-up effort from political communities. As one participant put it, there is a tendency among citizens in Europe to "excuse *ourselves* for not being informed... But when are we going to be informed? Who is going to give us this sphere of knowledge when we cannot define things like EU citizenship?" (Bulgarian Female, EU Group 4, Sweden). How do we build a bottom-up effort which can enhance citizens' awareness of transnational and global citizenship and mobility trends?

While this issue remains a challenge, an important first step by researchers would be to investigate emerging community building processes along with the issue of mobility in more depth. Due to the rather sensitive nature of this topic, qualitative research, especially ethnographic study might be required to really interrogate how the different categories of citizens—stayers, temporary, seasonal and permanent mobiles—understand how they are affected by novel community building processes. The resulting study might tell us something about the similarities and differences between notions of national and EU citizenship. This would then not only tell us something about citizens' preferred 'information' channels, but could initiate a broader, comparative research agenda which could shed light on the extent to which processes within the EU echo broader developments linked to global migration flows and the cosmopolitan outlook of (chiefly) Western travellers (see for example Skey 2011).

At the same time, if we interpret young citizens contribution to, and recognition of, contemporary processes of differentiation and exclusion from a citizenship studies prism, the emerging contradictions seem to reflect extremely well the inherently 'contested' nature of *political* community building processes. It is, after all, precisely this issue that grants citizenship models their political role and one that *must* redefine the active/passive citizen categories if and when a new model is introduced (Heater 2004; Bosniak 2008; Isin 2008). In the EU's case, young and educated EU mobiles' and stayers' as active/passive citizens' note-taking of national and mobility differences might then be a 'blessing in disguise'. It is, after all, a prerequisite for starting a new conversation among citizens about what an EU community *ought to* look like, compared to what citizens think it resembles today. In this respect, the promotion of learning—and, elsewhere, transnational—mobility programmes, might just achieve its intended EU citizenship goals (European Commission 2017). However, the evidence clearly suggests that we are nowhere near bridging the resulting differences between mobiles/stayers or indeed more deep-seated regional default lines among EU and national citizens. Indeed, there is still no conversation to be had between these groups.

However, there are indications, which suggest that these differences are already under quite a bit of strain—at least where young peoples' approaches to the EU's emerging community is concerned (Ross 2015, 2019). If and when a conversation about these differences occurs between citizens on a larger scale, it can grant an otherwise chiefly top-down and elitist model of citizenship—such as the EU model today (Magnette 2003; O'Brien 2016)—a more vibrant character. This is exactly what EU actors were hoping for when they introduced EU citizenship (European Commission 1993). While we are not quite there yet, the apparent fragmentation between active and passive citizens may also offer some encouragement for transnational and global 'political community' advocates.

Second, traditional models of citizenship and migration have been turned on their heads in the EU's case (Hansen and Hager 2010). Due to its almost exclusive reliance on EU mobility, serious questions were raised in this book about the *genuine* significance of EU citizenship compared especially to the more established national affiliations of member state citizens. It is just too obvious to note that EU mobility has little, if any bearing for stayers' senses of EU citizenship. In fact, based on the evidence, EU mobility might have the opposite effect—it is likely to strengthen the primacy of national citizenship for stayers. By comparison, even if EU mobiles' senses of EU citizenship is enhanced following periods of EU mobility, their resulting pro-EU attitudes are not permanent. They last while citizens reside aboard and as long as they do not integrate into the host country or indeed until they decide to return home (similar conclusions reached by Favell 2008).

Once they do so, the significance of EU citizenship in the eyes of previously mobile citizens seems to evaporate. In fact, EU mobility seems prone to enhance previously mundane national sentiments—and possibly for the longer term than it could ever do so for senses of EU citizenship. After all, experiences in the host and home societies only ever likely to accentuate that nation states organise citizens' everyday life in a mobile Europe, from opening bank accounts to registering with a doctor (Favell 2008). For now, temporality may explain why so many participants—and based on the survey data, so many formal EU citizens—are less likely to consider their EU citizenship a reality or separately from their national affiliation.

If we do accept and decide to retain mobility as a key to activating EU and, increasingly, *inclusive* national models of citizenship, we must also recognise that it is bound to highlight the primary role of national political frameworks first and foremost. After all, if and when considered relevant, senses of citizenship are highly context-dependent (Ross 2015, 2019). In order for future researchers to contribute to the broader debates about whether "the glass of EU citizenship ... is half full or half empty" (Sanderset al. 2012: 222)—we require further, EU-wide quantitative data with indicators that can account for the dimensions of citizenship and different experiences of EU mobility. Using this data could then help establish a more definitive model of mobile citizenship in Europe. Similar strategies can then be applied to data collected from elsewhere to aid cross-regional comparability.

At the same time, EU policymakers could complement EU mobility rights by placing an emphasis on the benefits the EU offers, directly, to its mobile citizens. Perhaps a good starting point would be to reach out to citizens who reside in non-neutral and often antagonistic member state contexts—of which we seem to have more and more lately. For instance, 'Brexit cafes' were introduced to assist EU residents' securing their residency rights for after the UK exits the Union in an informal and friendly setting. These cafes are the source of useful information to EU mobiles and also facilitate novel opportunities for exchanges between EU mobiles and a specific group of stayers—the 'aspiring Eurostars'. Perhaps similar initiatives should be introduced in other member states and with administrative and financial support from the EU.

Perhaps other types of global pressures, such as heightened migration flows or regional conflicts are more common concerns in the rest of the world. However, global challenges have propelled higher levels of regional integration elsewhere too—and far beyond the usual 'western' periphery of our fascination with a 'globalised' citizenship and migration landscape. For example, Southeast Asia has special provisions in place to encourage internal economic mobility within the region (e.g. Cheng and Momesso 2019). With the EU serving as the most advanced example of a regional community, its approach to a distinctive, EU citizenship policy might one day serve as a blueprint for other regions.

Finally, notwithstanding the richness of quantitative and qualitative approaches to research, our understanding of contemporary citizenship politics in the EU would greatly benefit from more mixed-method research. This book underlined that there is an urgent requirement to incorporate the findings of qualitative evidence about the citizenship ideals of policymakers with EU-wide data on actual national and EU citizenship attitudes and behaviour. It is only by attending seriously to both the top-down and the bottom-up aspects of citizenship models that we can further the ongoing debates between EU and citizenship studies. The resulting literature is bound to enhance our understanding of what is *really* at stake in current attempts at forging a dynamic bond between a transnational entitiy, such as the EU, its member states *and* the citizens.

REFERENCES

Bellamy, R. (2008). *Citizenship: A Very Short Introduction*. Oxford: Oxford University Press.

Bosniak, L. (2008). *The Citizen and the Alien: Dilemmas of Contemporary Membership*. Princeton, NJ: Princeton University Press.

Bruter, M. (2005). *Citizens of Europe? The Emergence of a Mass European Identity*. London: Palgrave Macmillan.

Cairns, D. (Ed.). (2010). *Youth on the Move: European Youth and Geographical Mobility*. Germany: VS Verlag.

Cheng, I., & Momesso, L. (2019). Rethinking transnationalism in a global world: Contested state, society, border, and the people in between. *International Migration, 57*, 107–201.

De Vreese, C. H., Azrout, R., & Boomgaarden, H. G. (2019). One size fits all? Testing the dimensional structure of EU attitudes in 21 Countries. *International Journal of Public Opinion Research, 31*(2), 195–219. https://doi.org/10.1093/ijpor/edy003.

Delanty, G. (1997). Models of citizenship: Defining European identity and citizenship. *Citizenship Studies, 1*, 285–303.

Deutsch, K. W., Burrel, S. A., Kann, R. A., Lee, M. Jr., Lichterman, M, Lindgren, R. E. et al. (1968). *Political Community and the North Atlantic Area*. Princeton, NJ: Princeton University Press.

Duchesne, S., Frazer, E., Haegel, F., & Van Ingelgom, V. (Eds.). (2013). *Citizens' Reactions to European Integration Compared: Overlooking Europe*. London: Palgrave.

European Commission. (1993, December 21). First Report on Citizenship of the Union, COM(93)702 final, Brussels.

European Commission. (2017). *The Erasmus impact study*. https://op.europa.eu/en/publication-detail/-/publication/13031399-9fd4-11e5-8781-01aa75ed71a1.

Favell, A. (2008). *Eurostars and Eurocities: Free Movement and Mobility in an Integrating Europe*. Oxford: Blackwell.

Favell, A. (2010). European identity and European citizenship in three "Eurocities": A sociological approach to the European Union. *Politique Européenne, 30*, 187–224.

Fernández, Ó. (2005). Towards European citizenship through higher education? *European Journal of Education, 40*(1), 59–68.

Franklin, M. N. (2004). *Voter Turnout and the Dynamics of Electoral Competition in Established Democracies since 1945*. Cambridge: Cambridge University Press.

Guiraudon, V., Ruzza, C., & Trenz, H. J. (Eds.). (2015). *Europe's Prolonged Crisis: The Making or the Unmaking of a Political Union*. Basingstoke: Palgrave Macmillan.

Hansen, P., & Hager, S. B. (2010). *The Politics of European Citizenship: Deepening Contradictions in Social Rights and Migration Policy*. New York: Berghahn Books.

Heater, D. (2004). *Citizenship: The Civic Ideal in World History, Politics and Education*. Manchester: Manchester University Press.

Igarashi, H., & Saito, H. (2014). Cosmopolitanism as cultural capital: Exploring the intersection of globalization, education and stratification. *Cultural Sociology, 24,* 1–18.

Isin, E. F. (2008). Theorizing acts of citizenship. In Engin F. Isin & Greg M. Nielsen (Eds.), *Acts of Citizenship* (pp. 15–43). London: Palgrave Macmillan.

Isin, E. F., & Turner, B. S. (2007). Investigating citizenship: An agenda for citizenship studies. *Citizenship Studies, 11*(1), 5–17.

Isin, E. F., & Turner, B. S. (Eds.). (2002). *Handbook of Citizenship Studies.* London: Sage.

Isin, E. F., & Nielsen, G. M. (Eds.). (2008). *Acts of Citizenship.* London: Zed Books.

Isin, E. F., & Nyers, P. (Eds.). (2014). Introduction: Globalizing citizenship studies. In *Routledge Handbook of Global Citizenship Studies* (pp. 1–11). Abingdon, UK: Routledge.

Isin, E. F., & Saward, M. (Eds.). (2013). *Enacting European Citizenship.* Cambridge: Cambridge University Press.

Kahanec, M., & Zimmermann, K. F. (Eds.). (2010). *EU Labor Markets after Post-enlargement Migration.* Cham, Switzerland: Springer.

Kriesi, H. (2014). The populist challenge. *West European Politics, 37*(2), 361–378.

Mackert, J., & Turner, B. S. (Eds.). (2017). *The Transformation of Citizenship: Boundaries of Inclusion and Exclusion.* Abingdon, UK: Routledge.

Magnette, P. (2003). European governance and civic participation: Beyond elitist citizenship? *Political Studies, 51*(1), 144–160.

Magnette, P. (2005). *Citizenship: The History of an Idea.* Colchester: ECPR Press.

Marshall, T. H. (1950). *Citizenship and Social Class and Other Essays.* Cambridge: Cambridge University Press.

Medrano, J. D. (2003). *Framing Europe: Attitudes to European Integration in Germany, Spain, and the United Kingdom.* Princeton, NJ: Princeton University Press.

Mitchell, K. (2012). Student mobility and European identity: Erasmus study as a civic experience? *Journal of Contemporary European Research, 8*(4), 490–518.

Mitchell, K. (2014). Rethinking the 'Erasmus Effect' on European identity. *JCMS: Journal of Common Market Studies.* https://doi.org/10.1111/jcms.12152.

Moravcsik, A. (1998). *The Choice for Europe Social Purpose and State Power from Messina to Maastricht.* Abingdon, UK: Routledge.

Muxel, A. (2009). EU movers and politics: Towards a fully-fledged European citizenship? In E. Recchi & A. Favell (Eds.), *Pioneers of European Integration* (pp. 156–178). Cheltenham: Edward Elgar Publishing.

O'Brien, C. (2016). Civis capitalist sum: Class as the new guiding principle of EU free movement rights. *Common Market Law Review, 53*(4), 937–977.

Recchi, E. (2015). *Mobile Europe: The Theory and Practice of Free Movement in the EU*. London: Palgrave Macmillan.

Recchi, E., & Favell, A. (2009). (Eds.). *Pioneers of European Integration* (pp. 156–178). Cheltenham: Edward Elgar Publishing.

Ross, A. (2015). *Understanding the Constructions of Identities by Young New Europeans: Kaleidoscopic Selves*. Abingdon, UK: Routledge.

Ross, A. (2019). *Finding Political Identities: Young People in a Changing Europe*. London: Palgrave Macmillan.

Sanders, D., Magalhães, P., & Tóka, G. (Eds.). (2012). *Citizens and the European Polity: Mass Attitudes Towards the European and National Polities*. Oxford: Oxford University Press.

Schmitt, H. (2005). The European Parliament elections of June 2004: Still second-order? *West European Politics, 28*(3), 650–679.

Skey, M. (2011). *National Belonging and Everyday Life: The Significance of Nationhood in an Uncertain World*. London: Palgrave Macmillan.

Sloam, J. (2014). New voice, less equal: The civic and political engagement of young people in the United States and Europe. *Comparative Political Studies, 47*(5), 663–688.

Sloam, J., & Henn, M. (2019). *Youthquake 2017: The Rise of Young Cosmopolitans in Britain*. London: Palgrave Macmillan.

Strudel, S., & Michalska, K. K. (2012). European citizenship in action: EU movers as voters. In E. Recchi (Ed.), *MOVEACT "All Citizens Now": Intra-EU Mobility and Political Participation of English, Germans, Poles and Romanians in Western and Southern Europe*.

Van Ingelgom, V. (2014). *Integrating Indifference: A Comparative, Qualitative and Quantitative Approach to the Legitimacy of European Integration*. Colchester: ECPR Press.

Van Mol, C. (2014). *Intra-European Student Mobility in International Higher Education Circuits: Europe on the Move*. London: Palgrave Macmillan.

White, J. (2011). *Political Allegiance after European Integration*. London: Palgrave Macmillan.

Appendix: Research Methods Notes

This book aims to provide an empirically-driven narrative of notions of national and EU communities and senses of citizenship (Chapters 3–5), this appendix provides some reflection about the research methods adopted to the collection and analysis of primary data, i.e. the focus groups. Similarly, some consideration of my role as a researcher of a topic that is closely intertwined with my own personal and professional positions as an EU mobile citizen, primarily residing in the UK (at the time of the research project). And, finally, this section includes a display of the profile of each group.

A.1. Rationale for Focus Groups

The primary focus group evidence used in this book explored how citizenship is *actually* perceived and realised by a subgroup of citizens—the young and educated—in their roles as EU mobiles and stayers. There were two main reasons for selecting focus groups as the main research method for this project. On the one hand, focus groups are seen as particularly suitable for carrying out exploratory research in a sensitive field of study (Bryman 2016: 501). Considering that citizenship, identity and political participation are unlikely topics for everyday discussions, making *real* sense of the perceptions of EU mobiles and stayers would have been difficult using survey or interview data. Focus groups are not

© The Editor(s) (if applicable) and The Author(s), under exclusive license to Springer Nature Switzerland AG 2020
N. Siklodi, *The Politics of Mobile Citizenship in Europe*, Politics of Citizenship and Migration, https://doi.org/10.1007/978-3-030-49051-5

only appropriate in imitating broader sociocultural processes and inter-actions from everyday life, but also allowed for the expression of diverse views and facilitated interaction and 'collective sense-making' among the participants (Bryman 2016: 512–515).

On the other hand, the interaction, reasoning and forms of reflec-tion present in the focus groups were expected to provide more in-depth data than possible with other methods. Participants were welcome to go beyond the questions I had prepared and often probed one another for holding certain perspectives. The resulting interaction among them was expected to highlight the issues *they* consider most important and produce insights that would be harder to access using any other research method (Bryman 2016: 501–502). In this sense, again, the essence of the focus groups was to allow for this book to develop definitions and prac-tices of national and EU citizenships to emerge, which chiefly reflects everyday life (in response to some scholarly demand by, for example, Duchesne et al. 2013; Ross 2019; Sloam and Henn 2019).

The focus groups covered three main topics. First, they explored how participants defined their national and EU citizenships, and whether EU mobiles were more likely to identify themselves as EU citizens than stayers. Second, they investigated participants' approaches to the three dimensions of citizenship; their sense of identity (EU, country of origin or host country), perceptions of dis/advantages as EU mobiles/stayers, and engagement in political participation at the EU, national and local levels. Third, the focus groups probed participants' views about their experiences of EU (learning) mobility and its impact on their senses of citizenship. In some cases, the focus groups questioned participants about the most appropriate and effective methods for promoting the idea of EU citizenship across member states.

A.2. Composition of Focus Groups

Participants for the focus groups referred to in this book were recruited via snowballing technique, using social media resources, posters, flyers and public announcements. They were aged between 18 and 30 years and required to have arrived in Sweden or the UK as a result of their exercising of intra-EU learning mobility rights, including both long-term study plans *and* Erasmus study exchanges. The interviews lasted for approximately 1.5 hours and the language of discussion was English.

Four groups of EU mobiles and one of stayers were conducted in each country. In total, these groups included 66 EU mobiles and stayers, 29 in Sweden (including 22 EU mobiles and 7 stayers) and 37 in the UK (including 24 EU mobiles and 13 stayers). Participants came to these countries from a variety of member states, including EU-15 and CEE states. They had spent different lengths of time in Sweden and the UK before the focus groups were conducted, ranging from one week to over four years. On average, participants in Sweden were aged 23.5 years and arrived 14 months prior to the focus groups. For the UK, the same figures were 21.5 and 2.5 years, respectively.

A composition and profile for each focus group was developed on the basis of participants' background (summary tables are included below) and the apparent dynamics between them that emerged during the discussions. The group dynamics were, inevitably, shaped also by my presence as the moderator. Additional factors shaping these dynamics included participants' social backgrounds, namely, language skills and the length of time they had spent in the host country, and whether or not the groups included participants who knew each other prior to the discussions—which was often the case in the UK groups but not so in the Swedish ones.

Focus Group Summary Tables

EU Group 1, Sweden

14 May 2012, Stockholm, Stockholm University

Interview coding/ Demographical information	Italian Male	Portuguese Male	German Female	French Male
Age	28	26	23	21
Gender	M	M	F	M
Country of origin	Italy	Portugal	Germany	France
Highest Education	BA	BA	BA	A-levels
Length of time (months)	42	9	18	4
Subject	MA History and Political Science	MA Political Science	MA Peace and Conflict Studies	BA Political Science
Year	MA	MA	MA	BA on Erasmus
Other country	USA 1 year, Spain, 1 year, Portugal 3 months	Belgium- 6 months	Namibia 2 months	No
Social group (self reported pre-interview)	No	N/A	No	No

EU Group 2, Sweden
14 May 2012, Stockholm, Stockholm University

Interview coding/ Demographical information	French Male	Bulgarian Female	German Female	Italian Male	Portuguese Male	British-Hungarian Male
Age	26	25	22	27	23	21
Gender	M	F	F	M	M	M
Country of origin	France	Bulgaria	Germany	Brazil	Portugal	Hungary
Highest Education	BA	BA	A-levels	A-levels	BA	A-levels
Length of time (months)	1	9	42	10	10	9
Subject	Pre-Masters Language course	MA Social Anthropology	BA Political Science and Economics	BA Political Science	MA Marketing	BA Mechanical Engineering
Year	pre-MA	MA	3rd year	3rd year	MA	BA on Erasmus
Other country	Canada, USA	USA 6 months, Netherlands 3 years, Austria 6 months, Germany 6 months, Sweden 9 months	France 6 months, UK 2months	UK 10 years, Brazil 16 years	South Africa, 3 years, Finland 6 months, Spain 6 months	Finland 2 years, England 11 years, Hungary 8 years
Social group (self reported pre-interview)	N/A	No	International community in Stockholm	No	N/A	Yes

EU Group 3, Sweden
16 May 2012, Stockholm, Stockholm University

Interview coding/ Demographical information	Hungarian-South African Female	German Female	Lithuanian Male	French Male
Age	25	22	25	23
Gender	F	F	M	M
Country of origin	Hungary	Germany	Lithuania	France
Highest Education	MA	A-levels	BA	A-levels
Length of time (months)	24	10	36	10
Subject	Media and Communication	Mathematics	MA International Relations	BA Urban Planning
Year	MA	BA on Erasmus	MA	BA and MA on Erasmus
Other country	SA 7 years, Spain 1 year, Canada 2 months- moving back after studies	No	Finland, China, UK	Brazil 3 months
Social group (self reported pre-interview)	Yes- not specified	No	European	N/A

EU Group 4, Sweden
28 May 2012, Stockholm, Stockholm University

Interview coding/ Demographical information	Italian Male (1)	Italian Male (2)	Polish Female (1)	Polish Female (2)	Bulgarian Female	Romanian Female (1)	Romanian Female (2)	French Male
Age	24	22	23	21	20	27	24	23
Gender	M	M	F	F	F	F	F	M
Country of origin	Italian	Italian	Polish	Poland	Bulgarian	Romanian	Romanian	French
Highest Education	A-levels	A-levels	BA	A-levels	A-levels	BA	BA	BA
Length of time (months)	4	5	6	6	0.5	21	23	9
Subject	BA Politics, Erasmus	BA Physics	MA European Studies	BA Culture and Literature of English speaking areas	BA Political Science	MA Media and Communication	MA Media, communication and anthropology	MA Geography
Year	BA	BA on Erasmus	MA	BA	BA on Erasmus	MA	BA	MA
Other country	N/A	No	Belgium 1 month	frequently visits UK (BF)	Greece 1 year, Scotland 2 years	Spain 6 months	N/A	Turkey 2 months
Social group (self reported pre-interview)	N/A	No	Students group and European women	No	Open-minded, sociable person	N/A	N/A	No

Stayer Group, Sweden
15 May 2012, Stockholm, Stockholm University

Interview coding/ Demographical information	Swedish Female (1)	Swedish Female (2)	Swedish Female (3)	Swedish Female (4)	Swedish Female (5)	Swedish Female (6)	Swedish Female (7)
Age	24	19	19	25	21	28	23
Gender	F	F	F	F	F	F	F
Country of origin	Sweden	Sweden	Sweden	Sweden	Sweden	Sweden	Sweden
Highest Education	A-levels	A-levels	A-levels	A -levels	A-levels	MA	A-levels
Length of time (months)	N/A	N/A	N/A	N/A	N/A	N/A	N/A
Subject	BA Political Science and Business Administration	BA Business and Political Science	BA Political Science	BA Business and Political Science	BA French	PhD Politics - EU institutions	BA Sociology and Political Science
Year	1st yr. UG	1st yr. UG	1st yr. UG	1st yr. UG	UG	1st yr. PhD	UG
Other country	No	No	No	Austria 4 months, Norway 5 months, Spain 2 months	Canada 1 year	6 months Belgium, 4 months Serbia	England 6 months
Social group (self reported pre-interview)	No	Lebanese heritage	N/A	N/A	N/A	No	English, women

EU Group 1, UK
26 February 2013, Egham, Royal Holloway, University of London

Interview coding/Demographical Information	German Male	Dutch Male	Italian Male	German Female	Italian Female	Romanian Female	German-Swiss Female
Age	28	25	20	22	24	22	23
Gender	M	M	M	F	F	F	F
Nationality	German	Dutch	Italian	German	Italian	Romanian	German and Swiss
Country of origin	Germany	Netherlands	Italy	Germany	Italy	Romania/Moldova	
Highest Education	MA	MA	A-levels	A-levels	A-levels	A-levels	A-levels
Subject	Politics and International Relations	Politics and International Relations	Economics with Political studies	Geography and Politics and International Relations	Geography and Politics and International Relations	European Studies	Politics and International Relations
Year of study	4th yr. PhD	1st yr. PhD	2nd yr. UG	3rd yr. UG	3rd yr. UG	3rd yr. UG	3rd yr. UG
Other country	N/A	South Korea 6 months	N/A	Canada 7 months, Chile 4 months	Australia 1.5 yrs.	Portugal, temp stays 5-6 months/ yr.	N/A
Social Group	N/A	N/A	Caucasian	N/A	No	No	N/A

EU Group 2, UK
27 February 2013, Egham, Royal Holloway, University of London

Interview coding/Demographical Information	Finnish Female (1)	Finnish Female (2)	French-British Female	German Male
Age	21	21	20	20
Gender	F	F	F	M
Nationality	Finnish	Finnish	French-British	German
Country of origin	Finland	Finland	UK	Germany
Highest Education	FB	IB	A-levels	IB
Subject	Politics and International Relations	Politics and International Relations	Politics and International Relations	Politics and International Relations
Year of study	3rd yr. UG	3rd yr. UG	3rd yr. UG	3rd yr. UG
Other country	Belgium 1.5 yrs.	USA	No	No
Social Group	N/A	White European	Armenian	No

EU Group 3, UK
27 February 2013, Egham, Royal Holloway, University of London

Interview coding/Demographical Information	Swedish Female	Swedish Male	Italian Female	German-British Female	Dutch Female
Age	23		20	21	20
Gender	F	M	F	F	F
Nationality	American Swedish	Swedish	Italian	German	Dutch
Country of origin	Sweden	Sweden	Italy	Germany	Netherlands
Highest Education	IB	IB	IB	IB	IB
Subject	Politics and International Relations	Politics and International Relations	European Studies	Politics and International Relations	Economics, Politics and International Relations
Year of study	2nd Yr. UG	2nd Yr. UG	2nd Yr. UG	3rd Yr. UG	2nd Yr. UG
Other country	UAE 3 yrs., Switzerland 1yr, USA 5yrs, Italy 1 yr., Sweden 10 yrs.	Netherlands	Italy 16 yrs.	Germany 17 yrs.	Singapore (holidays for last 2 yrs.), Switzerland 4 yrs., Netherlands
Social Group	N/A	N/A	No	N/A	No

EU Group 4, UK
1 March 2013, Egham, Royal Holloway, University of London

Interview coding/Demographical Information	Italian-Mexican Female	French Female (1)	French Female (2)	German Female (2)	German Female (1)	Italian Female	French Female (3)	Austrian Female
Age	21	20	19	20	19	20	19	20
Gender	F	F	F	F	F	F	F	F
Nationality	Italian-Mexican	French	French	German	German	Italian	French	Austrian
Country of origin	Italy	France	France	Germany	Germany	Russia	France	Austria
Highest Education	A-levels	French Baccalaureate	French Baccalaureate	A-levels	IB/ EB	IB	IB	A-levels
Subject	European Studies	European Studies	European Studies with Spanish	European Studies with Spanish	European Studies with Spanish	European Studies	European Studies with Italian	European Studies with Spanish
Year of study	2nd yr. UG	2nd yr. UG	2nd yr. UG	2nd yr. UG	2nd yr. UG	2nd yr. UG	2nd yr. UG	2nd yr. UG
Other country	Mexico 8 mths, Scotland 1 yr.	No	N/A	Canada, 2 yrs.		Russia 2 yrs.	Milan, Italy 13 yrs., Luxemburg 4yrs	N/A
Social Group	No	No	No	N/A	European	N/A	Yes	No

Stayer Group, UK
27 February 2013, Egham, Royal Holloway, University of London

Interview coding/Demographical Information	British Male (1)	British Male (2)	British Female (2)	British Male (3)	British Male (4)	British Female (1)	British-Swiss Male	British Female (3)	British Female (4)	British Female (5)	British Female (6)	British-Canadian Male	British Male (5)
Age	23	21	21	21	20	21	21	20	21	23	21	27	23
Gender	M	M	F	M	M	F	M	F	F	F	F	M	M
Nationality	British	British	British	English	British	English	British, Swiss, American	British	British	British	British	British Canadian	British
Country of origin	UK	UK (England)	UK	England	UK (England)	England	England	England	India	England	England	UK	UK
Highest Education	MA	A-levels	A-levels	A-levels	A-levels	A-levels	A-levels	A-levels	A-levels	A-levels	A-levels	MA	MA
Subject	Politics and International Relations	Politics and International Relations	Politics and International Relations	Politics	Politics and International Relations	Politics	Computer Science	Politics and International Relations	Politics and International Relations	Politics and International Relations	European studies with Spanish	Politics and International Relations	Politics and International Relations
Year of study	3rd yr. PhD	3rd yr. UG	2nd yr. UG	3rd yr. UG	2nd yr. UG	2nd yr. UG	3rd yr. UG	2nd yr. UG	3rd yr. UG	2nd yr. UG	3rd yr. UG	2nd yr. PhD	2nd yr. PhD
Other country	Greece 2 yrs., USA 1 yr.	India 6 yrs., Vietnam 1.5 yrs., Israel 1 yr., USA 1 yr	N/A	No	No	No	No	No	N/A	France, Paris 1 yr.	Madrid, 11 months for Erasmus	Canada 13, USA 4 yrs	No
Social Group	N/A	Jewish Community	Father is Spanish, feel attached to India	N/A	English	No	No	No	N/A	N/A	Pakistan	N/A	No

REFERENCES

Bryman, A. (2016). *Social Research Methods* (5th ed.). Oxford: Oxford University Press.

Duchesne, S., Frazer, E., Haegel, F., & Van Ingelgom, V. (Eds.). (2013). *Citizens' Reactions to European Integration Compared: Overlooking Europe.* Basingstoke: Palgrave.

Ross, A. (2019). *Finding Political Identities: Young People in a Changing Europe.* Basingstoke: Palgrave Macmillan.

Sloam, J., & Henn, M. (2019). *Youthquake 2017: The Rise of Young Cosmopolitans in Britain.* London: Palgrave Macmillan.

INDEX

© The Editor(s) (if applicable) and The Author(s), under
exclusive license to Springer Nature Switzerland AG 2020
N. Siklodi, *The Politics of Mobile Citizenship in Europe*,
Politics of Citizenship and Migration,
https://doi.org/10.1007/978-3-030-49051-5

Printed by Printforce, the Netherlands